The Logic against Humanity

ALSO IN ENGLISH BY MASSIMO SCALIGERO

A Practical Manual of Meditation (2015)

A Treatise on Living Thinking
  A Path beyond Western Philosophy,
  beyond Yoga, beyond Zen (2014)

The Secrets of Space and Time (2013)

The Light (La Luce)
  An Introduction to Creative Imagination (2001)

the logic against humanity

the myth of science & the path of thinking

MASSIMO SCALIGERO
Translated by Eric L. Bisbocci

Lindisfarne Books | 2017

Lindisfarne Books
An imprint of Anthroposophic Press / SteinerBooks
610 Main St., Great Barrington, MA
www.steinerbooks.org

Copyright © 2017 by SteinerBooks/Anthroposophic Press, Inc. Translation copyright © 2017 by Eric L. Bisbocci. All rights reserved. No part of this publication may be reproduced, stored in a retrieval system, or transmitted, in any form or by any means, electronic, mechanical, photocopying, recording, or otherwise, without the prior written permission of the publisher. Originally published in Italian as *La Logica Contro L'Uomo* by Libreria Tilopa, Rome, 1967 & 1991.

Cover image: *Hope* (2nd version, 1886, detail),
by George Frederic Watts (1817–1904) and assistants,
oil on canvas, 44 × 56 in. (Tate Britain, London)
Design: Jens Jensen

LIBRARY OF CONGRESS CONTROL NUMBER: 2017952434

ISBN: 978-1-58420-944-7 (paperback)
ISBN: 978-1-58420-945-4 (eBook)

Contents

Translator's Note   vii

PART ONE: THE MYTH OF SCIENCE   1

   I. The Problem from Which We Flee   3

   II. The Logical Forms of the Inner Decline   12

   III. Dialectical and Analytical Precariousness   33

   IV. Formal Automatism and Paranoia   54

   V. The Methodology against Science   73

   VI. The Meaninglessness of Semantics   99

   VII. Naïve Realism Codified: The New Analytical Logic   114

PART TWO: THE PATH OF THINKING   171

   I. The Search for the "I"   173

   II. The Lineaments of a New Science of Perception   182

   III. The Independence of the "I" from the Support   227

   IV. The Logic and Technique of Concentration   257

   V. The "I AM"   297

   Notes   308

   Glossary   309

This translation is dedicated to my wife

Nadia

the light of my life

Translator's Note

One of the difficulties in translating the works of Massimo Scaligero occurs when he uses the infinitive form of verbs as nouns preceded by a definite or indefinite article. Though this never occurs in English, it is fundamental to the living quality of Scaligero's thinking. Since the primary objective of his writings is to awaken a predisposition toward living thinking, I believe it is absolutely necessary that the active mobility of verbs, used as nouns, be maintained. For this reason, I have chosen to remain faithful to the Italian text by often using single quotation marks—when most appropriate—to denote the use of verbs as nouns in order to maintain the integrity of Scaligero's thought, e.g., *il percepire* = the 'perceiving,' or simply 'perceiving.' I have also occasionally used single quotation marks with respect to adjectives (preceded by an indefinite article) in function of inexistent nouns in English. An example of this is Scaligero's mention of *'un impensabile,'* translated by me as 'an unthinkable' (namely, something that cannot be thought). The use of double parentheses in this translation corresponds to his use of them in the Italian text.

Lastly, the reader will occasionally encounter the word *thought* (*pensiero*) followed by the word *itself* in single parenthesis—e.g., thought (itself). This was done not to mislead the reader into reading the word *thought* as a past participle (which in many of these cases would be a natural inclination) but, rather, to see *pensiero* as the phenomenon or activity of thinking itself. An example of this is "*...la persuasione di esprimere qualcosa che sia pensiero*" rendered as "...the persuasion of expressing something that is thought (itself)." Putting the indefinite article 'a' would reduce the activity of thought to a determined form, which, in this case, would itself also be incorrect.

This book intends to present the urgent need for human autonomy regarding the intellectualistic myths of the present time that feign, in scientific or logical guise, virtues of which they bear only the name: freedom, sociality, progress, pure experience, positivism, methodology, and so on. The author, with respect to the ideas expounded, cannot take into account any rebuttal that proves to be derived from an incomplete reading of the book.

With the expression "the logic against humanity" the author does not mean to designate logic adverse to the human being but, rather, the series of methods of present-day learning whose logical form is realized to the degree that it renounces the logical spirit from which it draws.

Part One

The Myth of Science

I

The Problem from Which We Flee

At the present time, the concept "I think" is immediate to any thinking being. There is no need for a spiritual practice of thinking or for a qualitative change. For us, as individuals, the thinking by which we orient ourselves in the everyday world—the ordinary level, or linear logic—is enough for us to believe that each of us is an "I" that thinks and that, therefore, somehow leads life and assumes initiatives and responsibilities.

Owing to the simplicity of this assumption, there are series of people responsible for culture that—acting in behalf of the human majority—believe they realize it. In effect, they do not pose this question to themselves. They do not worry about becoming conscious of such thought, since they believe it to be actualized in their intellectual work, for the simple fact that they produce this work.

These types of intellectuals do not believe that they need to stop and consider the fact that they are likely each the subject of their thinking, namely the "I" that thinks such thought. It is enough for them to consider it implicit in their discourse, to behave as if each of them were such an "I"; to verify it does not matter, as would the verification of a scientific hypothesis in a normal course of investigation. They can even be persuaded that this is not their task but, rather, that of psychology or of psychiatry—namely, that these can provide such proof. Then, they will understand it via that mystical faith, which, today, taken from religion, is transferred to the verdicts of science.

But do such intellectuals truly bear an "I" within them and does their thinking truly become justified by an "I"? In truth, the world's most reliable erudite scholars today worry about everything, yet they do not wonder how their thinking arises and if, at its origin, lies the one responsible that always validates it, called "I." Not to be dismissed is the hypothesis that such scholars are capable of so much analysis, precisely because they avoid knowing what within them thinks and is, therefore, able to produce the synthesis.

The irrelevance of and the disregard for the "I" could point to the absence of the "I" and, likewise, be an explanation for how much is happening in the present world that is confusing and unvaried in its chaotic nature. For this reason, in a single page we could summarize an outline of the ordinary facts of chaotic-ness, whose codification is due to the golden discursive–analytical embroideries of intellectuals well inserted in the system and who, in a refined way, even criticize its technicality and integral automation, but not to the point in which such criticism can jeopardize their personal state of affairs. Therefore, regardless of how much is happening in the present world that is confusing and monotonous, everyone ends up, in some way, cooperating by way of a routine action unconnected to its principle—an action perhaps devoid of the "I."

In the following pages, we will see how thought's measure of truth, or non-truth, cannot be but the presence, within it, of the subject to which it, of necessity, continually appeals—which should be the subject, insofar as it is independent of thought. For this reason, alone, thinking could manifest according to the virtue of its unlimited immediacy. Moreover, we will see that free thought cannot manifest wherever the "I" is not present. Within the current of thinking grasped by the corporeal support, the "I" is replaced by an altered likeness of it, inevitably identified with corporeity.

The Problem from Which We Flee

Precisely because the "I" identifies illegitimately with the thought of itself and thought identifies with cerebralism and, thus, the "I" with corporeity, dialectics and discursive systematics can indulge themselves without limit, without cognitive control, by taking on the problems of the Earth and of the cosmos, of the human being and of the psyche, of sociality and of economy, under the semblances of deductive precision and of terminological correctness, without really penetrating the contents to which they refer, because the "I," from which they seem to move is simply imagined, or imaginarily presupposed.

The misunderstanding, in fact, lies in the belief that the "I," or the "I think," are buried themes of idealistic philosophy, practically overcome by the current analytics, which today assumes a cognitive function in every field. The misunderstanding lies in the failure to imagine that it has to do with something other than philosophical themes—whatever its form, idealistic or realistic.

But would anything change if today's intellectuals decided to know the one responsible for thoughts and sentiments, known as the "I"? Would they begin an investigation that differed from the analytical and linguistic one by which they establish their own present knowing, or would they not believe it to be about extending that type of knowing also to the "I" and to thinking, so that, amongst the many themes acquired through the connection of words, they could also include the "I" and thinking? And do so any differently than what idealism did in another form, when it posed the subject of the "I," or of "I think," or even of thinking as an act of the spirit?

In reality, today's culture, with everything reduced to explanations and definitions, cannot but respond in this way. Those who could receive ideas about the "I," or about thinking, from specific manuals, would have nothing substantial to change within themselves. For them, it would be as if they learned nothing—nothing being the content, as well as the form of such notions.

In another sense, it is a situation similar to that of psychoanalysts and of spiritualists, who see in the "I" a kind of obstacle to the expansion of soul life, confusing the "I" with what negates it and takes its place as a bodily simulacrum or a group of instincts, to which they falsely bestow the name of "I": psychoanalysts and spiritualists who worry about repelling, about negating, and about exorcising the "I," nevertheless, without renouncing to be themselves the subject of what each of them thus do, namely without renouncing to be the "I," which just, at that moment, barely appears as the banisher of itself.

Thought—if we look at it without yet being familiar with the need to experience it within ourselves, but simply retrace its dialectical course—always leads to a point where it is not yet a determination, since it is about to take form from an original immediacy: a point that we cannot fix without losing, but with which we can each say "I think." This is indeed a further thought, but simultaneously the sign of a limit in which the mediation has the possibility to perceive itself, its *immediate being*.

The limit can in turn be considered, but such considering cannot again be reflective. Rather, it must cease to have a dialectical meaning, if it wishes to avoid leading back to the series of thoughts whose course it intended to retrace, all the way to the mentioned end point. To philosophize is, in fact, to stay legitimately within the limit, by intellectually conforming to it, and even speculating on its possible overcoming. Meanwhile, *dialecticism* is the art of consecrating it discursively, without even conceiving it as a limit but, rather, assuming it as a foundation.

It may become clear to the researcher how the limit is actually that of ordinary thinking, the point in which thinking ceases to be itself, in order to coincide with the dialectical expression. This limit is nevertheless normally encountered in the presence of the unknown, of the irrational, of the unexplainable, of the ghost of the unknowable, of the unthinkable, of the thing in itself, or of a "being" that we think without knowing we think it. The difference is that this limit—usually encountered externally or psychically—must now be encountered within the order of thought. It is the limit, however, from which we always flee philosophically or dialectically.

It is not the limit that is projected onto an outer problem, but one that is encountered within our very being, when we decide to observe the objective life of thinking within us. Therefore, we discover that no real thinking corresponds to the words by means of which, we, of the present-day culture, designate moral themes, or themes that do not belong to that physical–mathematical domain, for which the conversion of being into what can be counted easily realizes the coincidence of the concept with the object. Themes such as "unconscious," "soul," "freedom," "society," "sociality," "merchandise," "work," "capital," and so on, which we as human beings would be able to penetrate—if they were ideas for us that corresponded to the objects to which they refer—are not ideas, but only words with which we play discursively, since we lack the life of thinking that coincides with the reality of those objects.

Psychic contents operate as if they were ideas, since the articulation of consciousness within thinking does not occur, owing to the inner limit of thinking that—within the limit's domain—allows for the architecture of words, which feigns the range of investigation and of vision. Lacking the true ideal activity, we are possessed by that of which we speak, which is therefore not that of which we speak.

We can then understand that we are before the limit of thought by which today's culture is conditioned, and that what can be evoked as the tradition of an art of transcending the limit, is nevertheless assumed within the area ruled by it, because this limit, as it appears today, was unknown to the ancient world. The mental sphere of the "traditional" human being underwent a different limit, one that had a "noetic" value, indicating the direction toward the super-mental sphere, to which human beings could elevate themselves, since they essentially felt themselves grounded in it. They recognized, within the mental sphere—insofar as it was a sign of individual consciousness—a condition of caducity, there, where today, we live within the mental limit as if it were our true state: as if, within it, our task were to reduce everything.

That limit to thinking is also the limit to imagining, to meditating, to intuiting. Nevertheless, if we observe, it is thinking, namely the limit to thinking, which is itself thinking, but it is unaware of itself, as if it were in a state of unawareness or of sleep, with respect to its very self. It is as though consciousness arose only there, where it becomes estranged from itself. For this reason, it would make no sense to overcome the limit that we are meant to actualize outside the thinking by means of which it is formed, and within which it can be encountered.

It is not the projection of the limit into other areas of the soul that must be overcome but, rather, the limit itself where it is encountered and where it can only be overcome, for it is the point where the mediation of thinking opposes itself, by tending to operate as immediacy, so that pure immediate thinking cannot be cognized. For this reason, unfree human beings are advised by "teachers" lagging behind the times, such as Crowley, or Gurdjieff, or Krishnamurti, to free themselves in that "area" of the soul where the need to be free does not arise because the limit is not present, but only the effect of undergoing it—the mental area, the area of emotions, and the area of instincts, where it is easy but deceiving to believe that we encounter our own limit and overcome it.

The limit seems recognizable within the sphere of mental movements, of sentiments and of impulses, but it is elsewhere; it is, there, where we lack the power to look. For it is a question of looking at what a false ascetic is unable to behold—namely, thinking. Because one thing is the task of liberating thought from presumed prejudices, according to an unconscious mediation, which involves repeating an attitude from which prejudice arises again in other forms, another thing is to liberate thought by realizing the conscious coincidence between the mediation and immediate thinking. For this reason, the mediation is not the unimagined and perpetual resurgence of prejudice, but the act that overcomes the dependence on it.

Normally, when we have an idea, we do not notice the moment of its birth, for we are quickly attracted to its meaning. We do not notice perceiving something that is thought itself, which previously was not there, then, suddenly, arises out of the imperceptible. In reality, we perceive something that is noticed only by way of its "taking form"—something that, in itself, is original thinking, but normally not experienced as such, and nevertheless, thanks to a contemplative act, can be distinguished from the thinking that is already being thought, or from another type of thinking, just as one color can be distinguished from another. Here, the limit can be gathered, as well as the sense of what is needed for its resolution.

From a kind of sleep state with respect to its own movement, thinking can awaken by way of its immediate being, in which alone it can recognize itself. As experimenters, we can notice that the intuitive moment escapes us, for it is pre-dialectical. But it is pre-dialectical because it rises up from its real waking state. The experience that we can achieve is the recognition of the semi-dreamy state of ordinary thinking, with respect to a thinking that actualizes the real waking state. We can draw from an inner and living source, if we recognize the initial being of thinking within the intuitive moment.

The experience leads us to understand how, by and large, we are minimally awake and rarely attain moments of clear consciousness, because our normal waking state is based on a discursive process, not on the process of thinking. This sleep of consciousness is nourished on the dialectical plane by the cataleptic state of the latest philosophies with respect to the life of ideas, and, on the psychological plane, by the pseudo-masters who recommend "liberations," or resolutions of "complexes," conceivable by means of analytical 'mental picturing,' which can never be grasped as an instrument of investigation and which can, therefore, only be known within the products of mediation—no differently from what occurs in the mediumistic state, where each content is possible thanks to the loss of consciousness, for which, alone, that content can be of value.

If a science of thinking is to rise again for humanity, it cannot be the science of discourse. At each moment it must light up out of the idea from which it is born; it must not limit itself to identifying with its conceptual elaboration. If the philosophical or formal elaboration conditions the idea, the function of the human intellect fails. The work of the intellect rejects, in its development, lighting up with the initial *animadversio* (observation) of thinking, whose light, being a sign of the life of consciousness, is the prerequisite for the science of thinking.

When the intuitive moment is not the prerequisite of philosophical or logical research, this research can only move from a reflected idea, from a category, from a fact. Each of its developments becomes the use of the universal immediacy of thinking, of which it is not conscious, according to a requirement that is a representation, an empirical fact, a specific product of thinking, which does not have the foundation within itself, but elsewhere. Thus, with the weakening of thought, there can arise, alongside an even more organic dialectic, a corresponding logic, as a deductive technique regarding the object that it presupposes to itself—namely, the discursive norm of thinking.

There is an initial moment of any idea that we evoke or think, which does not manifest, except to simultaneously disappear, because it cannot be reduced to dialectical necessity. It is a moment of autonomy that does not allow its mediation to grasp it; it does not allow itself to be constrained, since it contains within itself, the reason for its immediacy, which only for a timeless instant coincides with the mediation, normally aimed outside its light. The art of logicians is to draw the science of thinking from thinking's oneness with itself, from which they draw. But we need to be able to conceive such a task, not to mistake the pure immediacy for the completed mediation—a mediation, from which thinking continually manifests as a lost light, the reflected form of the sphere of freedom into that of necessity.

We think because the autonomous moment of thinking is continually lost, insofar as it is reflected. Thinking is the sign of lost knowledge, but it simultaneously indicates the path of reintegration. In fact, we must experience the thinking process, in order to return to the moment in which it is yet to be. And for a long time, we must persist so as to move to that point by means of a will previously unknown. But the danger of the present day is that such a possibility becomes inconceivable due to thought itself that, philosophically, codifies the estrangement from its own source.

Precisely those who today seem to be investigative specialists of the thinking process and of knowledge impede what urgently needs to change within thinking. By losing the possibility to conform to its own source, thinking ceases to be the cause of a free 'acting,' even within the field of research that concerns its own activity.

A spiritual practice of thinking is urgently needed by the active core of human culture as the objective discipline that such a culture demands in order to take on its specific forms on the basis of truth. However, the most serious obstacle to such a spiritual practice, outside its possibility of being cultivated individually, in silence and in solitude, is the very logic of the culture known in present-day forms, as inspiration and as methodology.

Current thinking asserts itself, above all, with the force that opposes the recognition of its 'emerging' from the soul's original forces, and the possibility of investigating in that direction. Its logical–deductive form ignores the inner form, from which it nonetheless draws. The gravity of such a contradiction, and its meaning, are precisely the subject of the following chapters.

II

THE LOGICAL FORMS OF THE INNER DECLINE

1. THE BACKGROUND OF CULTURE

We do not need a special undertaking to realize how the fundamental impulse of today's culture is to be sought in human mental activity, rather than in its dialectical product. This product, in fact, appears as an expression of a thinking, to which readers or scholars should return, so that it can be resurrected as their thinking, according to an ancient practice of correct reading and meditation. They should be able to discover, within themselves, the inspirations that moved that thinking. They should be able to encounter, within themselves, the real conditions of the author's soul.

This encounter seems that it can no longer be a communication of real meanings, because the series of thought bearers has run out and they have been replaced by a legion of dialectical embroiderers, but also because readers capable of reading and reenlivening the contents of wisdom, both ancient or of a recent past, are evermore rare for the same reason.

No longer can the encounter be a contact with the values of the intellect, despite the activity of intellectual communities today bent on rendering the forms of culture "social," and despite the corresponding effort to popularize knowledge and to introduce its methodology in every field. In reality, such forms, regardless of the declaration of freedom by intellectual communities, can be recognized as being manipulated by politics and by publicity. Similarly, human beings that elaborate them and express them obey impulses other than those of a cultural spirit.

Nonetheless, the fact that politics and publicity have taken hold of culture and, therefore, of human life, does not mean that certain human beings, or individualities, direct politics or publicity and, consequently, culture. This would be desirable, but it does not occur. Instead, we can observe how some human beings who seem to direct political, financial, or political–economic or financial–advertising entities, can actually be carried onwards by the great mechanisms whose control levers they appear to hold. Actually, they are manipulated by what they seem to manipulate, as though impersonal powers functioned by means of those great leaderless entities, which are parties, anonymous societies, and advertising enterprises. 'Scientific–technical' dialectics functions as a justifier of positions that have thus been forming; it speaks through those who believe they possess them.

2. Discursive Faith

Those of us who believe that we reascend from cultural orientations to what determines them—namely to politics and to the propagandistic advertising spirit that is congenial to them—would not encounter the real causes there. We would need to reascend to ulterior causes, which explain the universality of the politically propagandistic phenomenon and its capacity to influence even certain scientific orientations.

The most practical investigation at a given moment would be the one that could turn to the psychological genesis or to the inner process of culture, which, in the end, could not but refer to a mental condition unique to present-day human beings.

From dialectics, which today— beyond the meaning that it had from Plato to the latest Western idealists—is an analytical structure valid globally by way of various expressions, and, at its level, accessible only to an analogous type of critical investigation, which is inevitably connected to the discursive form of its own hypothesis as a *principium negationis*, we would have to reascend to the typical mental act that renders it possible. This is the primary requirement of an investigation that does not risk being part of the phenomenon that it intends to identify.

To believe that we can control dialectics by way of more dialectics is the illusion of whoever is otherwise bound by the same error of the dialectics that one presumes to control. On the other hand, unless we master our own thinking, it is difficult to perceive a logical error without first repeating it within ourselves and, therefore, without being obliged to retrace certain involutions of thought, so as to be able to recognize them as such—which is to say, without the risk of being caught up in the error before managing to perceive it.

Nor does the error of thinking necessarily appear as a logical error; therefore, to notice it as an error is the movement of thinking independent of the logical construct, namely a movement, in itself, more important than the possibility of refuting the error accepted as truth because it is in standard logical form. Those who are won over by such a logical form are naturally led into error. It is not logic that persuades them, even if they believe that it does and they make use of this logic to support their profession of faith—but not their thinking, which is not there.

It is possible to intuit what truly operates behind present-day dialecticism, if we do not fall into the empirical–logical faith of being able to be told everything through the construction of the discourse—a faith that not only belongs to logisticians, but to all those individuals today who are polished with regard to the discursive construct. It just so happens that this construct normally exists, but it is only comprised of words, not of ideas. It is therefore a matter of

The Logical Forms of the Inner Decline

understanding what has substituted thinking, for which we can now point to present-day dialectics as the formalism, which is evermore knowing, precisely because it is devoid of thinking.

It is an arduous undertaking to retrace the thinking of someone who has well fashioned a discussion that is valid exclusively in the correlations of words, because it leads the thinking that retraces it, outside its own movement, within the weft of the correlations themselves—from which it is unlikely to escape, even if it is able to "proceed" indefinitely by means of them.

Either the thinking that retraces them is autonomous and, therefore, perceives the ensnaring, but must carry out a decisively intuitive act in order to grasp what truly moves behind a well-constructed discourse, or else thinking lacks autonomy and is thus grasped by the relational–associative mechanism, which compels it to its own movement. In this second case, thinking actually loses the possibility of perceiving the end of its own autonomy.

In reality, the creators of effective discourse—as a logical-abstract weaving—on condition of excluding the reader's autonomy of thought (which alone could identify its internal 'mythic nature') are moved by an impulse that is not their thinking, but an impersonal entity, the true creator of discourse. It appears that such an impulse knows how not to arouse thinking, but to communicate only itself through the progression of words with the stamp of logic, which is the semblance of thinking—a procedure which, in order to develop, must inevitably subject thought to itself, by expelling consciousness from it.

Thus, by means of a formally illegitimate dialecticism, we, as human beings, are trained to receive solicitations aimed at the automatism of our thinking, rather than at our real thinking. Real thinking becomes evermore laborious, while the progressive loquacity, founded on discursive mechanisms, facilitates the thinking whose own inertia is not important to understand but, rather, to codify.

We should not be deceived by the fact that such thought can follow the paths of philosophy or of science, because, as it will be shown, it is not thought capable of being aware within its own movement, but only within what occurs as the imitation of the movement—namely, the relation of words—binding to such a relation in a somnambulistic state as if to a certainty of consciousness, which, with time, is strengthened until becoming a cultural impulse.

3. THE PSYCHIC CONTENT

To an observer, it is inescapable how, in today's culture, thinking is losing the possibility to bear its own immediacy within itself, because, even though it nevertheless moves on its own by drawing upon its own inner force, in the reflective process it is drawn forward by the correlation of words, in whose logical plausibility it discovers paths already traced, which arouse within us an automatism that excludes its initiative; on the contrary, it demands its passivity.

Such passivity is not obvious; rather, it manifests in forms of activity, which can make it look like a dynamic that does truly not exist. Discursive automatism reaches much greater efficiency, the more it is estranged from thinking: the *dynamis* of thinking is removed from consciousness and used by something that is not the conscious principle capable of manifesting itself in autonomous thinking.

In fact, it is impossible to identify such alienation, except by setting the autonomy (originally proper to thinking) against it, so that such thinking can distinguish its conscious state from what is automatic–dialectical. But the subject that does not know the reflected aspect of thought as an extrinsic and negative being of original thinking, or autonomous thinking, cannot perceive the gradual diminution of thinking consciousness in the dialectical process, nor the corresponding loss of a true relation with the object and of the capacity to recognize the relationships between objects, or concepts.

If we examine which effective content in the autonomous–dialectical process takes the place of the ideational original movement—which alone could intuit the correlations between one reality and another—we will be able to ascertain that what is discovered is not a content of consciousness, but a psychic content, an obscure sentiment: a sentiment not aroused by ideas but, rather, by corporeal conditions.

4. FREUD AND JUNG

We believe we think things and situations and assume them logically. Actually, save certain rare instances of the exercise of pure rationality, we normally think what our "feeling" and our desire project onto them, without any possibility of noticing it. Discursive automatism is ready to pull thinking forward along a marked path, which is effectively trodden by instinct and by sentiment, followed by thought that has become inert. We believe that we are cold rationalists, but actually we are childishly instinctive. It is the ordinary psychological condition, of whose linear and practical knowledge humanity has been deprived by the fact that psychoanalysis has easily taken possession of the matter. The possibility for an objective and, let us say, pragmatic formulation of the problem to help us has thus been lost.

Psychoanalysis and analytical psychology have fixed such a problem in its state of insolubility, necessary to the development of their dialectics, complicating it by means of interpretations devoid of perception about the object that they presume to investigate, insofar as they stop at an object's series of images, unaware of producing it themselves by means of their reflective activity, as something that has a foundation elsewhere, not within itself. Therefore, by pointing to the "unconscious," they unconsciously point to the foundation that possesses them, without being able to identify its real nature.

And they elaborate this possession by way of a problematic, which—from the regular dialectical development to the formulation of therapeutic methods—expresses it with organic progression, conferring to it features of an authentic "universal," from whose authority it is felt they will no longer be able to escape.

The example of a theme developed and described as if it were "universal," without the guarantee of a fundamental experience (of noetic and gnoseological order) of what must be understood by 'universal,' reveals the sense of the pseudo-foundation of thinking, which is mathematically equivalent to the possession of thinking—not so much on behalf of a personal instinct as on behalf of an impersonal entity. Such an entity bears the characteristic demonic features whose movement, for example, the psychoanalyst (permeated by the presence of the "unconscious") and the psychoanalyzed experience without being able to grasp its identity and thus its absolute unrelatedness to the life of consciousness.

If the theme were simply logical and analytical, the possession would be less dangerous than the one possible by means of a psycho–analytical theme, whose dialectical expression does not refer to a formal element and an equally formal procedure, like the logical–analytical theme but, rather, to the content itself that operates as a premise, or prime axiom—namely, the unconscious.

The lack of foundation in the reflective psychoanalytical process and in its application is hidden by a specific language and by the dialectical apparatus that, without mediation, passes away into the therapeutic method, where deceit is not perpetrated through deliberate intention, but through an insufficient awareness of the relationship between thought and the presumed psychic object. The lack of experience with regard to such an object is compensated by the mechanism of dialectical therapy and by the fact that the certainty of such a mechanism arouses the immediacy of a temporary faith in the patient, incapable of drawing faith from another source.

The Logical Forms of the Inner Decline

The psychoanalysis of Freud and of Jung, which believes that it discovers the "unconscious," or at least interprets it and, in some way, operates on it, is itself the expression of the unconscious, but not of what it doctrinally describes and mythicizes; rather, it is the expression of what possesses its expositors, since they, by not mastering thought, allow something to work on them that is not thought, but feeling: the obscure intuition that immediately passes over into the determination of thought.

Dialectics is thought manipulated by subconscious feeling. Therefore, like thought, it loses the ideal penetrative power, which it replaces with an associative and pseudo-intuitive dynamic that belongs to feeling. Such a situation becomes efficaciously masked by scientific codification and by an ever-ready terminological coinage.

This subconscious feeling, which has been able to become the science of the psyche, observed by a conscious subject, cannot be confused with the source of pure intellectual intuitions, nor with true feeling. Rather, it is recognized as the psychic resounding of the nervous system and, in particular, of the neuro-vegetative system. The slightest alterations of the nervous system, as well as the irregular neuro-vegetative relationship with the metabolic system, are reflected in a gradation of ailments that range from light forms of neurosis to typical paranoiac and psychotic forms.

Psychology, having renounced its noetic–speculative foundations, has lost, amongst other things, the possibility of positively being an integrator or collaborator of psychiatry. It has come to psychoanalytically mythicize phenomena that can be reduced to corporeal facts, because of its incapacity to distinguish the "unconscious," as the psyche's zone of dependence on neuro-sensorial inherences, from the real life of the psyche and of its relationships with the autonomous forces of consciousness.

5. Misunderstanding the Unconscious

It seems that the founders and continuators of psychoanalysis move from the idea of the unconscious, but actually, they move from *feeling*, or better yet, from the dark feeling of the unconscious, which cannot be intuition or idea, because intuition or idea is always the inner element of a perception, or of a series of perceptions, namely the inner element independent of the perception itself, which, as we shall see, can have as a content, either a physical object or an inner object (an impulse, a feeling, a thought).

The perception of psychoanalysts cannot be anything other—with regard to a neurotic—than their clinical description, or their discourses, their confessions; with regard to themselves, it cannot be other than the sensation of their own bodies, or of their own psychic worlds. None of these perceptions can legitimize the *idea* of the unconscious with its known developments; if anything they can legitimize the *hypothesis* of the unconscious. In order to verify this hypothesis, however, one would need to experience forces of consciousness, an experience founded on the awareness of the life of ideas and the possibility of operating by means of this awareness.

If we observe, psychoanalytic investigation jumps from the series of clinical or discursive perceptions to a series of corresponding representations, treating them no more and no less than as real perceptions themselves and, consequently, as scientific concrete realities. From this arises its specific dialectic, which does not escape the limit of the initial representations, with any of its deductive formularies, because such formularies are developed from expressive and, therefore, unreal enunciations of those representations. In order to be real, they must correspond to the psyche's objective experiences, according to noetic laws, which psychoanalysis pretends to disregard, even if it seemingly refers to them. Jung, in particular, is able to give the impression of being familiar with the spiritual, recognizable to an expert eye as a mythical fact, with an aesthetic value at most, but dangerous for the relation of which it becomes the persuasive vehicle.

Meanwhile, a simply logical examination reveals, as being obvious, that this author lacks a theoretical and methodological foundation, let alone a correct intuition, for an understanding of the suprasensory element that structures the psyche.

On the other hand, the term "unconscious" designates a concept that wants to express an act of the consciousness that embraces something, which, because of its nature, tends to escape it. Ultimately, however, it does not escape it, because, in order to have it as an object, this consciousness must recognize it as a *minus quam* (less than) with respect to itself. Conversely, it is an impossible concept, because it implies that something, of which we are not conscious, can be cognized.

Each representation of the unconscious is an ideal activity that comes to envision a psychic process, as an ungraspable reduction or a continuation of the life of consciousness, of which it, as an ideal activity, is the only legitimate proof. Any investigation along these lines is nothing but the movement of the idea that, among other things, manages to conceive the "unconscious." But it can do this, inasmuch as it is the only activity of consciousness capable of conceiving something beyond itself, and consequently, of arriving at themes or enunciations which cannot eliminate it without thereby eliminating themselves.

The concept of "unconscious," estranged from such consistency, becomes misleading, because it is used to contradict its psychological meaning. That is to say, it is related to an object that seems to exist by itself, to have its own life, outside the idea from which it has solely arisen. In that way, what operates within the psyche is a content endowed with its own phenomenology, stimulated by a dialectic that has nothing to do with it, thereby revealing in this, its most unsettling aspect, and whose development nevertheless continues to be the series of projections of the unconscious's original idea, without having the possibility to recognize its effective genesis. For this reason, the same psychoanalytical dialectic ends up manifesting as an autonomous fact, which evidently codifies its lack of knowledge regarding the relationship between consciousness and psyche and, therefore, the very lack, within itself, of its own original relation.

The presumption of psychoanalysis to cure a psychic illness is not so alarming as that of establishing itself as a science of the psyche, since it itself, possesses all the characteristics of a psychic phenomenon. Its unconscious autonomy with respect to the original idea, and its dialectical process consequently automatic, place it at the level of natural facts. Once their objective alterity is acquired, they cannot but be part of the order of a pragmatic and even abstract necessity. Therefore, they cannot but oppose thought, as a negation of the soul's life or of the only reality that justifies an investigation like psychoanalysis and its manifesting as scientific semblance.

A consequence of the action practiced by Freud and by Jung upon today's culture, has been the decisive contribution toward the elimination of the "sacred," through the sacralization of the unconscious. Jung, who turned directly toward the theme, believing to have the "content" within it, distinguished himself in this. The consequences of such an action have harmoniously combined with those of scientism and of technological–analytical automatism, almost as forms of an identical mental impulse.

When human beings, representative of science, make use of their investigation to demolish the noetic element (to which alone the investigation owes its possibility of movement and its mastery) and they accomplish this by presuming to elevate themselves to the level of observing the facts of consciousness, there is no reason to be stupefied that average human beings—now conditioned (in everything) by what is prescribed to them by science—no longer consider the hierarchy of inner faculties and the value of ethics, and are consequently led to reject the "sacred," by harboring an obscure revolt from below toward all that is elevated, noble, and dignified.

The Logical Forms of the Inner Decline

It has now been a century; the concept of the "unconscious" has appeared in Western philosophy through three thinkers—Schopenhauer, Carus, and Von Hartmann. It is not wrong to see in these speculative assumptions of the unconscious, the filiation of the *caput mortuum* left out of Kantian philosophy, with the "thing in itself," inaccessible to human (and nevertheless real) consciousness—conceived solely by means of thought and also seen as impenetrable by thought. The *will* of Schopenhauer, the *unconscious* of Carl Gustav Jung and of Eduard von Hartmann are, in fact, mental presuppositions—namely acts of speculative consciousness that, at a given moment, limits itself and, beyond the limit, catches a glimpse of a "psychic" or "extra-rational" world. But, of this world, it can only see that of which it can be conscious, for which the concept of the unconscious is continually eliminated by speculative consciousness, to the degree in which, within the determination, it must cease to be unconscious of it. Thus, it is actually never there and, yet, it is continually presupposed, by means of a thought, which, in order to exist, must be conscious thought. It is a subject that would lead to grim consequences regarding these individuals responsible for human knowledge, who have misled the investigation of consciousness, by projecting outside of such consciousness, what they were incapable of grasping within themselves, even if they presumed to carry out such an investigation.

In effect, because of a weakened philosophical, or gnoseological consciousness, within the theme of the unconscious, naively and confusingly considered, dogmatism has been able to resurface and the carcass of ancient metaphysics (not metaphysics) has again been able to come to life. From the gnoseological powerlessness of Western speculation, the possibility arose for psychotherapy and psychology to exclusively take possession of the theme of the unconscious and for Sigmund Freud, at a given moment, to overturn the relationship. No longer could philosophy illuminate, from above, the investigation of the unconscious for psychology but, rather, psychology authoritatively took the reins of the research and drew its conclusions not only for itself, but also for philosophy, and even for religion. Then came Jung who extended this prompting authority of their ultimate meanings, to mysticisms, to traditions, and to metaphysics. The problem of the soul, forever shut off and alien to philosophical dialecticism, became the field of research of a dialecticism still less equipped, but furnished with scientific language and metaphysical presumption, in spite of its metaphysical incapacity and its inability to understand that we must enter the soul with the soul's essential force and not with psychoanalytical glossolalia. The decisive blows to the possibility of the culture of machines being connected with the forces of the world's higher guidance were thus fatally inflicted.

6. Dialectics and Mind Possession

The emotion that governs thought—to the extent that thought loses its original autonomy in identifying with the discursive process—and therefore utilizes thought by taking on its formal guise, while excluding its ideational movement, in order to prevail as it is unable to in the immediate emotional and psychic manifestation of itself (consequently managing to legitimize the instinctive life in the vehicle of expressive regularity) is *dialectics*. Dialectics is a term that by now—as we have already mentioned—due to logical reasons can no longer be used in the way that it once was from the time of Plato and the expounders of the Socratic logos, all the way to the European idealists, whose last (representatives) were still capable of intuiting, within thought, a movement that, in a germinal way, bears within it every logical form. Today, dialectics is the rhetoric of the realist, scientist or politician, but also of the psychologist, of the mystic, of the spiritualist—namely, the empty shell of rationality.

The present-day situation of dialecticism is formally the belief that it expresses something that is thought (itself) and, therefore, an objective assumption of a theme, while actually it has become the need of the mental sphere to express its own possession on behalf of an extraneous process, which is not an error in itself, just as a physical ailment is not an error; yet it operates in the world as an error, manifesting as a projection of thought: appearing as the form of a content of thought which truly does not exist. The dilemma is to discover which effective content operates.

When, for example, the connoisseurs of moral or psychological sciences affirm the possibility of attaining elevated experiences of consciousness by means of a narcotic, or a "hallucinogen," adequately divided into doses and used, they do not really express the thinking independent of such an experience but, rather, the thinking aroused by it, for they lack an inner activity capable of considering the substance's effect on the cerebral centers, since they place themselves outside these centers. But they unknowingly allow the physiological processes aroused by such a substance—as the producers of their very judgment—to act. Experimenters endowed with independence with respect to cerebral processes, who intend to experiment the effects of mescaline, or of psilocybin, or of lysergic acid, upon themselves—certainly not in order to attain a lucidity of which they should have no need—would perceive them as processes that rise up from the physiological plane against their faculties of consciousness, through an inversion of the relationship between mind and corporeity. They would thus have to fight vigorously against them. They would find themselves before processes that tend to disable the organ of thinking.

It would be naïve to argue that such a struggle would become creative for the spirit, insofar as it would stimulate a "furthermore" of its organizing power. For those who experiment responsibly in this field, things are exactly the opposite.

In order to express itself, the lucid inner activity, independent of physical corporeity, demands the cooperation of the cerebral organ at the functional physiological level, equivalent to a state of complete non-involvement with the thinking act, because only in absolute "immobility" can the brain realize its instrumentality with respect to such an act. In fact, each new ideal activity normally encounters resistance in the physical structure of the encephalon. Such resistance can even be projected in ideological reasons. Its overcoming cannot come from the possibility of the thinking person acting directly on his or her own cerebral organ, but from the fact that the autonomous activity of thinking, insisting on its own movement—regardless of the organ's opposition—ends up provoking structural modifications such that this organ ceases to oppose itself.

In effect, the instrumentality of the organ lies not in conditioning thought but, rather, in conforming to its activity. Therefore, mental habits, which instead are forms of conditioned thought, wind up coinciding with the processes of the brain, for which the brain acquires the power of re-proposing them to thought, and of imposing them to the point of automatism. In some cases, like those that we shall examine, this automatism will find its logic and its methodological expression, until becoming the impulse of culture.

The fact that the brain denies or rejects a new movement of thinking can be explained by way of the insufficient elaboration of the instrument on behalf of thinking, which is to say, by way of the temporary incapacity of thinking to realize its own nature with respect to the instrument. In that case, the physical person, race, health, temperament, and the physiological state condition thinking. The life of thinking is minimal. Precisely in such conditions there can take root, within the individual, the monistic–technological mentality, or even dialectical materialism, namely a complete system that demands to be learned and believed, like a faith, and not thought, nor grasped by a thinking capable of consciously retracing its own movement and, therefore, capable of noticing the original error of the system into which it has entered, through thinking. The error should be thought of as an error and not simply thought. *Yet, the error is original, whereas its deductions are exact* and the feeble thinker loves to live in deductions, in the *'already-thought,'* rather than in *thinking*.

When, however, the "physical condition" controls a thought that is incapable of logically–dialectically projecting its own possession, this possession tends to express itself directly in neuropsychic states that can be clinically identified. One thus has neurosis with its ordinary variants.

In essence, the intellectuals of today—pragmatists or scientists or materialists—are neurotics who seek to escape their anxiety through an act of faith: in myth or dialectical–technological dogma. What they truly lack is thinking, namely the substance of dialectics—that of which they instead believe they are themselves the special bearers or possessors. They are each instead a "consequence" or a person possessed, because of an inadequacy of thought.

In that sense, those who today appear to be brave renovators or revolutionaries are actually fearsome conservatives, insofar as they move from cerebralism, or from what constitutionally opposes each new thought, by representing the human being's past, the limit of nature that has become determinative.

7. Solicitations of the Cerebral Organ

In a balanced life of the psyche, cerebral processes would not be able to influence the thinking activity and much less project themselves into rational structures, which inevitably imitate the rational process. The opposite should instead occur, namely that a pure conceptual activity can experientially give thinking the awareness of being so much more lucid, the more independent it is of the cerebral instrument. Thus, a healthy thinking activity manages not only to make use of the organ's efficiency, but also to train it and to transform it, so that it responds always better to the need of expressing, in rational and linguistic terms, contents of an intuitive value. Such a possibility, to which the very logic of the thinking process should lead, is compromised by the automatistic deviation of the thinking activity and by the related suggestions of special conquests of consciousness thanks to external, or chemical–physical, solicitations of the cerebral organ.

Because of such solicitations, the cerebral organ loses its capacity of instrumentality with respect to thinking. It becomes relegated to a biological condition that precedes the one relative to its 'functioning' as an organ of conscious thought. It falls short of the structure's purpose toward which it has evolved and, by binding thought to itself, it uses it as a means by which to project its excitations. These are equal, therefore, to a regression of the psyche toward "primitive," or "infantile," and, gradually paranoid states.

Hallucinations are the obtuse language of such a regression, namely the phenomenology opposite that of the lucid experience of consciousness, which demands autonomy from cerebralism and the intensification of its waking state. Hallucinations, in either case, are the product of abnormal sensory stimuli. They are made up of the sensory–imaginative matter that the psyche continually expels as (something) unusable for its own conscious experience.

It is a sediment that one is wise to let lay at the bottom, because only by remaining in its true place, can it be used by consciousness, thanks to its inner forces, independent of the cerebral instrument. Specific physiological and biochemical stimuli can excite the contents of such sediment to the point of giving them autonomous life. In such a case, it is a situation that the subject has difficulty controlling and that can be objectively ambiguous on behalf of the investigator that lacks a true experience of the psyche.

The inferior imaginative–sensorial material, pathologically stimulated, projects itself in forms that have no objective value, since they are not perceptions that occur by way of the conscious principle. They are, in fact, possible only in relation to a diminution of consciousness, or to an onset of mental alienation.

The case of those who claim they reach elevated states of consciousness by such a path must be even more of a concern, because it is not a disordered imaginative material that projects itself before the hallucinated but, rather, a logical–speculative or logical–psychic world, relative to their everyday cultural–professional interests. In that case, they acquire lucid pseudo-intuitions and pseudo-visions as strength of evidence, which are mistaken for objective intuitions and visions, scientifically necessary. One is on the path of those cultured schizophrenics, philosophers, and mathematicians, which psychopathological case studies sometimes describe as particularly acute and coherent in their rational expressions.

It is useful to consider which deviations culture can undergo if some of them, endowed with scientific prestige and academic authority, succeed in spreading into the world—in legitimate systematic form—the results of their investigations carried out as a result of the breakdown of the psyche's relation with cerebralism.

8. THE ISSUE OF "HALLUCINOGENS"

The opinion according to which the psycho-pharmaceutical, or the psychedelic, or even the "hallucinogen," not only corresponds to the treatment of specific mental or psychotic events, but is also a path of the healthy individual or of the scientist toward profound psychic experiences or toward the realization of higher states of consciousness—once attained through inner disciplines—can be seen as a morbid consequence of this substance's activity within the organism of the person who asserts it.

The fact that scientific celebrities, doctrines, conventions, and conferences endorse such an opinion means little. It is not the official nature of a thesis that can decree its accuracy. The scholar, the scientist, the normal human being do not need psycho-pharmaceuticals to penetrate the realm of the psyche. They do not need substances that they acknowledge can be utilized in cases of mental imbalance.

Therapy by means of psycho-pharmaceuticals is always a mechanical action upon the nervous system, which should restore it from its abnormal state to its normal instrumentality. Meanwhile, in the case of an analogous action upon a healthy nervous system, any psychic result, apparently intuitive and effectively hallucinogenic, is not an inner experience—which can be carried out by the thinker and the mystic—but, rather, a pathological condition, whose morbidity and irregularity should not escape the psychologist.

Whereas the morbidity of some other toxic substance can even be perceived on one's person by the experimenter, the morbidity of a psychedelic easily escapes the self-experimenter, since, within the process aroused, the very consciousness that should monitor it becomes engaged. Yet, if consciousness manages to monitor this process, it cannot but notice within it an extraneous power that tends to overwhelm it.

The present danger is that scholars, already psychically involved, theoretically and scientifically justify a current condition that, in reality, they do not know how to see in its objectivity, because they have identified with it. An increase of inner activity cannot arise from a process of physical nature, except in case of an onset of pain, which would, however, be pointless to ask a drug addict about, when life itself takes care of procuring it every day. In the case of creative pain, or of a physical illness, against which one successfully struggles, the increased inner activity, always results from the capacity to overcome the physical limit in carrying out the life of the soul.

In the case of ingesting a psychopharmacological drug, the situation is the inverse. The physical process grasps the psychic dynamisms and projects itself in extra-normal images or sensations. There is no tension of thinking, no discipline, no moral effort. There is only the ingestion of the substance—a mechanical act. And then one waits comfortably on a chair for the spiritual capacity to awaken, without the spirit's initiative. One waits for something to happen that functions spiritually, in place of the spirit.

It could not be argued that the value of a substance's use depends on *who* uses it. The error does not change, because it consists in the principle whereby an inner experience is believed to arise from a process of the physical organism. From such a process, there can mechanically arise a psychic experience whose inner 'projecting' becomes a spiritual value, not because it is, but because the weakened consciousness of the experimenter assumes it as such. This weakened consciousness, which bears the illusory impression of a transcendence that invests it, is exactly what impedes the discrimination between truth and error.

The situation does not change even when the experimenter presumes to successfully utilize, by means of the ready forces of consciousness, what manifests in others as psychic trauma. The sophism is evident, because if these ready forces of consciousness are possible, they must be sought at the source from which they come, so that they can offer their own original content. They cannot be stimulated by mechanical solicitations unless they renounce their own self-solicitation and are grasped by something other than themselves—which is self-alienation, not a suprasensory experience.

This is not to say that psychiatrists or psychologists have to renounce experimenting with the effects of a narcotic or a hallucinogen on themselves if they are in the midst of such an investigation and believe self-experience is necessary. As we have mentioned, experimenters would find themselves before destructive processes that, within the nervous system, tend to annihilate their psychophysical equilibrium, namely destructive processes against which they should wage a dramatic fight. If they did not encounter such destructive effects within themselves, following the use of a psychedelic, but drew lucidity, wellbeing, or euphoria from it, it would be a sad sign for them—they truly ought to pass from the rank of a doctor to that of a patient. But it is difficult for this very recognition to occur. Today, the danger is that the sick person becomes the scientific diffuser of his or her own illness.

All experimenters are free to carry out experiments on themselves that they believe to be necessary. But we think that—particularly in the case of hallucinogenic substances—scholars should know what they are truly doing and keep intact an area of autonomous thinking, not seized by the phenomenon involved, in order not to mistake what they believe to be pathological in sick individuals for something good.

III

Dialectical and Analytical Precariousness

1. Discursive Neurosis

The need to train thinking according to the experience of its direct emergence in consciousness, so that its own generative force can manifest as a thinking reality, can be understood above all in relation to the mental state of the present-day human being.

Such a force, at a given moment of incommunicability, already underway, between culture and culture, between language and language, between logic and logic, between one current and another, between one human being and another, should end up being, in individual consciousness, the only organ that distinguishes truth from error. It should consequently become operative within the field of science and of the correlating methodologies, because it begins to operate within the soul of the researcher, for reasons that will become clarified in the following pages.

As a matter of fact, it will be shown that thinking, if its original process is experienced according to rules implicit to its immediate movement within consciousness, functions as an objective "sense" of truth, given that, in both the ideation and in the formulation of judgment, it can give the mental sphere a way to remain independent of influences that are unrelated to it. It has to do with influences that, though extraneous to the mental content, can assume a mental form: naturally without the modern-day intellectual, engaged in the expression of such form, becoming aware of it.

The latest psychologies believe they have identified the psyche's subtle forms within the human being, by directing the investigation toward the "unconscious," or toward an entity that (as we have seen) occurs to them as a simple hypothesis, and by connecting the possibility of the psyche's equilibrium to an agreement or to a disagreement with it. They believe they have identified our present-day pathological paths and, consequently, the paths of equilibrium in relation to the "unconscious": a ghost *depictus* (depicted) and, yet, presented as a real entity, lacking effective gnoseological and experimental proof.

Therefore, what has been possible is the curious fact that, by means of the prevailing psychoanalytical orientation, the attention of researchers has been diverted from a problem worthy of realistic attention and investigation, namely the one we presented in the preceding chapter and that can thus be briefly summarized. Given the premise that inner imbalance (psychic illness) can take mental paths, it is quite possible for it to be expressed in a form that is discursively legitimate. In other words, it is possible for mental illness, easily identifiable in its hysteric–neurotic and paranoid expressions, to manifest, instead, as a valid content if it has dialectical–logical regularity.

If such a problem exists, it is today undoubtedly the most severe, because it regards the possibility that mental illness, in dialectical–logical form, not only does not appear as such, but operates as an impulse of culture, a directive of life, philosophy, social science, psychological investigation: not as the consciousness of evil but, rather, as a consciousness so ruled by evil, that it functions as its organ of expression. Nor is it recognizable as such, insofar as it assumes the conceptual form normally expressive of intellectual contents.

We must not give up looking in an unbiased way at the real origin of certain monoideisms that govern present-day culture, nor of verifying if some of its "universal" forms really correspond to our human tendency toward the universal, or are not instead its impediment—though not the impediment in itself but, rather, what becomes a mental stance, a logical justification of itself, which takes on a scientific guise.

It is time for us to ask ourselves at what point is dialectics, as a discursive analytic, the expression of a mental state that corresponds to the normal relation between the brain and thinking, and when does it, instead, take on a specific logical and systematic form up to unexpected deductive–inductive acmes, precisely because it is the creation of a malfunctioning or sick brain.

In such a case, the analytic–discursive form manages to hide the error of thinking, precisely insofar as the error (in the formal process itself) manages to have its own codification as an expression. In fact, it does not occur to anyone to suspect a universally acclaimed social innovator, or a famous politician, or the initiator of a new type of psychology, or a commendable educator, or an economic minister, of being mentally ill, if in their works or in their discourses they demonstrate dialectical coherence and analytic penetration, since mental imbalance cannot be reflected in their specific elaboration. Meanwhile, such imbalance can hide within the internal substance of what they affirm, or of what effectively operates with the power of a psychic content, by taking on a logical regularity. It is an error that cannot be traced within the discourse, because, as an error, it is pre-discursive, or mental. However, it can be gathered in practical disasters, where it ends up manifesting. It is an error, which, in the correspondence of practical disaster to the theoretical announcement, could only be identified by a thinking that has not fallen into the dialectical automatism where present-day intellectualism has its congenial expression.

2. The "Functional Alteration"

The objective alteration of the cerebral system is what can be clinically identified in the physical organ itself, as well as in its neuropsychic manifestations. The functional alteration does not appear clinically. It cannot be grasped by psychiatric investigation, if it does not give rise to phenomena considered in the description of psychopathology.

Without presuming to return to the causes of such a type of alteration, which refer equally to the brain and to thinking, as well as to their reciprocal influence, it is enough for us now to observe that, because it is affected by such a type of alteration, the brain cannot but fail in its function as the instrument of thinking. Consequently, if thinking bears within itself a special discursive tendency, a typical inversion of relationship can occur: the brain uses rational thinking as an instrument to express its own state of affairs. Naturally, it has nothing to do with thinking as a conscious mediation; rather, it has to do with its reflected state, which alone can lend itself to giving the alteration the outward appearance of formal regularity, from which the real thinking mediation is excluded. Pathological mediation is possible in mental–dialectical form for the fact that the reflected expression, removed without residues from thinking, is expressed as though it were thinking: it operates with the authority of thinking. However, neither individuals affected by the alteration, nor those who allow themselves to be persuaded by its rational form, notice it.

The neuropsychic manifestation does not follow the emotional–instinctive path but, rather, the dialectical one. The alteration manifests in conformity with an intellectual–logical automatism, which gives rise to forms that are not recognizable as psychopathic manifestations. For the distinction regarding such a phenomenology can only be made by a thinking that is valid as a "clinical eye," namely a thinking that, even if it exists, can do very little at the level of a general analytical–dialectical expression, if, as the confusion between the essential and the nonessential, there now reigns that nocturnal shadow in which "all the cows are black."[1]

On the discursive plane, the distinction between the making of an altered mental state and that of a healthy mental state becomes ever-less possible, because the phenomenon of dialecticism of the present-day culture can itself be recognized as a product of the altered mental state.

In the following pages, we will see how mental automatism, detectable in the logical–discursive activities of a monoideistic kind, is most often to be assumed as a sign of mental disorder. It does not have to do with a monistic or universalistic vision but, rather, with reducing each and every topic to a single theme, according to a dialectical obsessiveness that is explained by the physiological persistence of the specific cerebral fact.

It is about becoming aware of how certain systems are born not on the basis of thinking, but on the basis of a physiological 'mental-ism,' and how it is inevitable, on the part of those who, being affected by it, simultaneously have a particular logical–dialectical tendency, to interpret culture, the human being, the world, according to a monochord or an obsessive thematic, in a materialistic–dialectical key, or even one that is psychoanalytical, or semantic or technological, and so on. Now, for more than half a century, humanity presumably proceeds according to the influences of a culture that, in large part, is the product of a mental disorder. Such a culture can make itself acceptable not only to the extent that it demands rationalistic automatism and formalistically anticipates the initiative of thought, but also because of its partial truths. True error is never obvious, since it would be quickly discovered, but it has that amount of truth that it needs to pass off as truth.

3. ABDICATION OF PHILOSOPHY

With the decline of speculative philosophy and the advent of analytical philosophy, what has developed dialectically, alongside the regermination of formal logic and of linguistic researches, is, in effect, an exclusively discursive type of general dialectic, because it lacks the substantial thinking which, from Plato to Gentile, had justified it.

It is a situation that becomes increasingly less comprehensible, especially to the experts of philosophy, and by means of them. And it is justifiable, if the same authors of systems that have acquired philosophical authority in today's world, all invariably reveal that they have lost the experience of the concept. In other words, their ideal production lacks the activity of the idea, the perception of the idea, and, therefore, the possibility of considering the being of an idea as real. And the contradiction is precisely that an idea's potential always animates the inner state from which such a pseudo-philosophy arises.

It is a philosophizing that, under a logical–dialectical guise, reveals (alongside the loss of the ideal process by means of which it continues to ideate) such naivety that it seems as if the centuries-old experience of philosophy has vanished into nothingness for such philosophers. We need only look at how the question of "being," the concept of existing, the subject of space of time, of nature and of history, and the question of logic are re-proposed, not with a capacity to begin again drawing from the real principles of knowing, but to begin again with the word having already become discourse and, therefore, with the discourse pregnant with long-standing philosophic knowledge and, thus, refined to the point of virtuosity, and, nevertheless, with an ideal content that, defoliated of dialectics, proves to be inconsistent.

It must be said that pointing out the experience of the concept and the validity of the world of ideas is not meant to lay claim to any speculative or idealistic position; rather, it is to refer us to *an experience of ideas*, in its concreteness, separable from any philosophical assumption, or better yet, valid precisely to the extent that it is not identified with any philosophy. It is the experience into which the centuries-old course of philosophy should have flowed, but which it has neglected. In what circulates today as philosophy, we can recognize the series of products of such an absence.

In reality, those individuals least qualified have taken possession of philosophy, namely those who barely manage to syllabize thought, but possess a ready-made philosophical narrative, precisely because they do not believe in the reality of ideas, or they do not believe in what they do. For this reason, they can, without ideal control, devote themselves to dialectical–logical reasoning, by adhering only to formal consequentiality, which, like ideas, assumes a series of abstractions, or the discursive void.

Today, this discursive void constitutes a prevailing world of intelligence, with internal coherences of articulations, consisting of a reflectivity identical to itself and sufficient unto itself, which can deal with all the problems of humanity without a true relation to the content, given that one is not present in such a relation—since the "I" cannot live in reflected thought.

4. Measure of Imbalance: The Alienation of the Concept

If one can establish that the present-day thinking of philosophy, of science, of ordinary culture, is a thinking in whose reflected expression the original intuitive element is excluded (an element that, alone, justifies 'being considered' thought), one is right to believe that each logical and dialectical form, at the level in which it becomes known according to its formal process, lends itself to taking on a content that is not its own, namely a content that is not ideal but, rather, psychic.

Devoid of its own inspirational element—which is the a-dialectical content of thinking, present, until recently, in a form rarely conscious, in a few idealistic philosophies and in the initial intuitions of the natural sciences—the "already-thought" in its entirety, today constitutes a formalism, valid per se, which can assume any psychic content, up to the psychopathic, through the word's non-relation to the concept to which it alludes, the only sufficient relation being that of discursive connections.

The danger of such a substitution of content is due to the fact that present-day culture lacks the experience of the concept. The experience that past thinkers possessed intuitively, modern thinkers could attain through the sublimation of the logical process, a process that today instead undergoes another elaboration. In reality, concepts are not lacking, but they are devoid of content, since they do not form the discourse. Rather, the discourse makes them its own and uses them. They appear as concepts, without really being so. Intellectuals of today do not truly think what they say. Instead, they give the value of thought to what they are led to connect discursively. Therefore, legitimate is the doubt that, if one can look at the inner content of the apparent concept, one finds (in more than one instance) the psychic element, or the altered mental element.

If this is how things stand, the problem that arises, concerning the expressions of modern-day culture, is to distinguish the dialectical–logical apparatus that functions with regard to a pathological mental fact from what expresses thinking's true relationship with reality.

Since it concerns a functional alteration that cannot be grasped by a clinical investigation, the problem is one of thinking, or of the analysis of thinking's procedure: not of the formal procedure but, rather, of the real or ideal one, since the formal procedure—precisely because of its deductive progress—is unable to establish a measure: just because it, being the mediation assumed in the exclusive relation to itself, can function as the most legitimate logical cover of an irregular mental process.

Therefore, the issue is, above all, one that regards discovering the thinking foundation. It is actually a matter of establishing which actual thinking operates behind a specific dialectical–logical system. We are directed toward a standard of truth, which cannot be a logical measure, or any measure of reflected thought but, rather, the proof of the relationship between a given system's ideal procedure and the very ideas presumed as a foundation. In other words, we are directed to a metaphysical investigation, not in the sense of ancient metaphysics, but in a peculiarly modern sense, as called for by the problematic proper to the coincidence of the concept with the object in scientific research. Such a coincidence, even when it appears in specific fields of investigation, is not recognized by formally rational thought, since such thought is actually unaware of its own conceptual act and is, therefore, dependent on something other than its own genuine movement.

Needing to identify the content or the background of a logical–dialectical expression, the investigation is metaphysical, in that it must be able to follow ideal connections as real mediations of an immediate 'devising': the one whose possibility today is called into question by destitute thinking. In spite of the doubts and denials concerning the reality of ideas, today there is no alternative for whoever intends to escape the series of deceptions of an intellectualistic procedure, which formally seems to be precise in all fields, but reveals that it no longer grasps anything of reality, outside well-defined sectors of the mathematical–physical realm.

It is a matter of ascertaining the germ from which a given type of thinking springs, since the germ can be the cerebral system's functional alteration, which has taken the place of the idea. It is difficult for the formal expression to be the revealer in that regard, because its regularity can likewise take on an ideal movement conditioned by a physiological functional process, and an ideal movement that draws from its own foundation, or from the pure idea itself. The investigation should be an investigation that regards the development of ideas in relation to specific ideal presuppositions.

In some modern systems, ideas are presupposed even if they are not enunciated, or not recognized as ideas. It is a matter of identifying them, according to an ideal–analytical method (whose technique is the theme of the second part of this book) in order to establish the germination to which they belong, namely if they belong to the physical germination—for which they are false ideas, or ideal movements pathologically activated by physical processes—or to the germination of the idea itself. The unfolding of ideas must, therefore, be capable of being followed even in cases where the rational procedure presumes to narrow itself exclusively to the logical–formal field, with absolute autonomy regarding the sphere of experience and of pure thinking. We will be able to demonstrate that it has nevertheless to do with a procedure of ideas, even when thinking is oriented in such a way as not to see itself except in oneness with logical structures of the discourse.

Such ideas, such thought, can be followed even if their producers deliberately and with scientific pretext stay away from them. It will again be possible to reiterate—in spite of the dogmatics of logical empiricism—that true logic is a formal domain of ideas. The idea of the necessary inference cannot but refer to the idea of the postulate and this, in turn, to the idea of the foundation. The initial relation is a relation between ideas; to establish it between opinions and between propositions is also itself an ideal movement. But we can gather here a symptom of the illness, if we believe that we can realize this relation as a relation between propositions, without gathering it as an ideal mediation that generates the very form of the relation and of each of its further movements, for which *we lack a relationship with the relation* within the same system by whose formal rigor we presume to operate. But it does not mean that such a configuration of the illness indicates all of its dimensions.

5. THE GHOST OF METAPHYSICS

From the tide of dialecticism today, deductive systems, elaborated according to logical principles independent of the ancient canon of reasoning, emerge to justify themselves with a resolute character of necessity, in relation to the formative process of the sciences. It is a canon to which in modern times, Kant, Fichte, Shelling, and particularly Hegel, and then, the neo-Hegelians directed new forces of investigation. These most recent ones (did so) in a form, which, by referring to the logic of thinking in movement that cannot be fixed in a categorical and syllogistic scheme, was no longer understood by the philosophers of analyses, who judged it to be naïve and outdated, and yet, they would have needed to understand its reasons.

But, in fact, if deductive logic is excluded as a formal science, or as a path of methodological knowledge urged by the further (albeit always one-dimensional) extension of science, and if the validity of this logic is excluded, except as an instrument of research or proof of specific mathematical sectors and in the field of natural sciences, the rest is nothing but dialecticism, or dialectics devoid of the movement of thinking that once legitimized dialectics.

The mere fact that an expression such as "dialectical materialism" was able to be coined—which, from the viewpoint of ancient dialectics, is a contradiction in terms—is not just the sign of a discontinued capacity to conceive the objective intuiting of thought, as an activity that has the foundation within itself, but also, consequentially, the possibility of allowing itself to be reascended to a sensory entity, to a physical support, namely the brain, the impulse generator of dialectics. It is the physical support, which, as a concept—and being only a concept, but not recognized as such—is a meager form of the intuiting that becomes negated. In fact, no one has ever experienced, objectively, or materially, such a support, which lies at the core of the materialistic doctrine as an established physical entity, but actually as an unconscious metaphysical entity.

However, dialecticism, which is the deterioration of dialectics, even Marxist, has a broad meaning. It has become the form of the present-day culture. If the physical sciences are excluded, no longer has any discipline a relationship with its own content, unless it deals with content, which, though ideal, formally appears with references to the sensory sphere, and, therefore, involves physical measurement—for example, an archeological object. In that case, the objective content that demands the objective movement of thinking, descriptive and rational, and therefore inferential, is an exact part of archeological knowing. But the exact description of the object and the deductive elaboration of its sensory notations, are not everything: the object has a historic–ideal and an aesthetic–ideal value.

Here, the historic–aesthetic–ideal content, in order to be observed, just as the object's sensory form has been objectively observed with the consequent logical series of its meanings, demands something more than the simple thinking capable of precise movement thanks to the object's physicality. It now demands a movement equally precise, but founded on the objectivity itself of the thinking that is realized, that is, on its pure intuiting, according to the method of ancient dialectics. Naturally, however, it could not be the repetition of ancient dialectics but, rather, the present-day logical thinking that knows how to experience itself independently of the objective support, therefore, better than devising formal rules for itself, discovering itself as the logos at the source of such rules, insofar as we recognize that it cannot be limited by its own discursive expression, contrary to what logical empiricism demands. Such thinking should discover itself according to its own relational movement, or according to its own capacity of the "initial movement" of thinking: what, before the discourse, having within itself the conceptual concatenation, also contains the relation between word and word, between proposition and proposition, and the principle of such a relation. But, naturally, it could get hold of itself in the pre-formal relational moment, to the extent that it was able to know itself through the formal expression.

In other words, thinking is correctly directed toward reality by the logic of sensory experience, e.g., by the concreteness of the excavated object, but it ceases to move according to reality when it lacks the sensory object as a reference, if, despite the methodology's support, it does not possess the movement by means of which it actualizes the methodological canon.

The sensory object, thanks to its simple existence, fosters the exactness of thought in the outer expression. However, if one observes, this exactness is thought's inner way to be. In effect, it is never the thinking that makes a mistake. Rather, its formal 'occurring' is always at the point of arbitrariness or the subjective assumption of the object. The exactness should be experienced as a characteristic of pure thinking, before it is experienced in its descriptive logical formulations. In this way, thinking can continue to express its own truthful being when its subject is no longer sensory, but ideal, aesthetic, social, economic, historic, and so on.

In that sense, as we will see with regard to analytical logic, the task of a logical person is not to ensure for oneself a series of "primitive propositions," or of axioms but, rather, to possess the technique of what can be called the "axiomatic movement" of thinking—which is the inner experience of the formal relation, or the suprasensory perception of thinking. It is the metaphysics obscurely presupposed by the new logic, which begins by negating it, and not wrongly, since it denies ancient metaphysics. However, it is not sufficiently aware of the mythic nature of the theoretical activity to which it unconsciously gives rise and subordinates itself as if to a metaphysics. Therefore, this metaphysics rises up as a ghost of itself. For now, *the materialistic–dialectical phantom and metaphysical specter* actually dance together with delight, intoxicated on the lymph of life drawn from thinking.

Since an archeological object, for example, has been mentioned, it is important that science justify the hypothesis that even if human history, in its essence, demands the search for outer data that prove it, its reconstitution cannot come from such data but, rather, from the intuitive perception of a synthesis, which is not the sum of those data, but the prior content which, attained, renders their evidence significant. Any restitution on the basis of outer data, documents, archeological evidence, texts, and so on can furnish only the knowledge necessary to dialecticism, whose own development is of interest, more than real knowing. Data can only have the function of confirming what must, above all, be intuited as suprasensory reality. This is the future path of science in every field. On the level of outer data, the prudent archeologist must, for now, always be able to imagine that the series of discovered objects lacks those essential data, decisive for the reconstruction of coherent meaning.

6. The Idyll between "Dialectical Materialism" and Mystical Cybernetics

Dialecticism is the predicament of contemporary culture worldwide. Therefore, the possibility to conceive metaphysical or moral qualities, which are not empty abstractions, is fading. The lesson of mathematical logic, in that sense, still does not teach anything, not even to those who cultivate it, if they believe that this logic and the thinking that expresses itself within it are the same thing. It is precisely such thinking that escapes logicians–mathematicians, and it escapes together with the meaning of their research.

Dialecticism is essentially a general analytical 'philosophizing' that today takes root in all fields by assuming the exact precision of deductive systems, regarding themes that are not immediately sensory nor that imply relations between quantities (except a few of their specific aspects). It therefore lacks the power of logic of its own content—which consequently always appears as "real science." But also, given its anti-metaphysical realism, dialecticism lacks the logic of its own cognitive process—i.e., being unaware (just like analytical reasoning) of the canon of the thinking implemented: the one, which once, beginning with platonic thinking, justified the *method* of dialectics.

It is the reason for which this analytical philosophizing lacks the capacity of synthesis: not the synthesis of its own propositions, but of the synthetic sense, which is the inner canon of the thinking called upon, namely the inner canon that it does not even imagine. Everything can be demonstrated, when it lacks the objective support proper to physical sciences, or when a rigorous formalism is not possible, but only a formalism relative to the non-sensory object, yet devoid of internal dialectical movement. Each sophism can be assumed as truth, according to a regularity of that discursive automatism, which has shown itself to be inevitably referable to the phenomenon of mental disorder.

The case of so-called dialectical materialism is typical. Along the way, it has well become something other than what Marx had initially intended, since he did not imagine the consequences of the metamorphic processes implicit in the system's self-compatibility, processes behind which the real content has operated cryptogenetically, namely that content which effectively had to be, or the one which, newly dialecticized in order to penetrate world culture better, can today meet, by way of occult affinities, with pseudo-Catholicism, with pseudo-democracies, with the whole world that has broken from its traditions.

Regardless of how this dialecticism proceeds, its syntheses are not real, since they presuppose a theoretic that could appear real only if it were elaborated as a metaphysics of knowing, which would mean, however, the elimination of the mentioned fundamentals of the system. But it is precisely post-Marxist dialecticism, itself, which has taken steps to eliminate them, not by virtue of overcoming, but on the basis of a pragmatic consequentiality with the impulse of which those were an expression. In fact, with the rejection of speculation, metaphysics and the transcendence of the original being of thinking (and, therefore, of its canon), the content's logical support has been explained as a semiformal system of axioms, by means of a logical–analytical formulation, which, nevertheless, has arisen by excluding the possibility of inwardly experimenting the theme (socioeconomic and scientific–historical), of which it has had to gradually be developed as a dogmatic theoretic not endowed with any other relation to it, except that of rationally considering one of its aspects that can be notably controlled. Of which, therefore, the real experience would arouse a really different thinking, if thinking were not preemptively seized by dogma, which is the original impulse that persists through all of the grindings and dialectical reshufflings of the system. But, even if the experience corresponding to objective thinking were possible for the dialectical materialist, we can truly say that not even for the economy would the physical–mathematical aspect exhaust its content. Meanwhile, it is obvious that the content of physical research, being an objective experience, involves a methodological formulation. Deductive sciences, when they refer to a specific research that is "real," have their unquestionable reason to be.

In other words, as long as it has to do with knowledge regarding quantities and sizes, synthetic operations are rendered possible by the laws themselves of deduction. Meanwhile, in the case of abstract entities, such as "matter," "capital," "merchandise," "history," "nature," and so on, the possibility of verification and of a logical connection must come from the objective synthetic power of thinking, before it can come from formal control. The synthetic power of thinking, however, is what the aforementioned dialectical materialists preemptively eliminate. Their denial of the suprasensory canon of thinking is the denial itself of any possible theoretic. What truly gives food for thought is the fact that the philosophy at the end of the past century and at the beginning of the present one has not been able to clearly identify such an infraction of the laws of knowing. Not even post-Hegelian idealism has been capable of this.

The logical failure of the materialistic–dialectical system and the simultaneous capacity of utilizing every logical form (true or false), argumentation and fact, by adapting dialectics to each occasion and even dialectically using its own contradictions, sophisms, and paralogisms—according to a discursive acrobatics that does not leave time for its followers to see the whole and to compare the initial dialectics to the present one—cannot but refer to an extra-individual impulse, to an element that, while identifiable in its psychic nature, refers to a transcendent direction.

The search for the true impulse that controls the whole phenomenon, even within democratic and conservative institutions, even within sacristies, is to be led beyond the doctrine. From the moment that an error cannot be identified on the discursive–analytical plane by a thinking that ignores the canon to which it appeals (a canon having nothing to do with factual and measurable contents), this doctrine actually proceeds according to the impulse within its own analysis devoid of contact with the alleged socioeconomic and scientific–historical content, until it establishes itself as a *limitless analytic*, such as to give the impression of an imposing logical system: which, however, faced with a thinking still capable of synthesis and of true logic, goes to pieces. But even if it does go to pieces, what remains behind intact and that nevertheless continues to act, is the impulse that is to be identified.

The problem today is not so much the fact that, in philosophizing and in logical reflecting, the thinking capable of actualizing its own internal canon fails, as it is the urgency of recognizing how in the specific case of dialectical–materialistic analysis—which nowadays lives by way of its own virtue, extraneous to the reality of the theme to which it presumes to refer—there operates a transcendent impulse of which this analysis is unaware and which has the power to also eliminate the possibility that its use of the normal instrumentality of the altered mental status can be recognized through its own activity. *It has to do with an enormous doctrinal apparatus that sustains itself solely on the non-relation with the theme that it presumes to deal with, namely the socioeconomic one.*

The logic of dialectical materialism, like that of all doctrines similar to or derived from it, is not only unable to have a mathematical procedure—if excluded are the physical and arithmetical references of a few parts of its structure—but it also lacks the speculative content, since it invalidates speculation as an activity independent of the sensory processes. Therefore, in reality, under the apparatus of the discursive coherences, it is devoid of content. As we have shown, the content is psychic. But, as such, while it refers to the altered mental status, it can equally reveal the activity of an extra-individual intelligence, which indeed needs the altered mental status to operate in the world according to a precise plan, which we actualize by believing to be its authors. It is the identical sense, recognizable by the discursive automatism that is cultivated by modern deductive logic, when it presumes to break off relations with speculative thought and traditional logic, in order to establish itself as an integral instrument of knowledge.

Behind such a situation, like behind the materialistic–dialectical one, we can recognize the hidden pressure toward a mysticism of physical reality—the gradual elevation of material objective reality, totally automated and cybernetically articulated at a super-individual level, such that, once and for all, we can believe in it, with the help of knowledge planned and secure, in which thinking can finally rest, so that this consciousness can function in place of thinking. It is a knowledge to which the *crepuscular faith* that has created the myth of matter and now caresses the vision of a society, mechanized and synchronized like a global empire of termites, can finally be dedicated.

7. Catechism and Contagion

By expressing themselves in a specific dialectic, the mentally impaired codify—both "directly," as in the case of psychoanalysis, and "indirectly," as in the case of dialectical materialism—their own set of circumstances and tend, instinctively, to achieve an analytical–linguistic regularity, which leaves their ailment intact.

Instinctively, or unconsciously, paranoid logicians are led to transmit their own illness, because only by infecting the multitude does their dialecticism fall under the order of normality, or the order of a general necessity, indispensable to them as a form of ethical value: facilitated in this by the press, by radio–television, by publicity, which today seem to function as its specific instruments.

The collective recognition of an objective "truth" (insofar as it is transmitted according to the logical–dialectical canon, operating as a faith) is what they need as a mystical support. In fact, we instinctively feel the non-reality of its dialectics. We instinctively look for extra-dialectical support. We tend to arouse the easiest faith, the one that today everyone devotionally grants to the results of a scientific–rationalistic investigation, without the need for proof.

Dialectical contagion is the easiest, because it takes hold of the mental inertia that tends to philosophically and logically justify itself by avoiding the effort of self-knowledge. Such inertia is precisely the principle of mental disorder, or the disorder that begins to become normality, insofar as it corresponds to a decline of thinking into dialecticism, and to dialecticism as a discourse independent of thinking.

Catechism thus assumes the function that today can be more normal to it, namely to operate by way of the faith that responds to the secret necessity of the altered mental status: to serve the processes of corporeity and of the subject matter mythicized and made cultural.

8. Cerebration by Mental Induction

The functional alteration of the cerebral organ, whose dialectical–logical thinking manages to become expression and therefore nourishment—as a possible transmission of illness to others—cannot be discovered by the person who suffers from it. Those who suffer from it and express it, ignore it. They have to instinctively negate its existence, since their very condition prevents them from supporting it.

Only those trained in meditation or in sound philosophizing (but how is a sound philosophizing nowadays possible?) would be able to perceive within themselves—if it should manifest in them—a functional alteration of the cerebral system, for they would perceive it as a physical opposition to the independence of thinking. In that case, they would know how to act, essentially, other than with possible physical remedies. They would be aware of the need to persist with energy in disciplines that render thinking independent of cerebralism, or of discursive formulations that are obligated and that mechanize. They would know that any automatic course of discursiveness would worsen the situation, unless they themselves were the creators of discursive forms according to an invention that does not contrast with the intuition of the therapy. And in case a professional engagement compelled them to a specific mental automatism, they would know how to find simple and efficacious ways to render thinking independent of *cerebrations* that would eventually tend to manifest. Moreover, to thinkers capable of such a discipline, it would be unlikely for them to have to confront the problem of a personal functional alteration.

Normally, as it has been said, those subjects who suffer from it fail to notice it and convert such a condition into a mental activity that they believe to be free and that can, therefore, manifest the feature of organicity and productiveness. In that case, thinking essentially expresses its own conditioning, or dependence on the mechanism of the impaired cerebral activity. However, an outer appearance formally manifests whose task is to conceal such irregularity by means

Dialectical and Analytical Precariousness

of the most plausible legitimization. In effect, the dependence of thinking on cerebration, and the functional alteration, reciprocally correspond to one another.

We must look, even hypothetically, at the 'coinciding' of the thinking process with cerebral automatism (cerebration), as a possible explanation for the excess of discursive–conceptual mechanization and systematic analysis of which the present-day culture goes on being substantiated.

The pathological character of such a cultural attitude is to be placed in connection with the fact that, regarding the greatest fluctuation of consciousness toward analysis, there corresponds no fluctuation of consciousness, of equal clarity and intensity, to counterbalance it toward the noesis thus aroused. This noesis is aroused, in fact, at a level of consciousness not realized, nor imagined. For this reason, an underlying "unconsciousness" is cultivated, to which the conscious activity that it itself generates is contrasted, namely a contradictory condition that nowadays constitutes the normality of the intellectual experience and thus implicates, as normal, the phenomenon of the altered cerebration.

The analysis presupposes and postulates a synthesis, and the synthesis a noetic capacity, which is the a-dialectical consciousness of dialectical thinking. The maximum polarization of the forces of consciousness toward the outer world is carried out thanks to a corresponding inner polarization, which needs to be recognized, so that the equilibrium between thinking and the world that is thought does not disappear. An adequate capacity of synthesis does not, instead, correspond to the abnormal analysis. It is not the synthesis of analysis, possible to the same analytical thinking, but the synthesis as a relation of thinking to the movement to which it has given rise. Such movement, which belongs to thinking, escapes thinking and, by escaping thinking, it belongs to cerebral automatism, which is to say, it forms part of the picture of mental disorder.

IV

Formal Automatism and Paranoia

1. The "Content" as Pretext

As we have seen, mental disorder can occur without being clinically identifiable. It can be an event that is simply "functional," not attributable to objective injuries of the cerebral organ. But precisely because of this, mental disorder, unable to express itself even in other organs, manages to manifest neuropsychically. In subjects less prepared, this neuropsychic manifestation, assumes psychiatrically recognizable forms, such as hysterical-neurosis, paranoia, and so on, while, in subjects, mentally prepared—to the extent that they are endowed with a modern-day kind of logical apparatus—it explodes in an ironclad and systematic dialecticism. It is ironclad because the mental disorder (on the strength of its physiological foundation), having a persistent nature, projects itself as a psychic content onto the dialectical theme, impressing upon it the impulse of persistence, namely obsession.

The most serious problem to consider at the present time is that the mentally impaired can communicate their own alteration through the formal architecture of discourse, having a way to take on, in a legitimate guise, any theme, from the physical sphere to the psychic and to the spiritual. The era of extremely persuasive dialecticians coincides with that of the mentally impaired.

Formal Automatism and Paranoia

As a mental illness, the alteration of the cerebral organ becomes hard to recognize, when it manages to project itself in a logical and scientific form, because with such form, it is not objectified in an alterity that can be valid to the subject as a sign of its own illness, but it expresses itself to affirm itself. In fact, it makes use of a language that is the legitimate language of the present time, one that has become more valid than the content which it uses as a pretext—the real content being psychic, demanding dialectics, not thinking. It is the form necessary to the mental disorder, which operates according to a level that eludes the subject's consciousness and, given the mental level rendered normal by it, escapes general human consciousness.

The present age is perilous because the errors of thinking are nourished by the impeccable dialectics of the mentally impaired in every field. The legitimization of illness is possible through new forms of discursiveness, which circulate in each and every cultural environment. They are, in particular, forms that have given rise to rationalism, by ultimately becoming the linguistic analysis and research of the exact systems of the inferential process.

Methodology does yet not manage to be an end in itself. But on the level of mathematical theories, it expresses its autonomy somewhat legitimately. Unfortunately, linguists and logicians, with a philosophical–mathematical inclination, believe that they can exert such autonomy by applying mathematical reasoning to "real" themes, until making this reasoning appear (in itself) more important than such themes, despite assuming it like a mediation for them. Thus, the method overwhelms the content, for which alone it has arisen. The methodological production manages to have an autonomous need of its own, even outside the field of mathematics. Regarding various problems, one nowadays only witnesses expositions or conferences methodologically inspired. The layperson remains dazzled by it. Psychic induction, the principal of mental disorder, operates by way of an overwhelming deduction, without achieving contact with an effective content of thinking—neither on behalf of the expositor, nor on behalf of lecturers or listeners.

The illusion is that there is content, to the extent that a subject can be formally developed. But the content cannot be present for the simple fact that its name is used. When the name as such becomes significant, it has effectively lost contact with thinking. Therefore, it enslaves an inferior form of thinking, which corresponds to a content that is very different from that to which it seems to refer. A psychic content is able to appear as thought, by immediately becoming logical nominalism. Actually, problems can be addressed without minimally touching upon their substance. The appearance of the maximum determination becomes the guise of the absence of thought and, therefore, of the absence of content.

This is not intended to be a criticism of symbolic logic, but of its potential to lend itself to an illegitimate use on behalf of today's intellectuals—a use for which ever-fewer thinkers are needed. There is nothing more pitiful, for example, than a history of philosophy directed by way of the analytical–structural method. Structuralism, of a formal–deductive filiation, devours any investigation that does not have, as an object, quantities and measurements.

The coincidence between the maximum logical refinement and mental automatism becomes possible relative to a technique of discursive formalism, devoid of an effective penetration of the content, which exists, but only as an alibi. Dialectics becomes a perfect guise for mental automatism, or the codification of illness, from which the subject cannot be freed, because the dialectical expression is not a catharsis, as the artist's aesthetic activity can sometimes be regarding an instinctive–emotive content. In the contemplated phenomenon, the dialectical expression is not the objectification or the expulsion of a process, with respect to which a minimum of independence has been maintained. It is not the liberation from illness, but its legitimization—or better yet, the activity itself of the illness.

Thus, in the artistic field, one thing is for the "demoniacal," the "horrid" and the "chaotic" to be recognized and objectively projected in images, by means of which a creative force enchants them in the form that redeems them, another is for the artistic production to be itself the expression of something "horrid" or "demoniacal" or "chaotic," from which it does not know how to free itself, and to which it indeed guarantees aesthetic legitimacy.

2. The Mechanism of "Alteration": Dialectical Psychism

Legitimate, therefore, is the hypothesis that the brain (as an organ of thinking and as a support of dialectical consciousness) can, through excessive dialecticism, undergo a "functional" alteration, which leads it to intervene in the determination of thinking: for which it ceases to be the mediator, thanks to which thinking transforms intuitive experiences into a conceptual–discursive expression. Such experiences can indeed be stimulated by the sensory sphere, but not because of this can they depend on it.

For the experimenter who recognizes the principle of self-experience regarding this type of investigation, thinking's independence from the cerebral instrument should not only be indicative of the instrument's functioning, but it should also be expressive of a thinking activity that is able to distinguish between a psycho–physical environment and a pure, mental one. This capacity of distinction should be considered a sign of the normal relationship between thinking and the brain, and an inner prerequisite for controlling the same relationship.

If thinking's dependence on the organ is provoked by a functional alteration, this cannot be gathered directly as such. Rather, it can be recognized in an ordinary aspect of discursiveness, the unambiguous automatic one—namely, the cerebration that tends toward the monoideistic manifestation of dialectics that is congenial to it. It is thus important to know how to look behind the logical and organic expressions of present-day intelligence in every field. Ordinarily, we are not outsmarted by the expressions of a naïve and unsystematic thought but, rather, by those of the intelligence that creates (according to an ironclad unambiguousness) the discursive vestment of the series of its contents.

Following the course of present-day logical–deductive formalism, a neuropsychic process can manifest as an organic architecture of concepts, without a real organic content. This architecture, in fact, is of words—the real relation between words is psychic, but formally it is logical and dialectical. The slightest activity of thinking is grasped by cerebral automatism. It is the reason for which present-day logic makes it easy for dialecticians today to assert their absence of thought, certainly not through formulations of a logistic kind—of which they truly are incapable—but through discursive structures that imitate and resemble them.

Actually, the whole of post-Hegelian dialectics—if certain forms of idealism are excluded—lends itself to misunderstanding the discursive vocation of new intellectuals, because a gnoseological and logical language, a scientific and critical language, can be used by them dialectically, devoid of the internal substance of thought, of which it is the form. It is a language that, in its neutral relation to itself, does not involve any effective mental viewpoint, but only a psychic expression.

While analytical philosophy aspires toward consistency and a reason to be, drawing from mathematical logic and requiring of it secure instruments for its inferential tendency, dialectical materialism is always confined to themes, which, because of their content, would demand moral and speculative penetration and, therefore, logical–intuitive thinking. For this reason, it is always more engaged in ideo–phraseological activism, whose progressive automatism presupposes the loss of any relation whatsoever to the themes by which it moved.

Formal Automatism and Paranoia

The misunderstanding of Marxism, like that of post-Marxist and socialistic filiations of every gamut, none excluded, is precisely to propose themes of supreme human importance, towards whose understanding it begins by suppressing the organ of knowledge, almost as if its hidden mission were to prevent the human being of today from penetrating such themes. We cannot help but be moved by a given psychism, when we are theoreticians and simultaneously deny the metaphysical canon of thinking. What therefore remains as a sign of philosophy's deterioration is not so much the fact that a "dialectical materialism"—namely, an idealism of matter—has been able to arise, as the fact that philosophy has not identified it for what it was and, therefore, has not expelled it as a discursiveness, foreign to our own world.

Dialecticism always has psychism within it, not thinking. This psychism is capable of assuming the form of thinking needed to arouse and to nourish the psychism of others, not their thinking. The form of thinking is subjugated to a content that, in its mediation, is irrelative to it, insofar as it contradicts thinking as an autonomous activity. It is the sign of mental disorder.

Reflecting the initial pathological dependence of thinking on the cerebral organ, dialecticism cannot but tend to represent it scientifically as a normal state of affairs. It thus legitimizes the hypothesis that the brain thinks, namely that it is matter evolved to the point of being able to think. And this hypothesis, at a given moment, transmutes into an axiomatic formulation, as if it were scientifically proven. But today this very science, by way of amateur investigations fortified with mathematical precision and with the sophistication of technical means, tends to affirm this, by circumventing a logical account of the argument. On the basis of this, it would nevertheless have the duty to present this assertion as a hypothesis, which it never had the chance to prove. In fact, the only possibility for it to accomplish this is eliminated, from the get-go, by materialistic dialecticism.

3. Monoideistic Constriction and the Retroactivity of its World Vision

On the basis of such a formulation, dialecticism is led to an interpretation of history, nature, culture, and the sense of life, whereby it projects the psychic condition of which it is the unconscious expression. It discursively establishes a new science of the human being centered on an economic theme, which becomes the abstract foundation of measures intended to ensure the existence of that evolving animal organism with which the human being is identified. The economy falls into the hands of theoreticians, who lack the intuition needed to penetrate economic reality, but who can pretend to penetrate it, by means of pliable dialectics.

A mythical theoretic projects itself in an economic praxis, which, nonetheless, by means of the disasters that it provokes, should foster the objective recognition of its unrealism. This does not take place: an ironclad political power, in fact, according to the typical paranoid course, is prepared to justify each failure and transform it into a starting point for further experiences, rectifying negative consequences by imposing an additional sacrifice onto the subjected masses, or by managing to obtain support from countries whose social unity works toward corroding the foundations.

If mental disorder did not govern the process, failure would be instructional, since it would reveal the inadequacy of the thinking called upon, namely the impossibility for the economy to undergo political paralogisms. But the plan cannot but obey its own logic. As a projection of the monoideistic content, it cannot but insist on its own movement. A feature of the obsessive content is, in fact, not to allow itself to be revised, since it lacks the autonomous activity of consciousness. Consciousness bound to dialectical automatism is capable of criticism, or of "self-criticism," not in regard to the obsessive content—because it would be unable to notice it—but in regard to the forms of its manifestation. Therefore, cultivated is the illusion that the doctrine can evolve in time

Formal Automatism and Paranoia

and the errors of application are able to eliminate themselves on their own.

In reality, despite dialectical metamorphoses, the psychic substance of the doctrine remains unchanged. The subsequent gravity of the crisis is continually compensated by the intensification of political conditioning, which, if necessary, mobilizes art, culture, science, and propaganda. While it forces the masses into a more intense productive rhythm, under the monoideistic pressure of redemption—by continuing to lack any relationship with the economic reality of which it presumes to be the theoretic—it simultaneously gives life to a supportive suggestion through the alteration brought to historical sciences so that they can respond to the doctrine's present-day aims. The retroactive projection of meanings regarding past events, devoid of a correlation with the present-day doctrinal content, is organized according to the logic of an automatistic scheme.

The pathological character of this projecting into the past, into history, into myth, into folklore, into all the sciences connected by the need for research, the sense of a doctrine born from a break with metaphysical meanings of the past, appears evident, if the historical content is thought to be the one that can reach us. For it is one with its own meaning, or with its own ideal necessity, as a spiritual expression of a given era, which the historian should aim at intuiting, not at eliminating in order to replace it with a belief—the product of a typical present-day mindset.

What is worth noting is the non-worry of being perceived as distorters of history, based on the certainty of an inevitable persuasion of the cultural and academic–university world which has nowadays entered into the climate of dialectics that is unconsciously substitutive of thinking—a dialectics which can easily adapt to any theme that presents itself with features of necessity and of solicitation of the mental automatism.

4. THE ECONOMY SLAIN WORLDWIDE

It should nevertheless be pointed out that the ultimate state of dialectical materialism is typical and somehow, symbolic. It is not a particular event of present-day culture but, rather, its true expression, naturally opposed by expressions formally diverse, but of an identical content, all resulting similarly from a common dialectical, reflected process and from a devotional faith in rationality and in the infallibility of science.

It is inevitable that the substantial materialism of culture, on the economic plane, gradually converts into the total automation of the productive process and into the unambiguous and acephalous grouping of economic complexes according to a mechanical organization no longer moved by ideas, but by methodology, technology, and applied psychology, which replace the individual element of responsibility and of creativity in every sector. The acephalous grouping actualizes the irresistible tendency to organize itself in the form of the state or according to state power, in order to replace, by means of juridical standardization, the absence of intuitive organizational virtue and simultaneously to impose itself as the power from which the free individual need not escape. With this, the Marxist ideal and the bourgeois ideal can finally unite, with post-Marxist dialectics as the mediator. Technological faith unites them.

The possibility of operating according to a reality in its becoming, which can continually be intuited dynamically, is erased by the need to produce according to methodological schemes that are reducible to a mental automatism, or to a mental disorder, whose unconscious aim is the total subjection of humanity to economic needs: the economic ideal having been identified with the meaning of life itself. The power is concentrated in the economic organism deprived of life, so that, as an economic fact, it can govern something that has suppressed the economy, and, as an economic fact, makes human activities subservient to itself.

The economic fact, from a means, becomes an end, not only by way of Marxist materialism, but regularly by way of the economic materialism of the day, or even by way of systems that seem to oppose Marxism—such a fact being the product of a thinking, common to both parts, which is incapable of grasping in economic reality something not numerically measurable.

While in one area of the earth, Marxism has had to die a logical death, precisely because it has been translated into economic and sociopolitical structures foreseen by its dialectical death, in other vast areas its cadaverousness spreads and is rekindled with automatistic–technological life, which tends to actualize its second death, by way of new socioeconomic structures. Marxist cadaverousness, worldwide, is the logical gradual completion of a nearly centuries-old dialectical and analytical–methodological process, ultimately furnished with mystical necessity by neo-Soviet ecclesiastical reasoning.

5. The Cult of the Unconscious: The Beginning of Mental Breakdown

The system of automatic dialecticism, as an expression of mental disorder, acknowledges a possession of consciousness on behalf of influences unrelated to it—with which it identifies—believing itself to be autonomous and thus operating as if it were in a state of hypnosis.

The group of extraneous influences would not be detrimental toward consciousness, if consciousness took on, by means of a precise technique—for which the reader is referred to the second part of this book—their force as its own force that needs to be freed from the altering form. Yet, they arrive at controlling it by means of its unconscious identification with such form and, therefore, by means of the alienation of the force that we call the "unconscious": with a sense that is essentially different from that established by psychoanalysis, which places the "unconscious" at the foundation of consciousness.

For us, the assumption that consciousness has its principle within itself, since it does not draw it from any physical or psychic support, is experientially based. From the physio–psychic mediation, it simply draws the possibility of emerging dialectically in individual form, nonetheless according to its own original being. The experience of this original being, as a solicitation of a higher form of consciousness, is possible thanks to a technique that excludes the theory of the psychoanalytical unconscious, by identifying its obscurity and non-reality. The identification neutralizes the negative character of the unconscious, whose danger consists precisely in being able to ascend to a mythical authoritarian entity, since a power, in scientific terms, is attributed to this entity—a power upon which consciousness depends regardless of being superior to it.

As we have seen, our dependence on an unconscious that is able to manifest in apparently legitimate dialectical forms—these being a special immediacy of the mental disorder—can also take on a philosophical and psychological guise. In this second instance, it has to do with psychoanalysis, given that it is a doctrine based on the unawareness of consciousness's identification with what is foreign to it, which it dreams of projecting before itself, since it is governed by it. Psychoanalysis, governed by what is foreign, becomes in fact a psychoanalytical doctrine.

Thus, the cult of the unconscious has no limits, because it is not only that of the psychoanalytical unconscious, but, above all, what, as an illegitimate *ethos* of culture, is formed and spreads by way of dialectical induction, provoking an essentially psychic contagion, which, in turn, reverberates as a mental disorder and expresses itself in further dialectics. Much of the literary and artistic production of today has such a source.

The nourishment of such dialectics cannot but be continuous, because it does not come from thinking that is free—which continually needs to execute an act of disengagement from the series of mediocre thoughts—but from a persistent mental–cerebral condition, since it is physically based. The cerebral condition becomes a psychic fact with a mental–dialectical expression. It is a condition that undoubtedly results from a series of anterior processes, which refer to a general crisis of human thinking.

That which is the presumption of the dialectical automatistic system—that the brain, or matter, thinks—is actually the result of a way of thinking already conditioned by the cerebral mechanism, or by the fact that the brain's physical processes intervene irregularly in the genesis of thinking, their task being, instead, to create an absolutely "immobile" support.

Schematically, it could be pointed out that, in the vicissitudes of the human intellect, at the threshold of "historical" times, a thought whose expressive necessity conforms to the memory of an original, but lost, spiritual dimension can initially be recognized. With time, such thought always tends to identify more and more with the cerebral mediation, by way of a specific experience of the physical world and thus of the conceptual system corresponding to it. It is the beginning of the philosophical era, which has perhaps concluded during our time, because of the complete physicalization of thinking. Descending below this physicalization of thinking, it cannot but become an expression of animality.

When the conceptual activity ends up coinciding with the cerebral mechanization, this mechanization inevitably predominates, and with it, so does the human being's animal nature, if the relationship is not balanced by an opposing activity of thinking, free of cerebralism—which is the pure intuitive possibility or the power (intrinsic to thinking) to consciously retrace the process of its own quantitative assumption of the world. Because such a rebalancing action does not occur, the cerebral "mechanism" predominates by eliminating the intuitive residual power. It appears to actualize a more secure scientific knowing, but it is actually the mental disorder in action. Behind the semblance of scientific systematization, a mental deterioration, resulting from the prevalence of cerebral mechanics over the thinking process, takes place. It is as if the telephonic apparatus, instead of transmitting the conversation, intervened with its own breakdown and consequent noises to replace it. The comparison is insufficient, but valid.

The cerebral breakdown cannot be recognized as the breakdown of an objectively visible devise. Cerebralism would be unable to change if consciousness succeeded in having an objective relationship with it. Unfortunately, its alteration is the product of errant thinking, of an age-old process of rationalistic deterioration, which can trace the crisis of the "sacred" in the West and relate to events such as the persecution of the Templars, the premeditation of their extermination, and the alteration of the truth regarding their historical function, namely to the breakup of powers (temporal and religious) with Tradition, and to the preconditions of the loss of thinking's metaphysical element, which will gradually lead to intellectualistic philosophizing and, consequently, to dialectics void of intellect.

6. Sensory Excess and its Codification

The altered cerebral organ brings about the typical automatism of thinking, which requires a logical–analytical guise; but, at the same time, the cerebral organ, in turn, becomes altered by thinking that does not conform to its own laws. The breakdown is reciprocal. Naturally, this situation is not so much about the objective process of analytical logic, as the not-so-conscious and, therefore, rhetorical use of its method.

The laws of thinking, not being physical, require from thinking a relationship with the physical organ, which is its use according to the order to which its biological formation has complied. For this reason, thinking's use of the brain, in order to be correct in the physical sense, cannot but be metaphysical. And it is such, in fact, in its pre-dialectical movement, without which there cannot be dialectical movement. Mere dialectical thinking, however, cannot be adequately conscious of this. The breakdown occurs precisely, there, where the dialectical process, realized by means of the cerebral organ, lacks the capacity to operate according to the a-dialectical principle from which it moves. It loses the force of such a principle, which is to say, its autonomy with respect to the organ. Therefore, it is only abstractly conscious of itself.

The reasons for the loss of thinking's autonomy in a metaphysical and, consequently, cultural–historical sense, cannot be included within the scope of the present treatise. They have been the topic of our other studies, to which we refer the reader. We are now interested in revealing that one of the reasons for which the cerebral process prevails over the thinking process—the beginning of the mental disorder, codified by the scientific persuasion that the brain thinks, or is the organ of thinking—is the excess of sensory perceptions resounding in the human mind, without an adequate conscious counterpart. In the age of linguistics and of rigorous semantics, this insufficiency of consciousness is a serious matter. The excess occurs both in the form of everyday experience, with regards to a pragmatic–technical level of present-day civilization, and in the form that is actually scientific, focused on the exclusive factuality of phenomena. In both cases, sensory experience is not integrated by a corresponding inner activity, or by anything more than a simple methodological awareness. It actually has to do with the inner activity aroused by the sensory experience itself, in 'its manifesting.'

The excess of sensations and of mental pictures connected to them cannot be balanced by a thought, which, analytically and speculatively, is the abstractification of this mental picturing, not its overcoming or its integration. From the viewpoint of perception, it is inevitably a continual charge of outer impressions without an inner response. And, from the mental picture's perspective, it is the continuation of the unilateral cerebration not retraced by the thinking forces set in motion. The cerebration becomes automatism and, as such, begins to cause mental disorder.

In intellectuals, such alteration can take on different forms of compensatory expression, which they will consider to be new art, or avant-garde thinking, or cosmic science, or nuclear science, but it will be evil put in a position to peacefully and ethically continue its work. It is not a healing but, rather, the intellectual expression of evil. On the other hand, if mental automatism discovers precise possibilities of rationalistic expression, it necessarily appears as a monoideism that persists according to the assumed social, or sociopolitical, or psychological, or philosophical thematic nature, to the point of obsessiveness, an obsessiveness whose pathological character is not betrayed, thanks to the logical–linguistic apparatus it has available.

7. Pseudo-scientific Paths of Science: Technology

Thinking has truly lost an original art, namely an art by means of which it could remain the spirit's organ even by way of scientific–rationalistic experience. Thinking has not been trained to encounter sensory perceptions with adequate internal forces, when the human constitution has required the strictly physical experience of reality.

The investigation has been conducted in function of the phenomenon and not of the human being. What took place within the investigator's soul as a result of his or her physical 'experiencing' has been ignored: and this 'ignoring' has projected itself outwardly as the exclusion of the inner correlation with the phenomenon, for which the phenomenon in its abstract outward appearance has been validated, and human knowledge has begun to depend on it. The phenomenon has been consecrated and the logic of science has been subordinated to it.

Formal Automatism and Paranoia

Investigators of the physical world have lacked the inner help that should have come to them from the spiritual currents of religion and philosophy—currents which, except on rare occasions, closed themselves, respectively, within the administration of their own revelation or of their own speculation, dismantling what would have been the task of real contemplation and of real speculation, namely to assist us at the threshold of the era of natural sciences, to illuminate, gnoseologically, our experience by providing us with the suprasensory counterpart of the research unilaterally directed toward sensory phenomenalism: to reconnect the thinking engaged in research with its own original force, so that thinking recognizes within its own inner movement, the *real content* of the experience.

The fact that this has not occurred explains the opportunity that pseudo-philosophy and dialecticism have had to provide the theoretical, gnoselogical and logical counterpart to new human experiences: separating these from their own internal logic and eliminating their phenomenological meaning. They have elevated the phenomenon to significance, by establishing the metaphysical inverse. It is the inverse because it is essentially anti-metaphysical, but compelled to a metaphysical status by its inescapable character of normativity regarding the assumed contents.

Pseudo-philosophy and dialecticism have provided an analytic, which, once and for all, removes the possibility of a connection with its own internal process from the experience of the natural sciences. For this reason, scientists actually proceed obtuse and alone. The *phenomenon* has begun to condition their research, to the point of becoming its content, independent of the thinking of which it is, therefore, necessarily structured.

Scientists—having engaged thinking in the phenomenon without the possibility of experiencing it as an activity of their own that is carried out in the phenomenon until they assume it as true—have ended up regarding, as real, the phenomenon, devoid of their (thinking) activity. They have been deprived of the most important act, namely recognizing that (of themselves) which is real, operating within the experience of reality. Satisfied with attaining the exact and quantifiable concepts of phenomena, they have not noticed how the event that determines the concept's connection to the object, has gone on losing the ideal nexus between concept and concept, therefore, the concrete content of consciousness with regards to the scientific activity itself—which is to say, the possibility of arriving at the perception of the phenomena's type of forms according to the process of contemplative observation intuited by Goethe.

Thus, instead of "forces," they have had empty concepts, which correspond to measurable quantities of chemical or physical "facts," separated, on the one hand, from the life of nature and, on the other, from their own sensorial and thinking activity. They have forgotten to owe their experience to an inner movement that precedes the methodological form. And when, during these last decades, they turned to thinking to create a philosophy of science for themselves, they were able only to have the thinking already grasped by the phenomenon and a deductive logic ready with its abstract formalisms to reproduce discursive thinking's quantum bond to the phenomenon.

In passing from sciences that initially investigated nature to the current ones, scientists have been unaware of not having anything more to do with the thinking that initially allowed them to experience the physical world and, by means of which, they have been able to create a unitary sphere of science, which includes biology, physics, organic and inorganic chemistry, rational mechanics, and so on. Illusorily, they have entered a new world of investigations, by means of which they believe to have acquired a more precise and authoritative relationship with physical reality. Meanwhile, the opposite is true. This tends to escape them as never before, leaving them with only the technical–methodological structures in hand, or the cybernetic corpse of the outer sphere, in which they truly move as rulers, while losing evermore ground with respect to the reality of nature and the cosmos.

In that sense, cybernetics, which, within given limits, could be a useful sector of specific researches, rises to a symbol of integral technology, by connecting the processes of automation that have arisen as developments of old disciplines, or by realizing the interdisciplinary aggregation of new specializations—rocketry, econometrics, biochemistry, biophysics, psycho-cybernetics, astrophysics, and so on. A cybernetic cosmos is being created for the human-machine that will smile compassionately upon those who do not want to recognize it as human, because, technologically, it will have its ethics, its legalism, its spiritualism, its religiosity (we know that in an Italian city there are centers of automation and of structural analysis underway for the exegesis of sacred texts), even its traditional reconstructions.

Cybernetic technologists now have everything. They lack only the thinking with which they initially had dealt by way of the phenomenon. For the phenomenon took it away from them. And today, a deductive logic is underway to sanction such a removal. Today, technologists, who still believe that they operate by way of science, mistake the thinking that is swallowed by the phenomenon and abstractly reconstituted, for the thinking that initially gave them the means to cognitively access the reality of the phenomenon. This is ultimately the sense of analytical philosophy, of so-called epistemology and of all present-day dialectics—namely, that we allow these to bestow content and form.

What presumes to be the most rational use of the thinking forces, in short, has become the least logical use, because it is unable to observe both thinking (as a phenomenal, pure form) and the essential process of sensorial perception. It lacks the fundamental possibility of positivism regarding the source of the cognitive process.

The least logical use of thinking on behalf of the logic that presumes to be the most rigorous cannot but be related to the deterioration of the cerebral organ. As a condition of logic, it is also the condition of dialectics, which nowadays cannot but depend on that, even without being its direct filiation. The deterministic–formal character of deductive logic, in fixing the discursive mechanism to the conceptual relationship, alters the relation between thinking and the cerebral organ, which is the vital relation, founded on the autonomy of thinking. Once autonomy is removed from thinking, such thinking is confined to an irregular relation with the physical organ, in that it must conform to an automatism that is foreign to it and that corresponds to cerebral automatism, or to the altered physiological function of the organ, not to the organ's instrumentality with respect to the thinking act.

Mental disorder is ultimately the event that refers to thinking's unilateral use of the cerebral organ, both because of an excess of sensorial perception and because of formal discursiveness, which is the codification of such excess. In its relation to the cerebral organ, thinking behaves by violating its own laws—namely, laws identical to those identifiable at the foundation of the organ's physical structure.

V

The Methodology against Science

1. Analytical Tenacity

We have acknowledged mental breakdown, which until now has been in question, as a phenomenon inevitably connected to our unawareness of it, in that consciousness identifies, without residue, with the dialectics in which it has its formalization. Only its identification could be the beginning of a healing. But it is difficult, even for human beings not yet affected by such a breakdown, to realize that the intrinsic character of the culture that they trust, is attributable to the specific psychic condition of intellectuals engaged in that culture, and solicits in these unaffected individuals the same harm on account of dialectical–logic. Even they are actually in danger.

The breakdown is the unconscious loss of thinking's autonomy with respect to its own organ of expression (the brain) and the beginning of a rational activity's dependence on the mechanism of physical supports, in turn, excessively activated by outer solicitations, without a corresponding conscious elaboration. The same scientific investigation begins to no longer have an authentic relation with its object, given that this object is established from outside on the basis of a validity, quantic and mathematical, which corresponds to thinking's renunciation of its own self-movement in the perceptive and cognitive relationship, for which the quantitative value is ignored.

With the unconscious alteration begun, the conceptual activity loses its synthetic power and its capacity of autonomy, by following courses that are dialectically bound, which it assumes as its free determination. Meanwhile, these courses are determined by influences unrelated to thinking.

The loss of synthetic power typically signals the collapse of thinking which it attempts to compensate with analytical efficiency and an abundance of the critical–bibliographical apparatus. With regard to formal dialecticism, the capacity to relate linguistic expressions is mistaken for synthetic activity. Whereas, it should be the capacity of having, as a synthesis, the movement carried out in the relation. This, however, would involve the experience of the concept, which present-day philosophy has lost and now no longer even conceives as possible.

Any dialectician or logical person can carry out formal syntheses of analytical discourses. But more than the synthetic power of thinking, what comes into play here is the capacity of leading the discourse, by means of inductive–deductive operations, back to its postulates, or initial formulations, or even the final ones: an automatic movement in its reversible inferential nature, which does not engage the life of thinking. More than the autonomy of thinking, it demands cerebral mechanics: above all, since thinking is limited to it, discovering within itself the best of its rational expression and identifying the exercise of knowing with the phraseological praxis. Having come to the first formulation, or the final one, there is no escape from it, since it is devoid of a conceptual passage. But the path that we believe to have thus carried out in the inferential sphere is irrelevant from the viewpoint of knowledge, insofar as it lacks synthetic coagulation—namely, meaning.

Cerebral mechanics, thanks to its fundamentally physical nature, favors the inclination of discursive thinking to remain in line with analytical insistence regarding its own content. The revolutions and innovations of such thinking, in fact, are always external and abstract. At times, they are violent and destructive in their formalism, but never substantial. On the research level, they lead from science to technology. They cannot give science a new impulse. Meanwhile, the path of science, from Galileo onwards, has always been an intuitive 'proceeding,' by means of sensory observation. False innovation and false revolution are the phenomenology of the mental state that can lead back to the functional alteration of the thinking organ.

Thus, the automatic dialectical dogmatism of the pseudo-revolution and the technological dogmatism of pseudo-democracies inevitably meet, by virtue of an identical econometric vision of the world.

2. The Compromise of the Religious Tradition

Cerebral physicality's prevalence over the current of thinking, whose relationship with the mental disorder we have seen, explains, amongst other things, the loss of the wisdom tradition in those appointed to religious life, namely those seized (as if they were in a sleeping state) by developments of the culture of machines, and, in that sense, intimidated, incapable of saying the correct word. And, in order to demonstrate a metaphysical certainty that they actually no longer possess, in the face of an impending technology, they are prepared to accept all its conditions, even within the circle of a cult and of a ritual, whose form is true only provided that it remain untouchable in its correspondence with its own original content. It is the sign of a rhetorical relationship of consciousness with a sphere that—being superior to it—should actually be recognized by such consciousness as the sphere of everlasting inspiration, namely the one with which it, instead, no longer has anything to do. If, in fact, such a communion were to hold up, we would be able to draw cognitive certainty from it in the face of each new event or problem in today's world, without being limited to compromises with the formalisms of linguistics and of technique, in a sphere where they are not truly necessary but, rather, demand to be kept in check.

To modern-day religious people, the strength to confront the intrusiveness of the mechanism and the series of amoralities that it involves should not come from compromises but, rather, from actually drawing on the spiritual sphere of which they speak and of which they appear as presenters. The Tradition, in that sense, should be the art of being eternally new, since they (modern-day religious people) are ancient, by virtue of principles. Therefore, in light of this Tradition, no outer and factual novelty ought to prevail with its monotonous appearing, codified in formal systems.

The Tradition should, by means of formal systems, arise as the courage not to reach compromises with the modern idolatry of the sensory realm, or with its corresponding methodology. It should operate as the courage to work against everything and against everyone, not through the spirit of conflict, but through the awareness of an orientation that the modern world has lost and demands from the depths of its automatic–technical misery: through the love of those who today desperately seek this orientation, insofar as they are unable to believe that the sacred is fiction, that it is not the very meaning of existence.

3. THE CULTURE OF ILLNESS

By expressing itself in the great systematic and analytical dialectics of the present-day, mental disorder involves, by means of these, the spread of its own process in the collective mental sphere. In effect, the culture of mental disorder today appears normal. It spreads by way of widely circulated publications, scholarly texts, and works with a specific university character, save rare exceptions.

The culture of mental disorder cannot but provoke disorder in those who allow themselves to be shaped by it. In reality, when certain specialists declare that thinking is a noble secretion of the cerebral organ, they are not wrong, because such an assertion is itself the thinking secretion of the condition of their cerebral organ. The pathological state legitimately becomes exact thought. And, nonetheless, even in such a condition, an act that is incorporeal, an act that cannot be identified by physiological processes, or logistically quantified, takes place. However, the deficiency of thinking consciousness is such that it does not manage to grasp this symbolic *minimum* of its own contradiction.

Such a deficiency, fortified by the mechanization of life (whose aim should have been the independence of human activities from material necessity, in order for a contemplative consideration of everyday actions to be possible to them) is established so that, as mental inertia, it easily dies into rationalistic automatism, which will call the zone of freedom and of clarity that it has renounced, "unconscious," and it will identify it with the zone of instincts, reaching that perfect confusion, in scientific and analytical guise, which will permit the cult of evil itself. It will allow the various paranoid, eccentric or violent expressions of new exemplary human beings to be considered forms of evolution and of greater autonomy.

4. The Bereaved Science of Logic

Dialecticism (as the deterioration of dialectics and thus expressive of contents more psychic than mental), simple analytical and systematic intelligence, discursive structuralistic automatism, signaling the breakdown of the relationship between thinking and the cerebral organ and, therefore, of thinking's loss of independence from the nervous system, are present-day phenomena.

They are attributable, on the one hand, to the decline of dialectics into dialectical materialism and of this dialectical materialism into post-Marxist dialecticism, which is its disintegration continually recomposed according to the structural analytics of fragments and nowadays, in themselves, anti-Marxist, but unconscious, and, on the other hand, to the modern resurrection of a logic born (it has now been twenty-five centuries) and exhausted as an orienting function of thinking. For, thought, having recently been identified with the measurable world, actualizes, here, an abstract connection with the object, which it assumes as concrete, and which consequently requires an awareness of its own movement, beyond the procedure of ancient logic.

The new logic, besides fixing its own analytics in mathematical structures, aims at codifying the thinking that binds itself to the sensory realm—even more than the thinking of the original natural sciences—by assuming, as real, the coincidence of the concept with the 'measurable.' And, without reascending to the real concept, it contemplates, as thought, the abstract projection of this coincidence. With this, it renounces the true logic of the process, or the experience of the concept, which has rendered the object knowable. The concept that has actually operated remains unknown to it. The new logic does not show any signs of the slightest awareness of such a concept, which operates and even remains behind the discursive screen. For this reason, it assumes, as real, the dialectical reflection of sensory phenomenalism, devoid of the concept that has rendered it possible.

Ancient philosophizing used to move more from the internal intuition of the concept than from its determination. For the modern person, *the willful determination of the concept* as an act solicited by the new type of experience of the physical phenomenon would be necessary. Such determination has not been possible, except in intellectualistic and abstract form. Nominalism has risen again theoretically. Thus, the experience of the physical world has lacked phenomenological orientation and, today, in its new method–technology phase, definitively devoid of the science of the concept, it is like a body without a head, which proceeds toward objectives upon which it experiments, but which it does not see. In reality, *modern scientists lack the logic of their own scientific experience*: which is not ancient logic, restored and modernized. It is not the current philosophy of science.

The return to formal logic during the present time indicates an insufficient awareness of thinking—with respect to the experience that it realizes in the physical world—devoid of the intuitive forces that it had available, even weakly, at the beginning of this (twentieth) century. It is a rhetorical return, because (as will be shown) it takes place at a level of rationality that is inferior to that of the principle of self-consciousness, aroused through the experience of the concept that abstractly coincides with the object. It is unsuitable to the demands of thinking totally engaged in the process of science and technology.

In fact, it has nothing to do with giving up on furnishing scientific discourse with formal rules, but with understanding the difference between formal logic, correlated to science, and the internal content of the scientific experience. Today, dialecticism tends to confuse the two forms of thinking—on the one hand, by altering the tasks of symbolic logic, managing so much as to elaborate formal intuitionist theories by way of algebraic structures and, on the other hand, by ignoring the possibility of objectifying the thinking that operates in the unfolding of physical experience.

One thing is the discourse, another is the *perception* of thinking that has entered the experience of the physical world and that actually demands its own method, independently of formal methodology, whose value is simply instrumental and expositive. This thinking, which is the essence of the experience, is, in fact, the intuitive and realizable movement of the research—what renders it true. It is unknown. It does not itself manage to be experience, because scientists do not consider this to be their task. On the other hand, they believe this to be provided by logical expression. At the same time, they believe they possess the content of the scientific concept as a content of thinking consciousness. In reality, the concept is assumed not according to the thinking that conceives it, and not even in its identification with the object but, rather, as a dead projection of this identification, in which there is nothing of the original movement of thinking.

Scientists of today are unconscious of their own thinking, which is something more than the thinking that results from an experience. They lack the capacity to distinguish between the logic necessary for the comprehension and further development of an experience, once carried out, and the essential thinking carried out from the depths of the conscious soul in the very same experience, so that it can be possible as research and invention. Not even a logic, which, with regard to its own formal process is itself unconscious of its own content of thinking, can provide this. Modern deductive systems cannot establish a unitary science of the forms of scientific thought, as long as they lack the concept of their own object—which is neither physical nor quantifiable—and, therefore, do not reach penetratingly where, *without knowing it*, the thinking engaged in physical investigation reaches, through its correlation with the physical object.

Methodology is the product relative to a content whose factual limits it is unable to overcome so as to translate it into formal terms, as long as it does not turn to a relation of thinking that is implicit in the content and without which this content could not be for us that given content, but contemplates only the relation's discursive modalities.

5. Machine and Methodology

Methodologists can themselves be experimenters, scientists that establish a relation with the phenomenon. But, today, it is the logistician, for the most part, that simply apprehends it, in order to transfer it to the sphere of deduction. In either case, however, they do not penetrate the relation to which they both turn. It is evident that, within the relation, they are not in possession of thinking in the act, which was the initial possibility lost by science at the beginning of this (twentieth) century. Rather, at their disposal, they have the deduced relationship (the initial moment of the new methodological orientation), from which they subsequently deduce (current moment), without science progressing a step, from an intuitive and creative point of view. This becomes obvious from the accounts of current logical–scientific literature.

The relation has not been grasped, but only its product, or the series of phenomenological notes, amongst which connections have been established from outside. From these connections, laws have ultimately been extracted. From these laws that do not correspond to anything living in nature (or in the concreteness of the phenomenon) but, rather, to the abstract correlation temporarily needed to substitute the incapacity of entering the reality of the phenomenon, they have moved by way of further operations, namely those producing today's technology.

The scientific transcription of a process, from a strict point of view, has no other value than that of documenting an incomplete investigation, due to thinking's lack of means. Yet, today, precisely this insufficiency prevents us from taking note of the actual situation, and it seeks its compensation in *new investigations*, which, for as much as they lack primal intuition, give rise to new experiences. But they lack the most important part: the *meaning*. Nevertheless, theorists, with this perspective of the experience, get worked up over finding meaning for it, with very sophisticated studies, propitiated by the system that supports the state of aforementioned things. For this reason, they would be gravely embarrassed if they truly chanced upon what they imagine seeking: the meaning, which would involve the system's annihilation. But they do not run such a risk, because the thinking by means of which they seek is precisely the one whose legitimization is derived from the loss of the meaning just mentioned.

Modern scientists operate by means of the relation's abstract signs, not by means of the relation, itself. That is to say, they operate nowadays as technicians: very up-to-date technicians. They remain within the limit, which permits them, at most, the objective projection of reality's abstractification, the mechanical production, and it continually annihilates their efforts to experience the living being, which is the level of the relation rendered extraneous to the investigation by them, and illusorily possessed in abstract notations.

The relation lost by scientists is nevertheless bestowed by mathematical logic as (something) possessed and appears in formal guise as a relation between signs, namely a formal relation that would be legitimate, if it could be derived from the perception of the relation of which they are signs. The relation, in fact, precedes the form and the form requires the knowledge of that of which it is the form. Therefore, when the current deductive systems exit the sphere of mathematical theories, we can say that they mythicize an inner or logical–formal, or philosophical, counterpart of science, as if they grasped the internal weaving of some of its structures, while they are really the tautological formal transcription of thinking's passive inherence to the phenomenon, without the possibility of perceiving its own movement and, thus, of penetrating the phenomenon.

All that is the world of machines (certainly necessary at a certain existential level, but absolutely extraneous to the interests of knowledge and that, today, nevertheless conditions knowledge and, thus, human civilization) as a projection of the inadequacy of thought with respect to the experience of the physical world, on the dialectical plane, is logic as formal automatism.

The error is not the machine, but the symbol that the machine embodies, since it is a sign of thought devoid of the productive power, which, in turn, codified and systemized, newly operates upon the human being, until demanding the integral automation not only of the means of existential functions, but of the existential functions themselves, the mental and the spiritual included.

6. Dialecticism, the Collapse of Philosophy

But the dialectics, electively theoretical, that spreads at this time as a discursive structure with historic, philosophic, moral, social, and socioeconomic content, finds itself in an even worse situation, because it suffers from the general state of analytical philosophizing, without the possibility of formal rigor that is not rhetorical, since its themes, being of an ideal nature, demand an intuitive activity which, as we have shown, is cut off as an unreal metaphysical element. Thus, dialectics with an apparent intuitive life, but actually devoid of idea, arose from Hegelian dialectics still founded upon an intuitive movement. And from the deterioration of dialectics devoid of idea, was born the current dialecticism.

In fact, the idea, as the pure immediacy of thinking, is attributed to an act of independence of the intellect from the thinking mediation, while dialecticism needs axiomatic presuppositions, mediations already completed and discursively fixed that avoid the experience of original thinking. In this way, it mistakes the dogmatic premise (i.e., the 'already-thought') for original thinking. It builds the systematic–analytical edifice on the moving sands of reflected thought and it degrades culture and corrupts peoples, by establishing the idolatry of what it assumes as having within itself a foundation, which, for it, is the impenetrable 'already-thought,' or the petrified 'already-thought'—namely, matter.

Dialecticism, lacking the internal correlation of thinking, because of its radical opposition to the pure intuitive element, needs the discursive correlation, or formalism, which nevertheless could not be formally logical, because, if it were developed with positivistic rigor, it could not but proceed until blowing up the entire system and, consequently, itself. Its content, not being ideal, is therefore psychic. As such, not having restraint in either a formal rigor, or in the concreteness of a theme, it becomes the correlator of words, for which it can be said that the only structurality possible in this discussion is simply the assonance of words, or the association of similar concepts. Here, it truly just so happens that black can be taken for white and vice versa, and that past history and culture can become retroactively transformed according to the dialectical decree of the present-day psychic influence.

Dialecticism has tried, amongst other things, to lead ancient Indian metaphysics back to its own scheme, particularly sankharian metaphysics, which, with its structure, lends itself better to discursive interpretation. But the reality is that discursive automatism, as a sign of the cerebral opposition to living thinking, is today a reality. It attempts to connect to itself that of the past, which appears formally akin to it, in order to reduce it to its own present-day psychic content by differentiating it (as it has already done with Hegelianism) from its internal identity, with which it could not establish contact. The system of Sankhara, given its formal preparation, lends itself to the dialectical reduction of content to an abstract monism politically usable by the present-day automatistic monoideism. But this cannot even connect logically with ancient metaphysics, since it is the projection of an experience of the physical world unaware of its own foundation and possible in the form modernly assumed, precisely because it is unaware of what is metaphysical, even if it is able to speak of metaphysics.

Greek and Indian dialectics, each quantitatively different and respectively consistent with distinct relations—one with *being*, the other with *essence*—were, in reality, thought in its encounter with the expressive necessity already intuited by it prior to the formal process. They were not the formal process, itself, which was never conceived as valid per se. Even Descartes, Hegel, Gentile—masters of thinking, to whom it would nevertheless be useless to return in order to grasp an art of pure thinking, which does not demand philosophy but the spiritual practice of thinking—were able to speak, in an era that was already intellectualistic, of a thinking founded upon itself, not identifiable with the analytics of discourse. What occurred when the discursive fabric of dialectics was gradually snatched from Hegelianism, while its ideal content, which alone justified it, became ignored and rejected, is an obscure and sad fact, which signals the beginning of the darkening of human consciousness. It can be recognized in typical impersonators, which, from Marx to Jung, have been able to universally affirm, by means of scientific and logical dialecticism, contents that apparently are mental, but, in reality, express a mental disorder.

It is important to mention that neither dialectical formalism nor, consequently, empirical–logical formalism, would have arisen without the degenerating of philosophy. By structurally making use of a few structures of symbolic logic, a formal technique and a genuine methodology could have been created on the basis of a pure science of thinking and, thus, as an expression of Spiritual Science.

At the beginning of the age of natural sciences, the scientist of the physical world lacked the help of a genuine philosophy of nature, once Kant eliminated the possibility of penetrating a phenomenon's essence and once Schelling and Hegel failed in the simultaneous task of creating an intuitive science of nature, which functioned as the art of approaching phenomena, above all, by allowing the investigator to follow what takes place on the stage of consciousness, as an inner counterpart of physical 'experimenting,' rather than by means of precise representations of their physical process. Dialecticism was possible because the best philosophers of the eighteenth and nineteenth centuries—still capable of intuitive thinking—fell short of a task sought after by human culture and for which, in one way or in another, they lacked the forces, as can be historically and philosophically verified.

Present-day disasters date back to this act of birth of dialecticism from the failure of dialectical thinking, which was the form of thinking still capable of conceptual movement and of an awareness of the concept as a foundation. Once thinking failed, the form continued on its own as analytical discourse. Therefore, today, once the formal experiences of logic and of mathematics, and the real experiences of physics and chemistry are removed—objective experiences on the exclusive plane of minerality and measurability—the rest of human experience is a dialecticism with the appearances of content, owing to the use of a scientific terminology usurped by the only experiences that justify it.

The psychic content of dialectical formalism has no relationship with the objects to which it refers. But a realistic investigation shows that its task is to prevent such objects from truly becoming known, being that no objects exist like those relating to the physical–chemical sciences but, rather, concepts such as society, liberty, capital, merchandise, price, sociality, and so on. It is the opposition to knowing, by means of the exclusive development of knowing's formal aspect: for which the object will always remain foreign to researchers, while they simultaneously nourish, within themselves, the belief that they possess it insofar as they speak of it.

7. Indian Dialectics: Unexpected Orientalists

The attempts on behalf of vigilant "orientalists" today to discover precedents to materialistic dialectics, even in Indian logic or dialectics, are to be seen as inevitable developments of the observed "mental disorder," which tend to project into the past a way of seeing that is a current phenomenon, but which does not regard the present, except as a symptom of its illness.

It is not our present task to show how ancient Greek and Indian philosophizing—admitting that the name of philosophy can be given to speculative Indian systems—was the form of a thinking that drew from inner experiences. In particular, the Hindu tradition in relatively recent times gave rise to systems of thought, which were only intellectual forms of the original metaphysical perception, and that today could be considered only in reference to such perception.

The logical formal element of Indian thinkers could not be the discursive counterpart of a realistic–primitive position—which is the substance of present-day dialecticism—nor could it be the propaedeutics of a philosophy of language that at a given moment became the condition of thinking. Inner perception was instead the prerequisite of thinking, the possibility of its formal movement. Madhusûdana's solution to the idealistic paradox, for example, has indeed a logical form, but this form is the guise of an intuition valid, first and foremost, in a mystical and ascetic sense. Thus, the thinking of Nâgiârjuna regarding the paradox of the "void" is valid, above all, as a technique of inner action.

The deductive–inductive process was not in compliance with the method of deduction and of induction in the sense of Western syllogistics and its formal developments. Rather, it moved from the contents of consciousness and of intuitive perceptions whose experimental value could legitimately operate in an axiomatic sense.

Even if that logic, with respect to the Tradition, acknowledged the descent from a metaphysical level to a "mental" one, it nonetheless maintained the relationship with the metaphysical. It played in the form, because it did not crystallize in formulas. It was not a propositional automatism, nor could it consequently arouse the automatism of others. It could lead form to antinomy and to paradox, insofar as it moved according to the informal light of thinking. It was not the formal guise of language separated from the content of thinking, the only one that could justify it. And when this "content" was the initial intellectual perception of the "void"—such perception being the source of the pure logical process—the propositions could not have been but allusive, paradoxical, obedient to a contradiction that, from the metaphysical point of view, precedes logical rigor. In fact, one thing is the formal rigor that tends to affirm only itself as a value outside the intellectual necessity from which it initially arises; another thing is that possession of the form used for the expression of certain thinker–ascetics, such as Bartrhari, Dharmakîrti and Prajñâkaragupta.

The polemics between the various currents are dialectical in their development, but they refer to spiritual contents assumed in opposite forms, idealism and realism: these being terms that do not correspond but indicatively to the meaning that they have for the analogous currents in Western Philosophy. Dialectical contrasts do not arise through a discursiveness that has risen to value. Rather, they focus on the relationship between two moments of consciousness, namely the pure intuitive one, and that of the word that expresses it. Thus, grammarian–philosophers are not rhetoricians or nominalists, but enthusiasts of the word as sound, in which the spirit expresses itself.

Certainly, the controversy acknowledges a crisis of "metaphysical" knowing, but it reconnects to the form of such knowing, not to the valorization of its lifeless remains. While Diññaga and Dharmakîrti consider discursive thinking to be a negation of the metaphysical act, for Bhartrhari, the discursive expression can be the legitimate guise of such an act, to the extent that it is intuitive.

When present-day philosophers of language and logisticians appeal to Indian grammarians as though to illustrious predecessors, they fall into a gross misunderstanding, because they mistake for empiricist–formal research what was then the elaboration of the form regarding an esoteric or informal content, which was especially important. It is the same reason for which dialectical misunderstanding cannot be extended to Indian thinkers, according to the recent attempt of nominalists in the guise of orientalists. For dialecticism, it is now possible to casually include within itself all of culture and of history, according to its monoideisms. Thus, the system of Sankhara, as has been mentioned, today becomes—through the action of unexpected orientalists—the pretext for a projection in reverse of present-day dialectical materialism. Examined has been the thinking with which he begins the *Vâkyapadîya*: "The Brahman without end and without beginning is essentially the Word, which immutable, is transformed into sensory objects: from it [arises] the origin of the world," and it has been believed that the Word is the spoken word, therefore, dialectics.

The monism of Sankhara is elaborated from the centrality of a principle that is the creative word, according to a process that lends itself to being presented in a similarity of sorts to post-Hegelian dialectics, thanks to the intuitive element's game of elimination. In fact, we need only substitute the term "Brahman" with that of "matter"—understood as the transcendent principle—and the materialistic–dialectical interpretation falls into place. Only it is forgotten that a relationship of words is established which excludes the content of which they were the vestment, in accordance with a procedure already used by Marx for the structure of his work, with regards to Hegelian philosophy. Born of it is the superimposition of a gratuitous meaning, absolutely devoid of a relation with the object to which it refers, but plausible for those who are no longer capable of thinking.

Dialectical materialists cannot worry about that content, because they do not even imagine it. Perhaps a logical spirit could help them, if they bear in mind that the cosmos of Sankhara, being identical to that of Nâgârjuna, presupposes the experience of the "void." That void was certainly not a void of air, nor even the image of such a void but, rather, a "perception" that would at least need to be put into question for scientific accuracy, since it turns out to be the foundation of that metaphysical monism. But it is a subject that is avoided, because its sense is obscure and impenetrable to the thinking that has fallen into dialecticism. It is the thinking that, closed off from its own original being, projects itself onto the support of names and onto the security that the tangibility of such support offers, unlike intuitive thinking, which demands meditation and creativity independent of the support.

With each value having been projected into words, automatic nominalists discover a way to continue thinking by constructing correlations between words, according to a need established by words.

They will thus encounter more names to which they will give the meaning prescribed by propositional automatism. For this reason, Sankhara, the great metaphysical monist, could be presented as an unconscious precursor of materialistic monism. Once the meaning that words had for those who once used them according to an inner light is removed, an edifice can be built by means of them whose sense is the opposite.

We have called dialectical–materialists in Eastern guise, "unexpected," because their orientalism is truly a non-sense, insofar as the content that they presume to be interested in is preventively denied. Its existence is refuted, because of the incapacity to conceive it. Given that Eastern tradition and culture can be explained only by means of such content—the suprasensory experience—what remains to be explained is the real intent of an intellectualism persuaded that the economic motive is an impulse of civilization. What remains to be of interest is a culture whose substance proves the exact opposite, namely the groundlessness of such a persuasion.

Proof of the attempt to include, within the historical–materialistic and dialectical conception, the Eastern culture whose intellectualistic forms contradict the materialistic vision (even when they express vitalistic and naturalistic positions), exposes the deception that dialecticians perpetrate not only to the detriment of truth, but also in opposition to the content that they presume to affirm, given that they tend to liken opposite contents to it. Therefore, such proof exposes the formal obsession of the doctrine, to which the reduction to the common dialectical denominator of all intellectual expressions suffices, without the relevance of their effective meaning, as long as the vast multitude of those grouped according to the absence of thought are supplied with the dialectical drug with which to obsess themselves in turn.

8. WESTERN PHILOSOPHY: HEGEL

Logic becomes a distinctive science when philosophy loses the teaching of universality and ceases to be the science of sciences. Dialectics splits from it and presumes to be the new philosophizing, moved by obscure impulses that assume political form and operate politically.

Emerging as a sign of philosophy's loss of unity and, therefore, separating knowing from knowing, dialectics then tends to reunite (on the basis of the common discursive–political denominator) the various sciences, the "moral" ones and the naturalistic ones, now separate, because they are deprived of the reciprocal relationship, or their original unity.

The sense of philosophy's 'dying' regards not only philosophy and the proliferating of dialectical forms in the various fields of learning no longer controlled by a spirit of philosophy, but also the orientation of culture and of civilization, the human custom. Such custom is no longer permeable by philosophizing. However, in deteriorating, it is codified and continually creates its specific contingent philosophy.

Thus, logic, by separating itself from philosophy, becomes a *unique science*: even it cannot do anything but proliferate. For this reason, logics, which strive to come together so as not to contradict each other reciprocally, or logically, are varied and specific. They tend to establish a unitary system. That is to say, they tend, unknowingly, to return toward what once existed and from which they became separated. By attempting to reconstruct a science of unitary logic, they essentially express the obscure impulse of the return to original thinking. But it is a problematic return, because they do not know which unitary source now truly connects them in the depths. Nor can they be united by ancient logic, ancient philosophy, as today they can be re-proposed: simulacrums of what they were at one time.

The reality is that the so-called formal logic that Aristotle founded as thinking's primary way to establish the concepts' normal connections, was superseded by modern philosophy and, with new rigor of thought, by Hegel in particular. Whereas the category of Aristotle is a concept fixed in its signification as the content of consciousness, the category of Hegel is the need to gather the same knowledge within its internal movement, as a noetic process. The fact that this need, then, is not realized in Hegel, because of an insufficient presence of the intuitive element in the dialectics of the same intuition, does not mean that it is not thinking's real orientation beyond ancient logic. But it is the orientation that could not have any ultimate purpose other than the metaphysical discipline of thinking.

The fact that Hegel did not realize the intent of his "Science of Logic," as a science, which, at its conclusion, postulated the spiritual practice of thinking, has meant, for human thinking, the impossibility of retracing its own movement when the experimenter of the physical world has engaged it in the analysis of phenomena. With this, we do not mean that Hegel's philosophy has been the cause of it. We only mean to observe that such a philosophy (incomplete with respect to the initial assumption) and the consequent possibility that its dialectical fabric was used by non-philosophical impulses, adverse to the reality of thinking, have been its sign.

Hegel intuited the non-temporal moment of thinking, but he did not turn toward perceiving it, because it would have arrested or transformed his 'philosophizing.' He preferred to follow its dialectics, so as to be able to describe its conceptual process and transmit it as an experience that could consciously be repeated. However, neither his disciples, nor successive philosophers, comprehended it as a pure intuitive experience, but only as a dialectical structure. Nor, therefore, was the internal petition grasped by a metaphysical experience mediated by pure thinking, which at a given moment rendered itself independent of the philosophical mediation itself. The philosophy of Hegel, conceptually exact, appears as an organic dialectical system, yet devoid of a noetic relation with the suprasensory element from which it originates and that would have, above all, been important for him to perceive and highlight, so that the ascetic necessity implicit within thinking, within the logic as logos, could result from the same thinking experience.

The resurrection of dialectics as dialecticism, and of logic as logistics, are thinking's regression in light of scientific necessity, the artificial resurrection of dead impulses in light of the demand of a modern investigation and of a conscious relationship with the physical sphere: the sign of reflected thinking incapable of confronting today's problems. The connection of this fall of thinking to the phenomenon of mental disorder at first sight emerges from the logic of present situations, from the logic of human relations, of relations between individuals, between groups, between nations, between continents, between cultures. It is the absence of real logic, precisely of that of which a person today would like to be so proud. The characteristic of various global situations is really illogicalness.

It is not enough for the substantial illogicalness of a particular logic, of the dominant ways of thinking, of the methodology of sociopolitical programs, of planning, of sociological, pedagogical economic theories, and so on, to appear by means of its catastrophic results. The catastrophe teaches something to the wise individual, not to the mentally impaired. The mentally impaired persevere. They devise new reasoning(s) for their catastrophe-bearing theories, especially if they have the political power by means of which they can publicly compel a community of submissive individuals to remedy, with an ever-greater contribution of work or of impositions, the consequences of the doctrinaire product of their impairment.

9. THE LOGICAL FORM OPPOSED TO THINKING

We cannot attribute to logical empiricism the erroneous thinking that lies at the heart of current political and economic facts, as well as of discursive–analytical culture. The fact that it is a sign and simultaneously a stimulus of automatic thinking, which removes us from our own inner source of reality and of truth, however, is unquestionable.

The unique position of modern deductive logic consists in presuming that logical discourse—to the extent that it can be edified within given limits by means of mathematical structures—can be led outside the mathematical sphere toward informal sciences in order to operate there formally. This would involve the truth of the content, be this content the method itself of logic as the discipline of formal disciplines, or be it as the logical structure of any other science. This is an incongruity, in that the truth of the form is not the product of the formal procedure but, rather, the product of the content's reality, just like within symbolic logic it is shown by formal analysis to have itself as content, e.g., when algebraic structures are employed in the verification of mathematical theories.

It is always a content that finds the rule for its own form. And already *in devising the exact form, its own form manifests*. Likewise, when the form as such is completed, the thinking that finds this form before itself is able to recognize it thanks to an independence from its own formal process. It is able to recognize this form not *in* propositions, but *by means of* them—namely, not to the degree in which that truth is outside it and it is able to learn from it (truth) something that it does not already carry within itself as a logical original activity.

If we leave aside the logical forms of mathematics and the mathematical operations that are useful in identifying such forms, a propositional calculus cannot but have limited usage. To believe that we can think by way of a formal language, in accordance with a movement that differs from that with which we are able to think and construct the formal system—so that it is necessary to dogmatically fix the norms of the discourse in which that movement thus becomes crystallized—means not to believe in the foundation upon which we erect that very system. It means to believe in a true 'determinable,' by way of words outside thought, in which we do not recognize the logical capacity that is nevertheless drawn from it, in order to attribute this capacity to preordained schemes: products of thought endowed with a relation of their own, not of thought. For this reason, the movement of thinking, capable of receiving the 'determinable' as true, would not belong to thinking, but to its logical form.

It remains unclear how the logical form allows itself to be recognized as true, without thought knowing that the recognition it realizes by means of the form is its own movement, and not the movement imposed on it by the form, according to a need of the kind relevant to the facts of nature.

Certainly, the possibility that movement is imposed on thinking from outside, as an error of thinking, becomes true, a true tenacity, through the 'appearing' of a discursive automatism that above has been related to the phenomenon of the mental disorder. But even admitting, without conceding, that the movement imposed on thinking from outside is true, one would need to learn what thinking has in particular, for which it can recognize what is formally true outside it to be true inside it.

10. THE LOGICAL AUTOMATION AGAINST SCIENCE

The logical form would, therefore, be endowed with a truth and an objectivity with which thinking would not have anything to do, but which it should simply grasp, once it is determined by means of analytical–deductive procedures. What leaves us perplexed is the fact that the most rigorous expression of thinking's form presumes to take place outside the experience of laws that objectively regulate the appearing of such form—a legitimate concern, if this thinking intends to attain a logical form whose objective is to expel it, since logisticians presume that its truth lies within that form, not in what produces it.

To proceed toward the objectification of the deductive forms is, in fact, only legitimate as long as we harmonize such an operation with an experience of the "architectonic" process of thinking, not as a psychological investigation but, rather, as a pure logical experience, which grasps its own fundamental movement and makes of logic what (after Kant and as was Hegel's intention) it should have been and was not—a science of thinking. Such a science (as will be shown in the second part of this book) would have ultimately postulated the spiritual practice of thinking. In fact, it can be shown that, on the eve of a conscious thinking experience—in order for this conscious experience not to be carried out according to its laws—what had to feign its identity by means of phraseology occurred: the general dialecticism of culture emerged up to its logistic and methodological acme.

What was truly prepared by those who had authority of it, namely a spiritual practice of thinking for the human being of the new times, should have responded to the need of thinking's experimental realism, which, in turn, should have constituted the inner and moral counterpart of the scientific–technical experience. But, because of the incompetence of mediators, given their expositive vain desire and lack of fidelity, it was possible for illusory dialecticism and logical automatism to encounter such a need.

In reality, according to the gnoseological requests implicit in recent scientific experience, ancient logic should have been overcome by not asking to borrow, from logic, mathematical structures, valid for it and for its connections with other sciences, thus, not in function of empirical and dogmatic reasoning, but in virtue of a conscious experience of thinking's intuitive element and, consequently, of its pure relational power: the matrix of all formal expressions.

It would be a matter of becoming aware of what used to operate in ancient speculation. A true beginning of logical rigor would have been to experience thinking as "being," which was indeed used in the forms of philosophizing and of scientific–natural investigation, but never observed, except as a dialectical and logical process.

Unaided by any mysticism, by any metaphysics, by any idealism —except the solitary light irradiated by Goethe—the scientific experience has developed without knowledge of the inner foundation of its procedure and without an awareness of the original autonomy of thinking, as if thinking were a secondary element and had nothing to do but passively comprehend phenomena, in order to codify them and ultimately learn by experiencing. Thus, the very significance of experimenting has escaped, namely the possibility, that is, of noticing what, from within, moved the 'experimenting.' Pure intuition has no longer been possible. It has been believed that the task of thinking was to photographically reproduce the phenomenon and, on the basis of the reproduction, to interpret.

The 'moving' of thought within a phenomenon, as an inner identification of its organic nature, has escaped, and it has been believed that the phenomenon manifested to thinking by way of its own virtue. Actually, the phenomenon moved thinking and suggested the relation between one sensory moment and another to it, as if the relation belonged less to thinking than to the object. For which, the phenomenon, deified and dogmatized, has begun to govern human beings, who nowadays have the thinking for which facts arise before them as true and objective, but they must not know that thinking somehow enters into this manifesting of facts.

Thus, the philosophy of science is not the thinking that discovers within itself the metaphysical forces by means of which it has entered the world, so that it can have further intuition, and the ideal and moral content of what it is carrying out. But it is the science of thinking, enslaved by phenomena or modeled according to them, forgetful of its own modeling capacity. However, we have seen how thinking, enslaved by phenomena is the principle of mental disorder, to the extent that the brain undergoes a unilateral pressure, crossed by currents of consciousness, which only occur by means of the sensory, but not as much by the awareness of such currents, according to the concrete relation of thought with itself.

And this is the odd situation of present-day culture and, particularly, of scientific logic, the one fabricated by analytical philosophers who abuse procedures that are justified only within the sphere of mathematical logic, namely that truth, measured and indefinitely measurable, is completely outside, because it can be grasped by a thinking that, nevertheless, is no longer there. Or it exists, but it finds before itself, already marked out, the binary of words and of logical construct, outside of which it cannot escape, because it has neither its power, nor authority. And when it believes that it escapes it, it deceives itself, for it cannot escape dialectical automatism by way of another type of dialectics, which is simply a juxtaposition of words. The autonomy does not belong to thinking but, rather, to the discourse.

The discourse that becomes autonomous with respect to thinking, the discourse that, with its logical forms, confines thinking and proceeds according to a series of inferences, certain of having thought within words—as if thought proceeded from a concatenation of words—is a sign of the cerebral automatism that conditions thinking, or the symptom of mental disorder.

But if the symptom multiplies and becomes the characteristic feature of the times, it is unlikely that a discursive expression of living thinking can still be possible, to which there corresponds, in readers or in listeners, the possibility of reliving that thinking. Because, nowadays, only what has connected itself, factually, to the specific words and forms of the discourse can have meaning. Thus, for those who, by expressing themselves, are not included in the game of general dialecticism and mental disorder—in which the specific coherence of the various intellectual groups is constituted, united in the contingency of the dialectics necessary to them, even to feign criticism of such a state of things—it is as if they had nothing to say. A wise person can be taken for a fool if he or she does not conform to the rules of dialecticism, which is not the form of the discourse as a form of thinking, but its mechanization.

VI

The Meaninglessness of Semantics

Discursiveness, no longer aware of the inner substance of thinking, believes that it, itself, by its own means, acts to reconstruct for itself, from the outside, an inner meaning, namely the one of which it instead continues to inevitably be the expression, and of whose direct presence, it unknowing makes use for its own process, by presuming to reconstruct this presence through imitation, from outside. This is an impossible process, in any case, because, by seeking from outside to furnish meaning to what, as form, is already meaning, it moves from an inner thinking that it ignores, and that it believes to have before itself in words, whereas it not only invariably has it within itself, but prior.

This is the contradiction of semantics, whose doctrine, today, moving away from its legitimate philological custom, presumes to have as an object what manifests only to the extent that it is not already an object. A science of thinking, or of the inner act that expresses itself as meaning, can exist, but not a science of meaning as an abstract activity separable from the thinking of which it is the mediated identity. Is semantics perhaps a science of thinking, or a methodology for the suprasensory experience of thinking? Anything but: if it were a science of thinking, it would automatically cease to be a doctrine of the concept's reflective meaning, abstracted from the concept, or a doctrine of what has a foundation only in thinking: in the thinking of whoever expresses a meaning and in the thinking of whoever interprets it. Apart from these, it is impossible for it to have meaning.

By tending to invert the original relationship between word and thought, discoursers essentially neglect to carry this out, and yet they carry it out as if it were possible for them. But, howsoever they wish to downgrade thought to the level of discourse and of its transcription into signs, they always depend on an inner thinking, from which they cannot escape. Therefore, in truth, they will never realize what unconsciously they would like, namely to establish a petrified forest out of the meanings of words, in which lost thinking is compelled to recognize itself.

In fact, another type of breakdown is possible for discoursers, in determined thought, not in the determination, as an act that escapes them. Semantic texts speak of the "influence of language on thought," without concealing the attempt to fix the being of thought in signs that symbolize the reduction of the spiritual to the contingent, and to the finite, yet according to a meaning unknowingly required of the very spirit that is still free, of thought independent of meaning.

Once on the path of analysis unaided by thought, which, like its original immediacy, is the synthesis that precedes the temporary coincidence with the multiplicity, discoursers are unconsciously inclined to identify the reflection with the discursive analysis and, consequently, to analyze everything. With their analytical automatism, however, they always analyze analyses, and analyses of analyses. Nonetheless, in such a procedure, they even attempt to include what does not undergo analysis.

The reflection can legitimately become a deductive form, if it moves from something that is certain, insofar as it is cognitively acquired in its entirety on the basis of experience. In the event that the object cannot be grasped in its completeness, because of its predominately conceptual structure, the reflection must draw from intuition, or from the life of ideas, all the way to a *conceptual perception* which, by managing to coincide with the thinking mediation, counts as experience.

Such an experience implies the distinction between knowledge attainable by way of empirical–logic and knowledge attainable by way of pure thinking. The latter cannot even be formally verified by means of the logical–deductive method. However, it can be verified thanks to the possession of that reflective mediation which instead—with regards to given objects—becomes directly and justly used for the purposes of examination by the logical–mathematical method. As will later be seen, the thinking mediation, to which logicians of today turn, is more important than its logistical product, *but it is the mediation of which they do not become conscious.* It is the mediation that, once known, leads to the experience of the conceptual object.

The mistake of modern logic is not to notice that the same mediation of thinking now demands a deductive method, now a pure conceptual method, thanks to an identical mathematical relationship with the object. The fact that we want to attain reliable criteria of investigation thanks to a system whose force is no longer logical thinking but the imitative procedure of mathematical logic—outside the sphere of the mathematical disciplines—reveals the inadequacy of logical consciousness.

There are objects that cannot be subject to analysis, without this being a non-sense. The analysis can be directed towards an object that is totally possessed, given that its concept coincides precisely with it and with its perception. The deductive method can be applied only to what is graspable in its entirety and objectivity.

When we are before an object whose totality escapes to the degree that we grasp of it only some aspect or effect or phenomenon, to analyze is to believe obtusely that we have before us the completeness of the object and that we can grasp this completeness by beginning to mistake, for the properties of the object, certain representations or deductions drawn from that of it which we begin to partially know. A phenomenon of living nature, a historical or cultural event, a fact of consciousness cannot be deductively penetrated, not even when they already appear to be proposed in dialectical terms. A formal ordering of the expression does not allow a grain of truth to be gained. On the contrary, it can constitute the crystallization of assertions devoid of foundation.

Faced with an object that it does not manage to grasp in its phenomenal completeness, nor therefore in its essence, the analytical procedure should fall silent and wait, in all logical honesty. The object must still be known and approached in another way: above all, through the experience of the correlation of the conceptual image with the datum, so that the correlation's movement can be continued on the basis of concreteness. (It is the technique of the thinking process addressed in the second part of this book).

We cannot analyze what is not yet an objective acquisition or a content founded on perception. It should also be this way for the experience of thinking. But discursiveness is what gives, as attained and attainable, knowledge based solely on its formalization, without noticing that it substitutes words and deductions for aspects which, regarding a given object, escape it, mistaking for perceived reality what it only manages to represent and report arbitrarily, to the extent that—as in the case of psychoanalysis—the representation of "unconscious" does not correspond to any effective perception of something called unconscious.

Therefore, semantics behaves as if it possessed the relationship between thought and word, or the origin of the thinking process. On this premise devoid of foundation, it builds a science, which, presuming to make use of various methods of linguistic investigation, from the metaphysical to the sociological, to the logical, to the terminological, to the psychological, and so on, cannot but have an analytical–deductive structure and discursive limit, even if it makes use of induction and synthesis.

If, in the premise not necessarily declared, it is implicit that semantics possess the relationship between thought and word, or aim to possess it, it should necessarily follow that semantics renews the intuitive art of ancient mystics, and possesses the key to the sciences of the soul,

The Meaninglessness of Semantics

or it is on the verge of possessing it. For, if we observe, that relationship is non-temporal and metaphysical. But it is obvious that semantics does not arise from a metaphysical or mystical foundation.

In the unfolding of a logical experience, there is a moment of thinking, in which it has not yet clothed itself in words and, nonetheless, lives of intuitive life: a non-temporal moment that already contains within itself the whole discourse, and yet, it still does not unfold within it. The more intense is this moment, the more the discourse—which has yet to exist—is potentially elaborated as if a form that awaits it were already constructed, since thinking is that determined thinking, identical to its own immediacy. This thinking knows how to choose its own form. Actually, it has already chosen it, because *form is inseparable from it*, but it is not a form that can be fixed discursively.

Form is not discourse, since the thinking that thinks, not yet clothed in discourse, already has its form. It is what semanticists would like to remove from it. *Discourse is the substance of form. It is not the form.* In fact, an identical thinking, endowed with its pure form, can be expressed in different tongues and in different languages, with different syntaxes. Form, however—namely what is authentic—is one.

Deductive logic and semantics behave as if they were familiar with the relationship between thinking and its form, and between this (form) and the discourse. It is as if very special investigators perceived the relationship between thinking as pure instantaneousness and the thinking mediation, as well as between the thinking mediation and the discourse. Actually, new logicians affirm that no metaphysics is valid and that we must begin from what can perceptively be assumed as real. We will thereby want to know these very special investigators capable of perceiving the metaphysical—since the relationship between immediate thinking and the thinking mediation is a non-sensory, therefore, suprasensory process—and of leading it back to a logical and semantic order. For, if they tapped into the metaphysical realm, they would have no need to linger in semantic *trifles*.

For this reason, with regard to semantics, it must be said that its actual doctrinaire development leads it (under the logical–dialectical apparatus) to lose the sense of its own limit and, therefore, to a situation that, seen in its internal meaning, is paralogistic.

Fortunately, some linguists still have doubts about the function ultimately assumed by semantics. On the other hand, the pretension of having a meaning be identical for all minds is invalidated by the preconception that all minds are the same. Or that they can react the same way in light of a discursive expression, for which, a meaning, rigorously determined, should be endowed with a universal objectivity, that asserts itself on its own, neither more nor less than a mathematical operation, which, nevertheless, is not the same thing. In fact, each one of us cannot but agree with the expression $2 + 2 = 4$, and yet, while identical for everyone in its "mechanical" aspect, or as an addition devoid of life, or as an operation whose objectivity is the being's cadaverousness reduced to a numerable being, it resounds differently in each mind, from the one that is most elementary to the one capable of noticing that such an operation is its intuition, active by means of those signs—such signs in themselves being nothing more than the reflected outer appearance of a light that is elsewhere.

Therefore, even from the level of a mere arithmetical expression, meaning, as the expression of the autonomy of thinking with regard to its products and objects, manifests a dimension of relativity, which is truly not negative. Rather, it is its authentic force, since it can speak to each person at his or her level of knowledge. Such relativity of meaning gradually becomes ever more relevant and operative, as it gives the linguistic structure a way to be the vehicle of its content. Fortunately, those who have really mattered, from Aristotle to Dante, to Goethe, to Sri Aurobindo, did not begin from just any theory of meaning.

The Meaninglessness of Semantics

It is said that today such theory appears necessary, methodologically. Yet, at the level of thinking's relation to discourse, it is important to recognize that, in spite of the efforts of logisticians to clearly distinguish a semantic characterization from the syntactic characterization of the deductive expression, there is no other justifiable science, from the viewpoint of formal rigor, than syntax.

A methodology cannot but renounce its own significance if it draws its own standardization from semantics and not from the science to which it refers, according to rules whose codification this science requires. A science of meaning is a useless science, or rhetorically useful to a spirit that no longer knows how to intuit and, therefore, no longer has anything more to say. It is the first symptom of escape from a legitimate limit: the attempt to standardize illicitly what, within its being, already expresses a norm, since it would not be, if it did not manifest as a product of its own norm. The meaning already exists. There is no need to devise a science for it, because it is to add something to it that, in turn—if the procedure is recognized as legitimate—demands the theory of its meaning. This procedure would never end, if it had to be consistent with itself. To believe in a "meaning of the meaning" means to begin the series of an indefinite progression, namely of the meaning of the meaning of the meaning, and so on.

The relation of a content of thought to its own expression is a choice of thinking, according to its laws to which the syntactic expression does not constitute a limit, just as the rules of handling a fingerboard and the bow of the violin do not constitute an impediment to the executive capacity of the violinist. Violinists can attain mastery of the instrument, precisely by forgetting the rules of handling the fingerboard and the bow, since they possess these rules without the need to stop and remember them.

Outside this modal legitimacy of the formal process, it is obvious that *thinking* chooses the expression by means of which to express itself, in relation to a theme and to its capacity of penetrating it. For this reason, a science of meaning does not have but the following alternative: either it is an art of reascending from the expression to the ideas and initial intentions of the author and, in which case, it cannot be but a transcendental psychology, for which, however, no one among the ranks of contemporary linguists reveals having the inner means (actually, they reveal having the absence of means). Or it is established as the mathematics of meaning, which proposes a universal scheme of grammatical–linguistic structures that count equally as a system of interpretation and objective expression for everyone, necessary, therefore, to every form of knowing, from philosophy to ethnology, to sociology, and so on, and in which case it can be recognized as a manifestation of the altered human mental sphere, namely as a sign of widespread mental illness, for it tends to standardize thought according to the integral automatism of what is no longer thought, itself.

In the same way that physiologists investigate the mechanism of perception—by following the behavior of specific organs and cellular tissues, without being aware of perceiving such organs and thus of already encountering what they seek beyond, thereby failing to recognize the only perceptions susceptible to the direct investigation of thinking, namely their own—certain cyberneticists seek to study the thinking process in a living brain, without noticing that they cannot find thought that functions in the brain, except in their own, not having any other relation between thought and the nervous system except their own relation, which they would therefore not need to seek in the brain of other people. In that very same way, semanticists investigate "meaning," without noticing that the relationship between the content of thought and the word cannot exist outside their own content of thought in relation to a given expression, their own or that of others.

The fact that some researchers, who believe themselves to be logicians in a strict, modern, mathematical, a-metaphysical sense, fall into such error, which is the error of logic, leaves one perplexed. A science that is founded on an error of thinking and that, nonetheless, expresses itself with a wealth of logical forms and by way of texts evermore discursively refined, cannot but be a sign, or a symptomatic symbol, an alarm signal. The systemic nature, most organized around an error, cannot be but a demonic formation.

Semantics presumes to establish itself as a science of signs expressive of mental contents, which leans on rules of symbolization, and which involves the analysis of the relationship between a mental process, the symbol to which it gives rise, and the symbolized term. American pragmatism and the researches of logical empiricism open the gateway to it, given that meaning is the ultimate sense of the discursive expression. Thus, for example, two authors, C. K. Ogden and I. A. Richards, in a text that has resulted in multiple editions, have spoken to us about "the meaning of the meaning," taking on the central idea of their pursuit of many cautious openings toward the needs of the loftiest sciences, of the soul and of the spirit, symbolic and anthropological, but leading them back to the need for a semantic awareness of their own: even when the so-called free discourse is distinguished from "scientific discourse."

It would have instead been wise to restrict the semantic field to the sphere of pure physical–mathematical sciences, or of sciences in which the concept coincides, without residuals, with the assumed object. Already in the field of biology and medicine, for example, things change, because a scholar possesses concepts that are inadequate with respect to the phenomena of life, or concepts that cannot completely coincide with their objects, which, because of their organic structure and vital function, elude the measurement that, instead, is integrally applicable to inorganic bodies. Therefore, the variability of meaning is important to the function of thinking with regard to the interpretation of determined contents and phenomena. To intuitive thinking, the same phenomenon means the possibility of a discovery, prohibited to others.

Only lucid mad people can believe they intervene in the most intimate relationship that we are able to establish with ourselves by way of thinking, namely a relationship between what we think and the word that immediately clothes it based on an unforeseeable choice, which is the level attained in our possibility to choose, or else the form of our freedom, in itself, irreplaceable. For this reason, the choice varies according to the level of freedom attained. We can better "mean" and intuit meanings, the more we are independent of the prescription of meanings, or of the norms of signification.

The conclusions of Richards and Ogden are unusual, but useful for comprehending the psychic content of the semantic point of view. Having been led by their research to the point of being unable to identify meaning with the symbolic situation, they are forced to direct their attention to another sphere, that of intuitions, of psychological processes, toward the assumption of a new sense of metaphysics. It is as if metaphysics, relegated to a deserted zone of past thought or of lost thought, were in wait for their reevaluation. "Each critical interpretation of symbols requires the comprehension of symbolic situations." A passage must also be left open to a "free choice of symbols," namely a passage on account of which all semantics disappears: the glimmer of light in the thick of darkness, that cannot but leave access to the hope that the meaning of human thinking exists, that it does not become suppressed by the science of meaning, that the relationship between thinking and the word is not compromised, that left to thinking is its inner autonomy, the possibility of actualizing its real nature, by means of the word that it unforeseeably devises, forming a 'knowing' that does not become its prison.

To intervene in the immediate and original relationship between thought and word means to interrupt it, to befuddle the human being, namely the human being who will not appear befuddled, given that he or she is rendered strong by the methodological mechanism that replaces the creative mobility of thinking. This would be thinking devoid of meaning, because it will have substituted the immediate relation (for which the word that corresponds to thinking is given to it as a sign) for the artificial relation extraneous to original thinking.

Even the thinking that corrects the construct of its own expression operates under the state of immediacy of its relationship to the word, namely an immediacy that always exists and to which the expressive mediation cannot interrupt the passage without ceasing to have meaning. Even when the expression or the syntax are wrong, that immediacy is valid, so that where it can exist, it itself rectifies and discovers the correct signs for its 'meaning,' which is the 'meaning' of each being in relation to the individual capacity of expressing him- or herself. Such 'meaning' cannot be codified according to abstract unity, without this being devoid of meaning.

Minds develop differently and each of us must be allowed to mean what we peculiarly are able to express, and to comprehend another person's meaning according to our capacity of understanding. Only such freedom of movement can give the highest expressions of thinking a way to direct minds that have a limited capacity of understanding and of expression. But the orientation is possible only if violence is not done to the immediacy of the relationship between thought and word, because within each lies the indication—weak or decided—of our freedom.

But those of us who have lost thinking want rules of expression, codes of signs, a logical and semantic Esperanto, in order to finally be freed of the responsibility of thinking, by drawing from our self-awareness.

Even more radically than empiricists, pragmatists, and positivists, we are convinced that at the heart of a doctrinaire construction, there must be the experience of the object of which one speaks: otherwise, we build upon soft clay. Therefore, confronting the problem of the relationship between thought and word, involves the concrete experience of the thinking process, an experience unforeseen by empiricists, pragmatists, and positivists, for it is not even conceivable, due to their obvious incapacity to distinguish the act of thinking from its discursive expression. For this reason, we must say that they are dreamy pragmatists and empiricists, since they presume to treat, scientifically, something that they do not imagine can be experienced.

The hastiness with which they believed to get rid of Hegelianism or Platonism (by saying this, we are aware that neither Hegelianism nor Platonism can today give any more help to whoever intends to experience thought) which, if nothing else, would have been able to establish for them a safe point of gnoseological reference, is a 'chicken that will come home to roost.' They are presently dealing with problems that, because of their logical development, demand the noesis of thinking, but they no longer succeed in distinguishing the movement of thinking from its discursive guise, semantically mistaking this for that. They operate by means of a principle that they do not know. Yet, they act as if they knew it. They act as if they were pragmatists and logisticians, while actually they are only discoursers, moved by a state of the discursive pedantry's obscure mysticism.

Any objection toward this criticism of ours, in homage to the need of a formal structure of knowing, can only be valid as a standpoint of the grammatical question and of syntactical analysis. It reveals itself to be a logical error, the moment it believes itself to be valuable beyond this limit and it presumes to justify the semantic intrusion into an inner process, which, because of its real function, requires to be left intact. This is disquieting, because it believes an abstract formulation—which from outside attempts to act as a normative element on the origin of the thinking process—to be legitimate: which is what it is, precisely because it already possesses what this foreign element presumes to bring it. The immediacy of the relationship between thought and word can in some cases be elementary, but its positivity lies precisely in the possibility of expressing itself, because, stimulated and developed, it can always arrive at the clear expression of what it wants to signify, if it truly has something to signify.

The Meaninglessness of Semantics

But what is the clear expression? Perhaps it is clear because everyone can understand it? In truth, the concept is one and the expressions are varied, but these expressions are much richer in meaning the more they bear within themselves the reality of the concept. We have already mentioned that even with regards to the expression $2 + 2 = 4$, minds act differently. There exist pages of Goethe on the theory of colors, which, in spite of their extreme clarity, were not understood by his contemporaries, save rare exceptions; and even later they continued not to be understood. Meanwhile, recently, such scholars have been able to draw the right meaning from them and even translate them into scientific and technical results, which essentially justify the exactness of those intuitions.

If we wish to arrive at the truth of meaning—to be expressed or understood—we must train thinking. We must turn to a science of thinking, before we turn to a science of discourse. It is autonomous thinking that can construct or penetrate meaning. Understanding, interpreting, signifying cannot be planned, without paralyzing the immediate 'springing' into consciousness of that of which they are the mediation. If deductive logic does not discover thinking apart from what is expressed in the word, semantics operates as a paralysis of the relationship between thought and word. But things would not change even if we succeeded in demonstrating that, there, within the mind exists thought and, here, within the word, exists meaning. It is like wanting to intervene in the relationship between the eyes and seeing, or separating the gaze from watching, with the presumption of wanting to make it see (according to specific rules) what it already sees, given that it contains its rules, within itself.

There exist ponderous volumes of semantics designed to impose themselves only by means of their dialectical and erudite size, and it would seem presumptuous for us to so simply want (without systematic analysis) to make the meaning of such a doctrinaire undertaking, collapse. But, as was mentioned in initial pages of this book, it makes little sense to refute a dialectic that has arisen from the identification of the dialectical process with its own reflective mediation, which is assumed to be the foundation, by a thinking incapable of recognizing its own foundation and, therefore, of drawing from the source of its own movement.

If by means of abstract normative elements we wished to intervene in the relationship between the legs and their movement, to presumably teach walking or to give meaning to it, no one would walk any longer, despite being able to write treatises on the art of walking. This is because the forces by means of which we walk are of an order that does not undergo intellectual intervention, or an alteration of its immediacy—an immediacy that contains a wisdom which dialectical thinking is far from possessing. For this reason, legs function better the more that such immediacy is guaranteed autonomy. In case a gymnastic or eurythmic exercise becomes necessary, it cannot but appeal to such immediacy. It cannot be the intervention of an intellectual process in movement but, rather, a special use of the movement, according to rules drawn from the experience of its immediacy: in itself untouchable.

Analogously, the immediacy of the relationship between thought and word is such that, from the outside, no thought, already thought, can substitute the wisdom of the relationship that thinking bears innately within itself in its manifesting of the word's immediate form. In reality, thought, to the extent that it is already bound to a discursive form, expresses an order that is inferior to the immediate thinking that is still unbound to any form.

A problem of meaning does not exist outside the strictly morphological–syntactical field, because the meaning that always appears is an entity carried out from within, according to a form uniquely justified by that from which it is born. It cannot be justified from outside, or arise by way of a process that is external to it and that, insofar as it places itself as the content, involves its own form, its own meaning. A variation of form is possible only from the inside. A superimposition of meaning makes no sense.

The Meaninglessness of Semantics

Meaning is the 'arising' of a thought's content in relation to the assumption of its own discursive form, or in relation to someone else's intuition. The determination, which draws from a rule, is inevitably arrested in its process. However, it cannot but have this rule outside its own content, as a morphological modality that is subject to this content, as it is to its own meaning. There is no one who does not see the limited usefulness of the rule, when meaning is already a form of thought, whose expression tends to be defined only according to formal norms at this point.

The determination cannot draw on any rule without renouncing its own identity, or without being the mediation of the content from which it moves. It should be something other than itself. It should pass over to another incarnation of itself, or it should be the determination that is annihilated in becoming the form of another determination: what it could not even (do) without its further self-movement—that is, without demanding its own content from itself. Thus, from the very beginning of this chapter, we have spoken of an "impossible process." The 'establishing' of a theoretic of meaning is the attempt to interrupt the possibility for meaning to exist. It cannot be codified from outside, for it is born of the spirit, from whose activity alone it can, once expressed, be recognized.

VII

Naïve Realism Codified: The New Analytical Logic

1. Formal Logic and Mathematics

The following analysis is not aimed at mathematical logic, whose legitimacy of calculations in a deductive role it recognizes, within the circumscribed sphere of its theoretical–analytical investigations. Rather, it is aimed at the attempt of modern language philosophers to extend the logical–mathematical process to fields of knowledge that, because of their objects and problems, require a movement of thinking that is not conditioned by logical forms but, rather, is completely independent of these, and which can therefore demand the logical form necessary from time to time for its expression, not excluding, when legitimate, the logical–symbolic one.

The issue cannot be the priority of logic over mathematics or vice versa but, rather, an awareness of the priority of the logical thinking act over its form, or logic, or mathematics, or logical–mathematics. The confusion that arises among modern logisticians with regard to the definition of the fields of employment and of inferential operation, meta-logicians, or meta-mathematicians, is reducible to an excess of formal consciousness and to a diminished awareness of the foundation—namely, of thought.

Naïve Realism Codified: The New Analytical Logic

The error is, nowadays, the presumption of new philosopher–analysts to organize the whole of logic in a logical–symbolic key. The formalization that they presume to nevertheless provide (apart from the formal disciplines themselves) even to the methods of "real" and "moral" sciences, is not a necessary logical apparatus, since it is found before thought structures, which, in relation to their object, already necessarily elaborate their logic. We do not want to deny present-day analytical logic the possibility of establishing itself as a unitary science of the various logical forms, but we intend to show how, in this case, the inference's mathematical form cannot be anything other than a particular moment of logic, nor can it govern its entire process without the disappearance of the gnoseological and scientific function that such a science requires. This science must be capable of possessing the awareness of the mechanical value of the proportional calculation and of the contingency of its use, that is to say, it must not establish its absoluteness on the basis of formal self-sufficiency.

We must, however, observe that, in the field of mathematics, the logical operations necessary for the elaboration of arithmetic and of geometry, as well as methods to make algebraic structures correspond to theoretical investigations, have a regularity whose awareness should constitute the sense of the limit regarding attempts such as that of establishing a "mathematics of ideals" or "the algebra of intuitionism"—what is unfortunately occurring already within the legitimate field of mathematical logic. In truth, even within the field of mathematics, the sense of the logical–mathematical limit can be lost. In fact, to lose the concept of the absolute immediacy of such intuiting, or of it being the condition of the lucid mediation to which pure mathematics tends, signals the dulling of mathematical intuition. The art of that immediacy can be incited by mathematics, but it cannot be identified with it, except on condition that it ceases to exist.

But the alarming abuse today is that of the new analytical logic, which, by attempting to identify with mathematical logic, aims to found the entire logical world on mathematical foundations, only because it has been able to utilize formal calculations practically regarding specific problems of the inductive technique, of probability and of causality. What has happened is that logic, which lost the power of being a science of thinking due to an insufficient awareness of the pre-logical process, found a new motive of consistency and self-legitimization in logical–mathematical structures and, based on these, it longed for the advent of a new logical cosmos, having been able to cooperate with undeniable fortune on the unforeseen developments of technological research and of logical–semantic doctrines.

We will have to explain how the principle of demonstrative structures, realized by the latest mathematics, cannot be legitimately brought into the field of logic where such structures operate not so much as to indicate the way for determined axioms to be true, as to derive logical coherences from postulated hypotheses. This principle can be adopted in specific cases and under the control of logic founded upon the analysis of the thinking process, since mathematicians themselves rule out the coincidence of the deductive mathematical procedure with that of a formalized axiomatic method. The subject of the second part of this book will consist of what can be the modern form of an analysis of the thinking process founded upon experience.

2. Logical Determination and its Loss

To apply a mathematical calculation to the discursive expression, so as to guarantee not only a definitive canon of marked precision but, also, as a result, an instrument of special methodological researches, is the positive aspect of present-day formal logic. But, in the light of what has been observed, the specific empiricism of this assumption—because of its inevitable dogmatic character, owing to the presumption of being totally modeled according to a logical–mathematical method that should, instead, simply constitute a particular moment of it—constitutes the further break-up of the human being with his or her inner person and with the living reality of nature. Because of the automatism of its procedure, it excludes the gnoseological awareness of its own functioning. Nor can it rise to a normative and axiomatic value, without losing the positive character of its own empiricism. This is the contradiction.

It is precisely the researchers of the positive, of the obvious, of the mathematical and of the tangible, in logical form, that risk creating the most organic superstition of the present time, namely the superstition of the word that can say something that is not but thought itself. If they aspire to the mathematics of expressive clarity, they have to realize that something must also be expressed, and this "something" is nevertheless thought, itself.

A truth, easily forgotten by logisticians, is that the word indicates not the thing but, rather, the thought of the thing, because such thought must reawaken in those who hear or read the word, until it refers the word to the thing. And if a choice of words and of relationships between words is necessary, this choice occurs by virtue of the thinking that determines the order of the words and of the propositions based on its very connections, to which the linguistic connections conform, according to the rules possessed and used by thinking for the purposes of its own manifestation, not according to previous and outer logical rules. Each logical rule, each enunciation of meaning, is a product of thinking, which thinking can utilize, but not undergo.

A formal science is not conceivable except as a science of thinking, from which, alone, linguistic rules valid for thinking can be derived, to the extent that it is aware of having existed prior to any proper formulation. And we will see how such a possibility involves a pure metaphysics of thinking, or a spiritual practice of thinking, because rigorous discourse cannot be constructed from outside but, rather, from within, according to a process of reflection that moves equally from intuitive immediacy and from the mediation set against the same logical expression.

A discourse, if exact, comes from thinking capable of expressing its own exactness, even when it believes that it constructs it mechanically, on the basis of fixed elements, whose relationships are used mathematically, according to the need of technical application. A logical discussion reflects the logic inherent in thinking, given that it is the spontaneous being of its indetermination, which is determined in the form. Formal error is always due to an insufficient awareness of the moment of the determination.

The opinion, according to which the formalization of the discourse—all the way to operations that are mechanically reproducible—can be carried out on the discourse from outside, because of pre-constructed "external" relations, is naïve and, thus, indicates an insufficient awareness of the logistical activity. The operation, in fact, occurs within the discourse by means of its objective relations, but such relations, in being determined, always contain the 'determining' from a sphere of indetermination. Nonetheless, such relations are carried out as if they received, from outside, the determination itself, since logisticians dream of producing this determination themselves (by means of those relations) and of, thereby, schematizing it. In so doing, they fail to notice the relation's 'occurring' within the logical moment of the determination itself. Logisticians fail to see the most important object—namely, its very own theme.

3. On Pure Determining: The Immanent Deducing

A distinction raised but not clarified by logician–analysts is that between the content of a discourse, as a methodological theoretic, and the content as methodological thinking that regards a theme. It is the distinction between thought as an exclusively formal research and thought directed at the logical structure of one of the so-called real sciences. But a more essential distinction that logisticians do not seem to discern is that between thought as pure logical discursiveness and pure thinking, or thinking as the weaving of all possible logical forms. Of this basic logical thinking, logistics should comprise a separate chapter. And we will show how only on such a condition can it aspire to be a formal discipline.

If philosophers intend to be logisticians, and if they are helped by logical consciousness insofar as they take on such a task, they cannot help but realize that, for any deductive operation, they indeed draw from specific rules that are familiar to them, but to the extent that they simultaneously move from an original non-formulated postulation, which is the logical order in the moment of its indetermination, namely the immanent deducing, which bears within itself the possibility of each formal relation. The 'deducing' of logisticians is, first and foremost, an inner operation, an essential experience[2] (empiria), whose regularity, however, seems external to them, for they are capable of recognizing it only in its discursive formulation. Originally, it is the deducing proper to the movement of thinking. By not noticing it, logisticians ignore a principle present in the determination of postulates, of axioms, of definitions, of inferential relationships, with which they are persuaded to actualize the order to which they aspire. They are unaware of overlooking that from which they move according to an essential logic—the original deducing.

Logistics—though claiming independence from metaphysics, from speculation and from ancient logic—thereby presupposes, in the thinking that it uses, a metaphysical kind of order, in that it thinks not according to ready-made reasoning, but in view of a reasoning that it intends to edify, by implicating the logos as the producer of the formal structure. It aspires to obtain this form according to a rigor that it is yet to have and that it therefore requires from thinking, not from the form still to be established. Actually, with regard to a conscious experience of the word, deductive logic could not exist without transcendental logic, nor could transcendental logic exist without metaphysics, nor metaphysics without the spiritual practice of thinking. The collapse of philosophy has been due precisely to its lack of what it has always presupposed: the spiritual practice of thinking.

Present-day deductive investigation aims to respond to its own formal calling and not to expire into a particular science of transitory logical facts, alongside other specific sciences. Nevertheless, it does not show that it wants to acquire an awareness of the limits within which it necessarily closes itself out of need for the object that it presupposes to itself and not so that such limits can be valid for thought. It does not succeed in preventing the form from escaping the formative force, and the treated object (in its abstract alterity) from governing the research, by annihilating the being without which it could not even begin to be—namely, thinking.

The analytical investigation could aspire to establish a formal doctrine only if it controls the cohesive force of its own structures, by drawing from an awareness of the pure 'determining.' Reasoning should be a particular moment of this awareness: it cannot but be it, even if, for now, it does not even imagine that thinking can manifest pure, free of words, as real thinking, bearing within itself the law of its own form. It should open itself precisely to what it specifically solicits, namely 'deducing' as an inner process. By recognizing the reflective determination as the mediation necessary to the formal process, regardless of its content, it would not be able to become aware of the pure determination. Formal sciences cannot exist without themselves being forms of an exclusive pure formal science, the relation of determinations: without therefore being essentially synthetic. This principle should also be valid for mathematical logic.

If logisticians do not relinquish the logical representation, they must realize how things can be uniquely designated by their names thanks only to the thoughts or the mental pictures or the concepts of things, expressed by means of names. A name can correspond to a thing, because it awakens the thought or the memory of it. Therefore, the problem with logic is not a problem of relation between names and propositions, but of relations between concepts, also in the case of semantic formalization.

Deducing is not a discursive activity, but, first and foremost, a conceptual one. To believe in the objectivity of the deduction means to believe in the objectivity of thought, which knows how to manifest its own formal and, therefore, linguistic rules, to the point of utilizing in given cases a propositional calculus, which, however, does not have to escape them. It does not become the determination. It does not eliminate pure determining, the principle of the logical form.

A real 'deducing' cannot but be the form of immanent 'deducing': of a thought drawing itself from another according to an *original relational movement*, which is the pure source of the inference within the rigorous formal construction.

4. The Inexplicableness of the "Interval"

Because words are not mere graphic signs or sounds, but symbols of concepts, with regard to the structure of non-formal or semi-formal sciences, logisticians are easily led to forget that the relation between words, as a relation of thought, demands, above all, a formal science of the concept. It is not enough for this relation to be actualized implicitly. The error, or the fall, of modern thought can be recognized in the fact that the philosopher or scientist makes use of this relation and even ignores its identity, believing that it exists in the syllogism or in the inference, in physical or metaphysical facts, and not in the thinking that recognizes it.

Nor is it sufficient for the latest idealism to have been able to indicate the relation, as an act of thinking, because to conceive this relation and to be able to philosophize on it does not mean to possess its movement: the only point of conceiving it being the *animadversio* (observation) of the experimental requirement that it postulates, that is, knowing it as form on the verge of being fulfilled according to its own law. This is the experience that we point out in the second part of this book. To ignore that water exists in a given place, and to know it without the possibility of obtaining it, is the same thing for those who need to quench their thirst.

To ignore the connectivity of thinking means to use it and to attribute it to outer symbols, which, nevertheless, as such, also manifest to the extent that they have been thought. Thinking is ignored in its pure logicality. When logistics, intending to actualize the rigor of the deduction, believes that it overcomes traditional logic by exclusively establishing a relational technique of propositions, it essentially separates the word from thought, by directing the concreteness to the discourse and ignoring where the concreteness, or the capacity of formally recognizing the discourse as true, has its source. Such separation is logically impossible, because there exists no mechanism of discourse that can be separated from the conceptual value of the words that comprise it and of which such words are symbols united by means of "intervals."

The interval is more important than symbols, because it is the presence of original thinking, the pure relation. A thought, or a concept, corresponds to each name, but the thinking between one name and another that unites them cannot be transcribed. It formally *appears* bound to names, but it is in itself a pure relation, pure thinking. In truth, the interval cannot be symbolized by anything. A logical phrase must always mean something more than the formal relation fails to say, even when the two logical forms—the "real" one and the propositional one—coincide, and in the verification of the "meaning" one can grasp a precise thought. Since this thought is never alone, it is connected to the whole of thinking, namely *to what goes unsaid.*

If we manage to understand that the laborious researches of an absolute formalism and of a system of relations, in themselves axiomatic, are metaphysical efforts, or attempts to render the formal structures transcendent, we will grasp the radical nonsense of the logistical phenomenon.

5. The Furor Deductionis and China

Having believed that they eliminated metaphysics, the Gods, transcendences and revelations, dogmatisms and idols, logisticians fail to notice that they have reproduced them for themselves in another way, namely by projecting, outside themselves, thought values upon which to depend by way of thinking, since they have not lost the inclination to depend on something, despite the anti-metaphysical revolt. Their lack of thought regarding the demands of a new experience of the concept and, therefore, of a new logic, leads them to an absolute unconscious idealism of logical discourse.

The idol rises up again as a formal value. And we begin to see its practical reflections, for example, in the attitude of a whole Far-Eastern population, among which the first and decisive philosophical germs were brought precisely by the forerunners of pragmatism and of that declared by us as unauthorized mathematical logic. For this reason, it has just so happened that this population—whose philosophical attitude had reached the thresholds of the twentieth century—still driven by traditional mysticisms and ultimately by dialectics bound to their modern set of problems, got to know Western thinking by means of a unilateral logical–analytical assumption. And, from this, it moved exclusively by way of its hurried cultural and social revolutions.

It was done in such a way that Chinese culture (whose situation during that period can be recognized as an anticipation of grafting consciousness soul forces) could primarily soak up an illegitimate deductive logic, ignore idealism and, therefore, not be able to make use of the real contribution of Western thinking, of which it could not but have a dangerously partisan image, namely the one specifically possible to a Bertrand Russell, to a John Dewey and to the prosecutors of their pseudo-philosophical preaching.

The Chinese have known neither Fichte, nor Schelling, nor Hegel. We note this not because we believe that idealism would have been able to give this population what it anticipated from the West, but because it certainly would have been able to act as an element of equilibrium against the possible unleashing of *furor deductionis*: which, instead, has been able to be unleashed, unimpeded, to the point of collective automatism, to the point of establishing the 'people–robot.'

This does not mean that Chinese Marxism is more dangerous than the Soviet one. On the contrary, precisely because Soviet Marxism knows how to continually reenter the normal methodological limits, required by the transformism characteristic of its internal dialectics, it achieves coherence with the immanent mental automatism, practically capable of all the pretenses essential to a harmony with other churches and other political systems.

By becoming a psychism of the masses, the identical automatism in the Chinese cultural soul can explode into recognizable paranoid forms, because the methodological scheme lacks the power to limit its consequences at the level of an instinctiveness of the kind unique to that specific human type.

It is the same reason for which even more deleterious than Soviet Marxism is the Marxism that moves forward in its benevolent socialistic and democratic forms, by way of a reformist legalism and within the hospitable vehicle of religion, methodically corroding the foundation of all institutions: by including in its absorbing process of planning, all the ethical–cultural, ethical–social, socio-economic systems already attacked by the *virus* of social redemption, because they are nowadays devoid of the content of ideas of the respective traditions.

It is evident that in such a process of ecumenical absorption, the system that more firmly possesses the logic of the disintegration of values will include others within itself. This is the strife that in the world today engages the leading churches and their specific dogmas.

6. LOGISTICS AND *PAVOR METAPHYSICUS* (METAPHYSICAL FEAR)

The actual separation between discourse and thought can be conceded, as a phenomenon of unconsciousness, to the 'philosophizing' that has lost its own noetic content and that, precisely because of this, is developed and rules as the dialecticism of the various doctrines, but it cannot be conceded to a discourse that presumes to be the norm of formally rigorous discourses.

Such rigor, even when it turns exclusively to the form of propositions and to their inferential concatenation, is not possible without an awareness of the inference's conceptual moment and, therefore, of its relationship with the canon of thinking that renders its rigor possible.

Logisticians object that it is not their task to take responsibility for thinking, or to identify the laws of discourse with those of thinking, or to consider thinking a subjective activity and, therefore, a theme of psychology. It is the weak point of current deductive logic, because it regards not the propriety or impropriety of the analysis, but that from which it is born and towards which it goes, that of which it is a transcription, namely the value. It is a value that is essentially logical, because it corresponds to the structural noesis of the content, which logisticians avoid by tending exclusively toward calculable forms of the analysis. They move there as if they were in a security zone, from which they do not wish to leave, for fear of having to lose it. But this cannot be the way to establish relationships with the forms of knowing, and between them.

As we have said, it is legitimate for logisticians to turn exclusively to inferential necessity, provided that they know what their operation logically presupposes. Otherwise, this operation, despite the legitimacy of the postulated hypothesis's use, is an airy-fairy construct, because it has, as premises, primitive propositions, whose validity, unable to spring from deductive operations, awaits instead to be recognized by these operations, but by way of an inductive-intuitive act that uses these according to what the formal operation requires from the very start.

Able to arise only from an intuitive and gnoseological fact, validity always postulates a logical, essential procedure, independent of calculations, even when it makes use of these calculations. Such observation is also valid in case logisticians oppose pure formalism without an object, or "logic without ontology." In fact, it is not a question of content in the ontological sense, but of content in the noetic sense. It has to do with content that should, to the greatest extent, be of interest to the logical analyst, surely not because of the deductive procedure, but because of the awareness of what makes it possible—the movement of thinking unbound to a particular object and that, therefore, has within itself the principle of each and every type of relation.

If analytical logicians, methodologists, intend to dedicate themselves to the rules of deduction, with the certainty of operating by way of science, they must, first and foremost, become conscious of the thinking that can become logical precisely because it is not obligated by a logic that pre-exists it. Nor can logisticians isolate the word from the thinking of which it is a symbol. For, even if they wanted to, they cannot, and when they indeed want to, they enter an area devoid of meaning, since they abstract from thinking's relation with itself, of which they make use, by projecting it as the discourse's relation with itself, whose exactness has indeed a discursive limit that they renounce knowing, by also renouncing to know that, beyond that limit, the exactness is apparent and can redress the error.

The word without thought is nothing, whereas thought without the word is a content that is in itself essential, capable of having its own formal movement as the original flow of the various possible forms, amongst which is the logical relation. From what we have been considering until now, it should be clear that it is not so much the logical–mathematical form that renders the content significant, once it is expressed, as it is the act of thinking of the person who comprehends it, recognizing it by means of such form. We have also seen how semantics is a doctrine such that 'its posing the question' of meaning renders it extraneous to the very act of 'signifying.'

Logisticians who intend to have thought that coincides with the word and with the formal relations, by excluding the pre-discursive movement of thinking used, lose the distinction between this thinking and its reflected aspect in which it operates, thereby obligating it to a mechanical relationality by means of an analytical development that thinking, as a synthesis, bears within itself already overcome. Therefore, those who conform to such rules are compelled to a diminution and alteration of their own true logical nature, above all, because they unconsciously end up opposing the discourse to its real sense, that is, the product of thinking to thinking.

The analysis that is truly thought (itself) is the synthetic highlight of the constitutive elements of a synthesis. Whoever does not possess thinking as a synthesis, cannot carry out the analysis. Analysis is the relief of the temporary separativeness of the multiplicity, which thinking does not need to justify or relate from the outside according to a contingent alterity but, rather, from within, according to its own synthetic canon, which already bears the relation within itself. However, thinking will not be able to actualize this relation if it is paralyzed by discourse, or forced to operate without its own synthetic vitality—namely, that from which the logical procedure can arise.

In reality, logisticians draw directly from the metaphysical content of thinking, but because of *pavor metaphysicus*, because of the subconscious fear of having to move in a field in which they do not feel safe as they would in a formal one, they ignore it. They cannot admit it. With this, they contradict the inner logical movement, because that content is present 'in their deducing,' as *an ideal, unconscious activity*. This 'deducing,' therefore, despite its mathematical paths, will indefinitely seek its object, as well as the justification for the inferential connectivity, without the possibility of recognizing them, despite moving amongst them.

One can object that, even if this were the case, it would not take anything away from the objectivity of formal deductive systems that have the intention of operating on a level of autonomy, from both the metaphysical sphere and the physical one. But it is what—if the closed field of mathematical logic is excluded—can easily be contested, because an unawareness of the ideal element in the formal logical process prevents one from recognizing how the 'manifesting' of the inference's meaning and, therefore, of the value of discourse, can be possible. This is the ideal value, even if the discourse is purely formal. Each discourse occurs so as to be understood, and it is understood to the extent that it arises as an idea in the mind of the person who understands. Rigorous discourse is ultimately understood because the idea moves within it.

To ignore the ideal deductive element, means to exclude the basic canon of thinking of which the formal canon should be a product. For this reason, despite logical rigor, error is inevitable. Such error can be formally demonstrated by whoever perceives it, and yet formally codified by whoever is its author, not only on the basis of the ambiguous immediacy of the premise, but also on the basis of the abstract coherence of the calculations of inferential structures, outside a real meaning.

The need to overcome the limits of Aristotelian logic with regard to the demands of modern thinking was just barely felt intuitively by Kant, as a position of "transcendental logic," and brought to expression by Hegel as the metaphysical structure of the new logic, but devoid of its own internal identity: unaware of the perception of the logical form's structural thought. What was then lost, is, today, doubly lost and even formally given as reconstituted. The product of that loss is present-day technology, devoid of a human subject: an exact technology, but one that excludes the inner order to which it owes its very existence and its exactness.

7. The Self-alienation of Thought

Logisticians are moved by the hidden dread of having to find another certainty than the one founded on propositions deductively connected. And to words and to propositions they bind relational values, which they end up believing to be objective, as if these possessed, within themselves, the truth and the capacity of relationship, so that their contrivance can function automatically to the point of mechanicality. They forget what moves from them, as producers of the formalizing activity, or of the fundamental mediation.

From the viewpoint of the canon of thinking and, therefore, from an integrally logical point of view, it must be observed that, there, where thought is brought to a maximum determination, it simultaneously expresses its greatest capacity to bind itself to its own mediation, or to its own complete alienation: up to the possibility of a system of signs without meaning and, nonetheless, inferentially valid.

Such a possibility, instrumentally legitimate on the level of mathematical analysis, actualized outside this level, becomes an error, if the clarity attained as a conscious self-negation of thought is attributed to a self-identity of terms or symbolic signs, and to their consequent relation, and not to the inner relational virtue of thinking, which has the possibility of re-forming its own mediation by means of them. Thanks to such clarity, it would be the duty of logical consciousness to carry out, from the very level of formal expression, the work of restoring thought to its own original movement, namely work demanded by thought insofar as deductive logic leads it to bind maximally to its own formal mediation. But for such work to be carried out, it does not demand fact but, rather, the logical–mathematical spirit.

There is no logical–mathematical fact that is such on its own. In logistical texts, it is not necessary to refer to a logical–mathematical *spirit*, but in order for this to be the principle of what is explicated in those texts, logisticians have the possibility of experiencing it through an awareness of the operations they carry out. Otherwise, they behave like primitives before objects or signs to which they attribute a value that they allow themselves to be moved by, ignoring (the fact) that the value and, therefore, the movement, begins from a determination of their thinking. For such thinking is capable of self-alienation, or dis-individualization, in which lies the germ of its maximum individualization, as mentioned. The capacity of self-alienation is, in fact, the very germ of self-determination, which expires into reflectivity, because it is unaware of itself.

For this reason, today, the discipline that assumes the highest rational–linguistic rigor, with the series of its methodological formulations, is able to ultimately become the expression of thinking's fall into the realm of truth that appears formalized, or the realm of obtuseness technologically codified, with its facts, its demonstrations, the proofs of its concreteness and, therefore, with its strong organic nature: in which, as a matter of fact, there lies only the cadaverousness of thought solidified in dazzling mechanical structures.

8. The Hidden Dangers of the Formal Apparatus: The Appearance of the Content

Undoubtedly, logic is not the theory of knowledge, but it serves as its instrument; and its only reason to be is to operate precisely as such an instrument, both in an analytical and systematic sense, and for the purposes of specific verifications of scientific discourse.

While in the mathematical field the arithmetical and algebraic operations that abstract from quantities or from objective contents are legitimate, this is granted to logical operations only if they express the art of experiencing the original mediation, or if they move from assertions of the canon of pure thinking. That which is the axiom of the mathematician, should be the thesis of pure thinking for logisticians, when they turn to a non-sensory content. The inference thus bears the effective formal necessity.

Logisticians presuppose pure intuition. They refute it, but unconsciously draw from it when their formal research is exact. It has, nevertheless, to do with short-lived exactness, since logisticians, unconscious of the pre-discursive moment, subject thinking's essential element to the scheme of discursiveness, which does not come to them from essential thinking, but from the thinking already governed and moved by cerebral formalism, namely by nature. For this reason, they use the conscious forces of thinking to the benefit of an apparent objectivity, whose sense is to continually annihilate those forces of consciousness: to even arrive at negating their reality. Discursiveness, derived from such contradiction, by impressing itself on the intellect of another person, has the power to deprive it of intuitive nourishment and to mechanize its expression—which is the expression of the present-day culture.

A curious thought, for example, is that of Carnap, when he affirms that, just as geographical coordinates facilitate the task of the scholar regarding the configuration of nature's spheres, so too can an artificial language be used as a system of reference to study a certain natural language or a class of such languages. The truth is that geographic coordinates, as a construction of lines not produced in nature, correspond to immobile physical entities, which can be objectively determined, whereas words, in any case, correspond to concepts, or to immeasurable mental entities.

The logical–mathematical structure of a specific language does not automatically give rise to 'its functioning' as a system of reference for the control of other languages, since it has nothing to do with a dimensional relationship, but with the inalienable mental relation, not only of languages with respective contents, but of the mental content of the one with the mental content of the other.

The logistical error is that of wanting to place symbolic logic outside the logical–mathematical field, without being aware of the limitedness of the language's structural coincidences that can be calculated with that of non-formal disciplines. A simultaneous error is that of wanting to place pure logic outside the field of pure thinking, or outside the thinking that gives a construct to such logic, since this thinking is its formal movement, its prime relation. The specific field in which logic can legitimately operate, unconsciously obeying such a canon—thanks to the coincidence of the formal relation with the type of relation implicit to the object—is precisely that of mathematics and certain sectors of physics.

Therefore, given the limitedness of the sphere of its legitimate usability, such logic cannot give rise to a science of language as the vestment of thought, without being an automatism that tends to replace the initiative of thinking, by offering it an easy formal correlation, which can take on any psychic content and, thus, operate as a legitimate vehicle of mental disorder. In fact, it does not express psychic illness as such, but the form that conceals it, appearing as the deductive vestment of a legitimate content.

The most difficult paranoia to identify is precisely the one that is clothed in logical form, given that the content, thanks to such form, appears as the bearer of its own legitimacy. The deception consists in the fact that such a content's legitimacy is, in effect, an appearance, since it is only supported by the formal apparatus, whose erroneousness, as has been seen, consists in its manifesting according to the needs of a determination that it does not possess: therefore, as if it were unrelated to any object.

The path of our liberation from the deception of present-day culture will consist specifically in discovering that, in more than one of the present-day empirical sciences, it is the formal apparatus that fashions the content of which it seems to be the vestment.

The formal apparatus does not rest on the content. Rather, this content arises from the apparatus. The content really does not exist. Sociology and psychoanalysis are characteristic in that sense. It is a dangerous situation not only because it lends itself to the logical–scientific expression of the mentally impaired, but above all because such sciences edify themselves, without the experience of the object to which they refer and which allows them to believe that they are empirical.

9. FORMALISM AND THE INNER CONTENT

The proposition of a philosophy of method and language requires an awareness of its metaphysical presupposition, because it manages to posit itself as a universal theoretic of knowing, when particular sciences and their specific methodologies already exist, which gradually produce language and clarify it, and each one from its particular domain can legitimately establish the relationship with others. When methodology wishes to be whole, as an archetypal science, it must be aware of taking on postulates that once belonged to philosophy, as a science of sciences. It could truly do this legitimately in an age in which philosophy has renounced its mission as the science of sciences and has lost logic as the science of thinking and, thus, as an integral methodology. But it is unable do it, because it does not notice the sense of its calling and the noetic task that it entails.

Analytical philosophers, logisticians should not find it difficult to realize that the error of thinking, outside the field of physics and mathematics, can appear in regular logical form, given that the form seems to refer to a mental content, whereas in reality this content is psychic, and that, thanks to the seeming independence of the inferential scheme from the content of thinking, the real situation of this can escape. A science of language could not be a formal analytic, with a theoretic function and, nevertheless, be divorced from a science of thinking. For, if it were an expression of a science of thinking, it would grasp its own limits. It would not presume to control thinking. It would not presume to establish itself as a philosophy of language, but it would be included in its legitimate morphological syntactical scheme.

The error of thinking can be grasped only by means of pure intuition, and such intuition, if it needs to be expressed, can also take on logical form. It is not, therefore, the logical form that confutes the error, but intuition, which assumes a logical form. This, once expressed, can communicate an intuitive content, not so much by virtue of formal rigor, as for the fact that the rigor is the guise of this content. It is its production. For the same reason, the reader's act of thinking makes the intuitive content its own, since such form does not paralyze its movement by automatistic means.

In reality, words cannot be used as mere signs by the linguistic system, because, as words, they are already signs within a content that is immediate to them, the concept being *sub-stanial*. The concept, in its mediation, implies a logical relationship, since its isolation makes no sense. The relation between these signs is *in primis* conceptual. It thus operates within the form, all the way up to a possible logical–mathematical form. The science of the concept appears essential. Outside it, deductive and semantic logic fall into the formalism of a non-sense.

A distinction in this regard is possible and necessary, namely between a content that can be attained through a mathematical–physical experience and, therefore, one that can be expressed according to a formal determination, and a content that can be acquired via a logical–intuitive path, according the conceptual relation abstracted from sensory data—for example, the concept of work, or society, or fraternity, or logic, or thought, or vital force, and so on.

Some logicians forget the limits of their assumption, when they discover the errors of logic in texts belonging to the philosophical–metaphysical tradition, since these are not in keeping with their current logistic measurements. The truth is that those philosophical–metaphysical expressions often correspond to real non-sensory experiences, as in the case of Plato, or of Quintilian, or of Thomas Aquinas, or of Hegel, for example. Logician–analysts do not object that it is an empirical–logical duty to refute each expression of thinking that cannot be guaranteed by experience (the deductive method itself being the formal experience) because, in that case, they would have to demonstrate that some of them experienced the lack of experience of the inner object on behalf of those metaphysical philosophers. This is the obscure and mythic side of logistics, namely not to admit that the non-sensory can become experience, while the use of logical–symbolic structures is actually even, itself, an extra-sensory act.

We need only observe that an inner experience can also be expressed according to a logical order, from which a formal system could be consequently drawn, a system, which, as has been noted, would itself be, nevertheless, taken on as an expression of the inner experience—a presupposition of a science of pure thinking, or of the form–thought that can be known before being known as a discursive determination.

10. Formal Unconscious Metaphysics

To believe that truth can be presented to others as truth, simply because it is expressed in logical form, has been shown by us to be the discursive faith of primitives. Such form is a means, or a support, for something else, something essential, which is thinking that is cognizant: that of which logisticians would like to do without. Therefore, in their research, these logisticians are unaware of not doing without it, and better yet, of wanting to make rigorous use of it, without succeeding, since they *mistake form fixed in its determination, for form that is determinant.*

Symptomatic, for the ultimate meaning of such logic, is the fact that logisticians are not conscious of the content to which logic nevertheless conforms. They should be able to look at this content, it being their very task to leave aside all content. Only an act of thinking, not a discursive determination, is capable of such an undertaking. The incapacity to identify the role of the formal undertaking in relation to an object that is itself the form, still independent of determination—whereby the determination normally becomes the content (regardless of what it is) to which the form becomes a mediator—shows how harmful it has been to logisticians to have deprived themselves of the experience of the concept and of the science of judgment.

For their operations, they use thinking that is formally more conscious, given that they lead it to a maximum determination, or to the maximum negation of itself, by binding it to values indirectly deduced from sensory experience, but which they tend to render independent of this experience, until conceiving a "logic without ontology," which, if positively observed, is a metaphysical petition.

It is a serious thing for formal modern logic to unconsciously establish itself as metaphysics, since it flies in the face of the initial proposition. Analytical propositions (having as their object the proposition itself as an abstract entity) require a synthetic activity that, carried out logically, leads to the world of ideas; or there where one could presume to leave aside content since it is the world of forms, whose essence consists in not being bound to any determination and yet, as such, is capable of being rigorously tested by thought.

The positive form of the inference could not but have such a course, from the calculation of the propositions to the syntactic or semantic value of the deductive expression, to the identification of the various types of implication and of their relationships, the effort to have the logical form maintain a nominalistic and linguistic character outside thinking, is to unconsciously escape the internal logic of what is being carried out: ultimately, a radical formulation of principles as much as that presumed by the syntheses a priori Kantian, because of the incapacity to understand the ultimate or primary sense of the research, namely a metaphysics of form. This metaphysics of form cannot be the discursive form but rather what, if experienced or acknowledged in its essentiality, would illuminate, from the sphere of its own immediacy, the sense of formal problems—the form already mediated, needing only syntactical analysis.

11. The Reciprocal Non-connection of Deductive Systems

A philosophy that had corresponded to its original mission would have had, as one of its particular tasks, to arrive at reflecting upon the language of modern science, among other things. In traditional 'philosophizing,' a philosophy of language has always been one of its special and subordinate expressions. Until recently, 'philosophizing' has been a 'reflecting' on human activities, on works completed and to be completed, for the purpose of identifying its ideal laws and transforming them into further cultural impulses.

Current analytical philosophy and the mutually related linguistic science are not the activity of the philosophy that, by continuing to maintain the threads of knowledge, acquires, amongst other things, an awareness of the new perspectives of science, but what legitimately tends to take the place of an already inefficient speculation by way of deductive systems—namely, systems which, nonetheless, are not exempt from gnoseological and ontological positions, that go beyond the inferential scheme and whose speculative character, however, logisticians fail to recognize. Combinations of the deductive–inductive method and of speculation (of which nothing is said) casually overcome certain contradictions. In the elaboration and in the reciprocal confrontations of logical–deductive doctrines, we witness—with regards to arguments such as "the ultimate object," or the function of philosophy, or the sense of physical experience—the unconscious surfacing of "Platonic," or Platonic–Aristotelian positions, or of mystical attitudes, owing to a rigorousness that invests form without taking thought into account and that, faced with contradiction, continually resorts to a discursive solution, and not to the act of thinking.

When contemplating the panorama of analytical philosophy, we notice that we are facing a logic of airtight compartments—logic without a metaphysical object but with a physical object; logic without a physical or metaphysical object; logic with a physical and metaphysical object—without gnoseological implications or with gnoseological implications in which mathematics grasps linguistics and in which linguistic analysis passes away into mathematics—with a philosophical bent, with an anti-philosophical bent. For each situation of knowing, we devise a new logical language, a new analysis, with new sutures, and if a logical form does not correspond to specific problems or situations, we resort to ulterior forms. We appeal to new axioms, and, to the practical act. We utilize a logical empiricism that corresponds more to the solicitation of urgent situations of thinking.

By reading the texts of logical-formal research, we have the impression of escaping, by means of a theoretic–deductive language, to a unitary vision, to a synthetic thinking that can justify the diverse analyses and their possibility to remain together, logically.

The reality is that, if we exclude the system of logical operations necessary to mathematics, no logic exists that can stand on its own, as a pure theoretic of the form. Pure form cannot manifest in deductive logic, in spite of its meta-ontological presumptions, since it is already the form of the determination. Its formalism compels it to the determination of its own object, which it, as a particular content, indeed excludes, but simultaneously assumes. Actually, it is obligated to assume, because of the inevitable substantiality of the determined form, even if it is free of content, bound to the fixity of the objective formulation. We could legitimately speak of pure form only in the case of "pure thinking" (to whose experience we refer in the second part of this book) and in the case of its methodology, which truly has, as an object, the non-determination drawn from the determination of thinking.

Logic that arises as a science unto itself, separated from other forms of knowledge, cannot exist: not so much for reasons of the type of "paradox of inference," as for the fact that such a science should primarily be a methodology of the logos, or a science of the concept—precisely that from which logisticians decidedly shy away.

What truly gives pause for thought is that such a non-connection of the logical zones, is noticed, as an existential fact, in the classic logicians of the present time, who also specifically have a logical preparation to sustain positions and attitudes, personal or professional, which between them, in contrast, lack a logical relation: a non-relation, or disconnection, that manifests in their incoherence of life, always logically justified. It is where we see the impossibility for logic (of which those people are nourished) to be the educator of thought. Such logic is certainly not formal logic, but the logic that, now resounding generally from an abuse of formal logic, in every field of culture, no longer has a hold on the reality of human beings, if we exclude the sphere of their technical–mechanical interests.

Logisticians do not object that such problems are not included in the field of their studies, since they were hired to discover rules for the exact and necessary deduction. Such problems are actually connected to the logical fact, through the inseparable unity of the word with thinking, and of thinking with the will, and of the will and of thinking with human feeling: therefore with all human 'existing.'

When in the form of discourse, we believe we gather that of thought which has an objective value, leaving to other sciences the task of attending to the value of thought as a presumed psychic and subjective fact, we have essentially succeeded, once and for all, in separating thought, already inert, from its life force. We have done all that today is needed so that the relationship with reality, with the forces of nature and of history, can only be discourse, reasoning: so that no science can any longer have a relationship with its own object, that is not logical formalism. For this reason, the substance and the meaning of life permanently escape human thinking.

12. Formal Appearance

Some prudent logisticians, however, do not forget that the field of formal logic today, being rigorously that of mathematical logic, cannot but be reserved for specialists and oriented only toward specific methodological researches. In reality, what negatively influences knowledge is the deductive formalism brought also into fields that do not require it. For this reason, it manages to operate as a nominalism sufficient unto itself, without a relationship to the contents to which it makes reference. Moreover, what is actualized by means of thinking—be it also due to a group of specialists—is the expression of the human mental sphere. It nonetheless resounds in human culture.

An error of codified thought is a *virus* that circulates in the whole cultural organism and, therefore, penetrates life. Formal language is seductive, corresponding to our present-day need to assert ourselves by means of an 'appearing,' to express ourselves without being, to create for ourselves a world of discursive certainty, to justify, by way of flexible analytical discourse, the forms of our dependence on the sphere of instincts. We replace reason with the architecture of phrases, since reason would confute our talking and our acting.

The penetration of the automatistic language into the various forms of knowledge is an obvious phenomenon. It is dialecticism that has only the analytical and relational assonance of deductive science, without possessing the relation between propositions, through a lack of an ideational connection within the content, and a lack of inferential technique within the form.

In various disciplines, the empirical–logical language is penetrated without restrictions. Automatic–logical semblance is sufficient for them. Analytics has become the guise of a type of intellectualism, which, from sociological–economic sciences to psychology to spiritualism, needs the inertia of thinking, in order to justify its own discursive pedantry. The new type of intellectual is essentially a rhetorical logistician, namely a dialectician–logician, but without the logical uniformity that alone could justify, at least formally, his or her discourse. Formal semblance is truly sufficient for all expositors that have a pseudo-science or a pseudo-doctrine to affirm, as well as an insufficiency of thought to hide, or a mental disorder to express.

For this reason, it can be observed, for example, how all Marxist or post-Marxist dialectics is essentially a discursive agglomeration that, in the light of scientific empiricism, would go to pieces, but stays intact by virtue of logical consonances that seduce the weak thinker, thanks to their analytical semblance, not their effective analytics. The presuppositions of such dialectics are not ideas, but anti-ideas, or mystical positions with an ideal appearance, obscure beliefs in the magical nature of material processes and in the inescapability of typical technical and social facts, for which self-movement and, consequently, a relation with the treated theme—which only has the function of pretext—are impossible for thinking.

13. The Nucleus of Logical–Analytical Misunderstanding

Ultimately, what is the theory of necessary inference? It is the aspiration of logic toward a formal system of relations, which not only constitutes a conscious analysis of the experience, but also knowledge's criteria of certainty. If logisticians truly thought what they have the intention of seeking, they would not be able to identify it simply by means of the necessary structures of logical discourse, or by means of their symbolic scheme but, first and foremost, by means of the movement itself of the inference. For the inference is, above all, the *inferring*, and this inferring precedes its discursive manifesting—not as a binary that compels thought, but as the very movement of its mediation. It is the movement that, experienced, turns out to be structurally relational in itself, that is, intuitive and deductive–inductive at the same time, because it is free in its internal need and it bears within itself the order that it dialectically believes to obtain by means of formal operations.

Inferential necessity is borne by thinking as one among its many possibilities of determination. It cannot be fixed as the logic of the proposition, without knowing that what is fixed is already contained within thinking, as one of its possible forms, of which it is essentially a postulate. It is a postulate whose structural necessity is thinking itself, not the proposition, which could be different since thinking can express the same necessity according to equivalent inferential forms.

The expression "necessary inference" is a contradiction in terms as it is used by the logical formal canon, in that it is not seen as a sign of the expressive necessity of an intuitive content in the act of mediation, but only as a form of the propositional unfolding. To say "inference" is already to say "necessary inference." It is like saying relational thinking. The expression is pleonastic, because, structurally, thinking is already, in itself, a relation and its reflective determination cannot separate itself from the form of itself, like it can from its own being. The inference is nothing but thinking that formally unfolds its own being, necessary not as a deductive determination but, rather, as a structural power of deduction. The science of pure form is not linguistics, since its movement is the *immanent deducing*, which belongs to the original nature of thinking.

By forgetting or not noticing this, logisticians work toward the constitution of a formal discursive cosmos that—establishing itself as a thinking technique, despite assurances of being limited to the formal field—rises to a metaphysical standardization and to an unconscious dogmatic theology, against thinking itself, by not acknowledging the thinking that fails to correspond to its theoretic formulary, namely by removing from thinking the original immediacy and the power of synthesis, so as to logically establish the paths of an 'already-thought' to be rethought according to its fixed and decisive alterity.

Thinking is used, but devoid of deductive virtue, precisely because it is enclosed within the deductive mechanism, therefore emptied of those inspirational forces that virtually express themselves as wisdom and morality: forces that do not seem to have a relationship with the propositional calculation, but which, in a higher octave, to the observer of thinking, end up being connected to the very order of thinking, of which that calculation should be the projection.

To believe that the logical–analytical process excludes morality can seem non-pertinent or arbitrary. A check can be normal in its outer form—amount, order, signature, and so on—and still be false to the extent that it is "a bad check." Analogously, a rational expression can be exact, but not correspond to any content whatsoever—neither outer, nor inner. But this is not the error, because a logical–mathematical operation can have a purely formal value, useful as an educational technique of mathematical thinking. In this pure formal value, a content of thinking is present, unbound to an object—physical, or ideal. The error begins when applying the proper rule of knowledge, or when attributing scientific efficiency to the formal expression, outside the concept from which it originated as pure theoretical necessity. The methodology cannot be an end in itself. Rather, it wants to be the logical sense of the experience.

Here, we stand before the crux of the logical–analytical equivocation. By becoming the guise of the scientific object, that formal expression must renounce its own structural autonomy, in the interest of a content, which, in turn, renounces, in the form thus acquired, its own internal logic, namely the thinking that has operated in the experience, in order to become a codified phenomenon, which can no longer be elaborated and integrated by thought, insofar as it already appears as a content, well defined and formally regulated. Each further investigation, or reconsideration, or deduction, is conditioned by the determinedness of that formalization. In reality, *the formalization does not provide inner meaning to the experience, nor is the experience the inner meaning.*

This inner meaning is indeed what is lost, even though it is inseparable from the experience. It is the a-dialectical thinking that (as explained in another part of this book) is engaged as a force of investigation, but known by the experiencer who is conscious only in the dialectical moment.

It is useful to observe that the original formal rule, though it does not correspond to any objective content, neither physical nor ideal, nevertheless has its own content as a formal standard, or as a form of its very self as idea, for which its true being is inside. It is not born of nothing. It is precisely this inner content that ceases to exist in knowledge analytically and methodologically elaborated, because it gives its formal being up to another content, which nevertheless lacks that for which it can be a real content, namely internal logic. The equivocation is that this other content expects such internal logic from the logical form, which, by leaving its own formal world, loses the possibility of this, to the extent that it, itself, renounces its own internal structure.

We must focus on this. The validity of logical standardization lies in the ability of the informal content's objective presence to justify the form. It has to do with a pre-formal, inner content, which, only if it manifests as inner and pre-formal, can it be the principle of the formal norm. Because if it, itself, had to already be a formal expression, it would, in turn, need to presuppose an informal formative principle, as its original content. Analogously, a specific methodology and a knowledge elaborated methodologically are true to the degree in which they contain, within themselves, the formative principle. But it is precisely this that they lose in becoming formalized. They lose it by becoming unaware of their initial impulse: an impulse, which during the analytical developments should guarantee the truth of the deductive process.

In order to identify the logical–analytical paralogism, it is essential to behold the meaning of the relationship between the formal standardization and the internal content, or the initial ideal substance. Furthermore, if we can conceive the inseparability of form from content, we can recognize how the discourse formalized by means of such standardization is then normally led in such a way that mistaken for the foundation is the object to which it refers—physical or moral or psychological—and this, again, because theoreticians of methodology are unaware of the pure formal content to which they initially appeal through formal standardization. Such standardization is carried out devoid of the original logical substance.

When we speak of morality, we wish to refer to the original correctness, or to the very principle of the logical investigation, namely to what—along the path, from the idea of standardization to standardization and from this to the discourse specifically formalized—is lost. From this arises the grave misunderstanding responsible for mistaking the analytic of the matter dealt with for the inner content of scientific knowledge, while we lose sight of the thinking from which the analysis had its start and that thus leads knowledge from a norm to the norm of itself, without ever being able to give meaning and orientation to such standardization: without being able to provide it with the content of truth, which is to say, morality.

14. The Morbidity of the Technological Vision

If the inferential procedure excludes thought, not only does it divest itself of meaning in relation to the conscious subject, but it also ceases to function from a logical point of view, becoming discursive automatism, or equally the cause and the vehicle of the mental disorder: nonetheless, keeping intact the semblance of the formal consequentiality, the illusory shell of truth.

Logic, as a methodology, can give rise to discourse that can be propositionally fixed, provided that it involves an awareness of the specific thinking that produces the methodological structure, so that such thinking is always free with respect to this structure and does not end up depending on the rules of expression that it formulates. It is important, from a formalistic point of view, for the methodologist to possess the logic of thinking that expresses itself as a methodological activity, so that such an activity does not coincide (as we have seen) with the automatism indispensable to the expression of the mental disorder. It is clear that the thinking summoned to work on the rules of deduction cannot itself be analytical–deductive.

This observation is valid even when the logical systemization refers to an objective content whose structure can be translated into technical values. The danger of the logical–technical procedure lies in its becoming objectively independent of the human subject and active on it and compelling its mental development, according to artificial necessity. Even if it is formally normal, such necessity, in establishing its exclusive relationship to the human mind, induces it to an automatism that cannot make up for the awareness of it and of any activity of real thinking.

In that way, so-called technicians or modern specialists—to the degree in which their rational activity coincides with the technological element—are paranoiacs in power, because they do not carry out any other logical activity, except the one imposed on them by facts which, in themselves, do not possess any real logic, except their own internal abstract and mechanical relation, which, as we have shown, has been created in contradiction to the original process of thinking.

The morbidity of the psychic condition of modern "technicians" consists in its operating according to a logic that does not come from the movement of thinking, but from its dead projection, which is revived in the mental realm as an opposition to the principle of the same thinking process. One day, the origin of the series of mental illnesses that today circulate like theoretical germs in the present-day culture will be discovered in this internal breakdown of the relationship of thinking to its own foundation.

To believe in an "invention" of operative procedures that progresses with the progress of science, means to consider such progress justified and directed by a thinking that has within it *the canon of its own movement* and that can provide itself with original formulations and, therefore, a logic of discourse, or a methodology, given that its relational capacity encounters specific objects. Such objects can be diverse and new in time, and continually demand that the relation be extended and modified, giving thought a way to establish "relations between relations" and between syntheses of relations, namely the synthetic power of thinking, which is its pre-discursive being that bears within itself every possibility of logic or exact discourse. But precisely this virtue of thinking, which is its experiential reality, the concreteness that can be translated even in logical–mathematical terms, is cut off by logisticians, not because they deny it—since they cannot negate what they do not know—but because they believe that it has nothing to do with their research. And they succeed in cutting it off, because the thinking compelled by deductive constructs to ignore its own movement, without which such deductive constructs nevertheless would not have arisen, is automated and loses its intuitive vitality, which alone could justify methodology and technology at their level, and, as director, prevents them from becoming universal systems that compel the human being.

We must point out that thinking, as a movement that is objectively original, capable of analytical order, because it bears within itself the unlimited power of relation, is not the original thinking bound to sensory necessity, but the thinking that begins to 'de-subjectify' itself in the exercise of mathematics or of logic, without nevertheless obtaining, by means of these, its pure form but, rather, only a provisory symbolic–discursive projection of it, namely the pure form demanding the conscious experience of its normal movement. The 'de-subjectification' is not for an artificial form of its expression, but for the expression of its real nature.

The objective consequentiality, presumed in the expression, belongs, above all, to thinking. Thinking demands it. Otherwise, logisticians would not demand it. The request for the formalistic order does not come from the meaningful fact, but from the thinking that (with regards to the multiplicity and the quantitative) tends to actualize, outside itself, the unity that it already bears within itself, but that simultaneously belongs to the internal structure of the world, of which the multiplicity and the quantitative are the apparent contradiction. It is the apparent contradiction, valid only for reflected thought, still incapable of actualizing within itself the internal order of thinking and thus demanding the systematic–logical surrogate, undoubtedly necessary on that plane, as well as its technological projection, but both equally reflecting a temporary limit of the human mental sphere.

15. The Limits of Structural Analysis

The regularity that the logistician intends to formally attain is a projection of the unlimited internal organic nature of thinking. This organic nature, which is not given to the human being gratuitously, but thanks to a precise investigation of thinking within thinking, is, in itself, identical to the inner organic nature of the world's structure. The physicist and the logician make evident an aspect that barely surfaces from the unity of human thinking and of the world's thinking order. The arrangement of the multiplicity is a temporary initial movement, which would be integrated by a rigorous awareness of it, since the objectification of the rules and of the laws projects the temporary limit of thinking, incapable of grasping the world's internal unity, onto the world and onto linguistics. It is reflected thought that does not escape the closed circle of subjectivity, no matter how many attempts it makes to elaborate a knowledge that can have a foundation within itself. This knowledge cannot have a foundation within itself, since, as a systematic order, it is the inferior projection of the inner order of thinking, or of the true foundation, while its technological version, undoubtedly useful within given limits, is the formalization of such a projection, which aims to be valid per se until establishing itself as *universal*.

The objectivity of science and of logic does not have a foundation within itself but, rather, within thinking. Without being able to regulate itself by means of such a foundation, that objectivity leads to the error of treating the object as a foundation. In the expressive act, thinking, seeking to attain order and the relationship between orders, which it has as its original power, actually limits itself according to the needs of the sensory world. Therefore, orderliness cannot regard the sciences of the soul, nor of the spirit but, rather, the methodological aspect of the studies that introduce them. The limit of formal logic is precisely this. In its practical application, it would not be able to exit the sphere of quantitative sciences, except by becoming conscious of its own procedure and by recognizing its contingent instrumentality. In that sense, technology would not eliminate us. Instead, we would ultimately use it.

Such recognition is the gnoseological act that alone could reconnect the deductive theoretic to the internal logic of thinking. Devoid of such an act, its whole system ends up being mechanistic, and where it appears minimally usable, it can be replaced by any other equivalent form of logical procedure. The impossibility of deducing without an initial axiomatic substance, or without the basis upon which to elevate the deductive edifice is obvious: this being an objection that naturally lacks validity regarding pure logical–mathematical formalism. It begins to be valid regarding its use outside the need of formal mathematical structures, or in relation to the scientific method in general.

If truth is knowledge rendered possible by the deductive procedure, it cannot lie before such a procedure but, rather, at its conclusion. But, by not preceding it, what holds up the edifice? Any means of the "pre-existing" of know-ability is incompatible with the anti-metaphysical and anti-dogmatic position of the new logic, whose pretense of making knowable (by means of deduction) what exists as a premise to a hypothetical heading, nevertheless means to place this 'knowable' outside both the premise and the deductive procedure.

16. Deductive Procedure and Intuition

As it has been said, with logical empiricism we find ourselves before the most abstract determination of thought, therefore, before the greatest commitment to a formal experience. But this operation stops halfway. It is arrested in words. It inheres to discourse, from which it does not escape. Thinking's element of autonomy is lost in technique. Discourses are many. Rules multiply, but the doctrine of the logical form does not seem inferable in a completed system. We are forced to admit, amongst other things, that methodology alone, as a particular analytic, can be fixed in a system, having furthermore to evolve with the progress of the science to which it refers. Being a particular science, it cannot operate as the logic of ancient philosophy, as the science of sciences. As we have already shown, it would be able to operate as such, if it were, first and foremost, a methodology of thinking, independent of formal and empirical phenomenology, but capable of following the original content of each phenomenology and thus of relating a rigorous discourse to a noetic principle that connects it with the ideal content of other discourses.

We cannot speak of the philosophy of science, but of special logical methods. Such methods cannot rise to a formal unitary science capable of assuming, within itself, all the possible developments of its analytics, since such methods depend on the various classes of phenomena and on languages that these classes demand in particular forms. It is, therefore, logic that would correspond to its task, if it could operate in each and every field as the unambiguous principle of expression, namely as the logic of the essence. Only in that case would it be logic in movement, according to a pure formal principle. It would be the *inferring*, not the inference as a scheme fixed in signs and symbols, separated from the thinking from which it is drawn. In reality, there is a 'deducing' immanent to thinking, upon which every deductive operation depends. For this reason, to turn directly to the source is the art of the thinker who does not wish to be limited to being a technician of the finished expression, and tends, therefore, toward a true formal science. As a matter of fact, there exists no real logical operation that does not proceed from intuition.

The mistake of logical empiricism is to be unaware of the metaphysicality of both the thinking set into motion in its method, and the thinking that operates unknown in physical–mathematical investigation. It is its inability to establish itself as the philosophy of science, and to thus be a logical system capable of being valid as a methodology of methodologies, so that research can be reconnected to the intuitive thinking to which it unconsciously appeals, *since only the reflected form of thought directed toward the object of investigation is conscious*. Intuitive thinking is nevertheless aroused, but our unawareness of it continually excludes its element of life, activating only its determined formal expression, drawn from such thinking and ultimately opposed to it.

Methodology thus becomes an impediment to the intuition needed by all genuine research. In fact, the most ingenious technical application, up to unforeseen developments of a given physical principle, is not the product of intuition, but of the methodology and the technology, which, according to the progressive inferential type of development, utilize the original intuition of the principle. Intuition truly remains the vital nucleus of scientific thought.

The excess of logistic formulation, outside the consciousness of the thinking engaged in it and, nonetheless, independent in itself, cannot but end up opposing intuitive thought, by tending to eliminate it. Logician–analysts are not able to acknowledge an intuitive activity capable of instantaneously penetrating the sense of problems that can be laboriously solved by means of linguistic–mathematical operations: or better yet, they manage to acknowledge that such an intuitive activity is possible, but fail to acknowledge that it cannot be substituted by logical–algebraic operations: thereby distorting the legitimate task of formal logic. The pure intuitive activity, where it is still possible, guarantees the correct use of such logic.

Intolerance of the intuitive–imaginative element corresponds to the unawareness of how much this element enters the formal structural process, as an essential relational movement. It is a symptom as grave as the excess of physicalism, of linguistic theories, of structural analyses, and of abstract formalism, not exempt from pleasure nearer to psychicism than to logic as if, to some, logistics as automatism had gotten control. It seems that the extreme inferential process had ceased to coincide with objective thought, or with thought that knows measure and number, relation and meaning. Extreme logical nitpicking runs the risk of losing the thinking that allows for an excess of reasoning and justifies it.

17. ANALYTICAL NAIVETÉ

The pure form of the inference, which seems to be the object of logical empiricism, involves a transformative force. There does not exist a form that, as such, is not a dynamic structural entity, or an immediate symbol of a force. A fixed form never occurs, except as a temporary abstraction.

Within the form, a formative force is virtually present that manifests according to its laws, which, however, *cannot be deduced from the finished form*. One thing is the formative force; another is the

Naïve Realism Codified: The New Analytical Logic

completed form (but thus fallen outside the form itself, as the symbol of a content that demands to be part of the inner order from which it has been separated).

If the relation is possible, there is no need to ask ourselves, "of what does the relation consist," because, as the being of the form, the formative force contains it. The question thus posed is metaphysical, even if logician–empiricists do not observe it. Consequentially carried out, they postulate a science of thinking, namely of the suprasensory canon of thinking, to which a rigorous logic cannot but lead. Deduction–induction and relation turn out to be the products of thinking. They cannot be established but abstractly, as paths that compel thinking according to a formal development, valid only in the autonomous ambit of mathematical research, but even, here, with limits proper to the required formal technique. This would be grave if they became unknown even to mathematicians, so that, by means of algebraic formulas, they attempted to grasp the intuitive element or, if we observe, non-mathematical, non-formal metaphysical content.

Believing that it overcomes traditional syllogistics and ultimately gives induction a modern meaning, the deductive procedure actually chains thought to a closed systematism, from which it risks no longer freeing itself, because it ends up believing the result of the deduction or the induction to be true, at the conclusion of deducing or of inducing. Deducing and inducing would proceed toward truth, which they do not possess, since truth is either at the beginning or at the end of the process. This truth, induced or deduced, will never be reached, because it is regularly projected outside the process from which it arises: it is never grasped within an analytic–synthetic movement. In fact, required only for the hypothetical–deductive process, it is not possessed in itself at the conclusion of the process. Rather, it is valid only as a point of departure for a new analytical process, which, in turn, projects a further truth attainable outside of it. For this reason, we will never know where to stop to have a fixed point of knowledge, a foundation in which to experience truth in oneness with itself, or as reality.

18. Automatism of the Limit's Determination

There exists no concept that is not connected to all possible concepts. There exists no thought that can be separated from unequivocal thought. A science of thinking must be able to contemplate the inner world in which, from a single source, the forms of thinking are inexhaustibly possible, so that the substantial relationship of one with the others can be known, since each form tends by its own virtue to reconstitute the original unity with the others.

It would have been the task of philosophy, which cannot be substituted by the fact that a single branch of philosophy separates from it and constitutes a field unto itself and, at a given moment, takes on a role that is valid as philosophy. It would be desirable for a new philosophy to be born under the sign of logic, but present-day logic is actually the manifestation of a thinking that tends to be valid only within the limitedness of the determination, assumed as an immediate absolute.

It is logic that rejects the sense of its own mediation, or metaphysical nature, due to a lack of philosophical self-awareness, which is to say, due to a lack of logical awareness of the ordinary connection of thought-forms. And, with this, we do not mean to say that it must renounce its formal procedures, but that it should justify them by means of itself, in relation to the non-formalized thinking that makes them possible and can give them a completed sense.

It is atomic logic, the logic of finite quantities with no relation between them, that is not numerical, or equivalent to the numerical relation. But what is valid for numbers makes no sense for words. The logical–formal canon cannot but be a way for the canon of thinking to appear. This canon of thinking can do without the former, but not vice versa.

Any translation into symbols of the discursive construct is valid only for an official research directed toward linguistic–technical objectives, and should, precisely by means of this, manage to identify its own ironclad limits. Consequential for logical empiricism would be to recognize the limits of its own proposition, given that it involves the recognition (beyond the limits) of a canon of thinking, whose power of synthesis contains all logical operations, since it contains the logic of its own movement, namely its autonomy, to which no logic could be opposed.

To move within the logic of such thought is an act that involves the inclusion and, therefore, the overcoming of the limit, which to objective reality, both physical as well as metaphysical, makes up each logical operation, as a limit needed by the discursive determination. It has to do with the limit for which logical empiricism will never be able to obtain the object that it proposes for itself, since it assumes the limit as a necessary form of thinking and, thus, removes from thinking the possibility of operating within the limit according to its own unlimitedness. Thus, by finding itself before the limit, it cannot resort to thinking but, rather, to a new determination of the limit, thereby giving rise to different deductive systems and, yet, without a relation between them. Thus, if such a relation were to occur, a relation of thinking would be necessary, namely a synthetic relation, not an analytical one. The ultimate sense of deductive analysis cannot be but a synthesis: not as a synthesis of analysis, but as an experience of the thinking of the synthesis. We must go back to knocking on the doors of thinking, with a renewed understanding of knowledge, if we want to arrive at a logic where what is present is suggested by its name: Logos.

19. Metaphysics of the "Relation": The Pure Axiom

Conscious formal research truly demands something more than placing propositions or judgments into relation according to passages necessary and, therefore, formally pre-determinable. This is an analytical operation, which presupposes its original one—the key to all the passages. One cannot be separated from the other.

If only concepts with their correlative names were possible, we would find ourselves before isolated entities, without any other possibility of a relation between them except the one that is synthetic and algebraic–semantic. However, the relation lies not between the names of concepts, but between concepts provided with names, since the original relation is immanent to the concept, if the concept's immediate form can be recognized.

The relation always precedes the deductive–inductive process that expresses it. In the conceptual determination, the interval between concept and concept, between name and name, is a "void," filled with thinking, which is not thinking bound to an object as a concept, but the pure concept, or thinking that has the possibility of establishing relationships between concepts, inasmuch as each concept calls for it. But, so that it, itself, can recognize this function, thinking should experience itself at the moment in which it is not yet identified with its own determination. The identification should inevitably happen continually, but on condition that the logician (the thinking person) knows it and, therefore, does not take on, as original thinking, what is already an objective determination, and only as a determination, is a logical expression, *since it contains the formal process within itself:* not outside.

This distinction is necessary. One thing is the thinking activity capable of forming concepts on the basis of representations of physical and non-physical things, and of translating them into linguistic values, by working on their logical form; another thing is the thinking activity capable of living the being of the concept and of establishing relationships between concepts, which is the immediate force of the concept, or pure thinking. The first is inevitably bound to the object and, therefore, structurally analytical. Each definition is thus an analytical judgment. The second is an activity not bound to any object or concept, but for this reason, capable of entering into the concept's pure form and of perceiving its relationship to other concepts, all the way to the fundamental relationship of the concepts. In this relation, *the deductive power immanent to thinking coincides with the formal principle.*

Not in a Hegelian way, not idealistically, but in a noetic sense, we can speak of an ideal activity that fills the intervals between concepts, between names with its immediacy and is thus determinant. Because, in itself, it is free of determination. In that sense, it does not operate outside the concept. Rather, it is entirely within the concept. For this reason, it can trace back to this ideal activity by means of a single concept. Within its power of synthesis is the concept's substantial force, where the concept is experienced in its identity with itself, until it expresses its own movement. This movement is the germinal form of the inference, in itself necessary, from inside thinking, not by way of a graphic–symbolic standardization from outside. It is the intuitive deduction that goes from thought to thought before going from proposition to proposition.

When specific signs call for a path to thinking, this thinking actually accomplishes something that it already has within itself and that it could accomplish with regard to a group of given concepts, or with regard to a problem, without any formal prescription. In fact, this prescription is its very own production: made static, measured, having become alterity, yet it is its production.

We have the illusion of possessing this power of relation within the inference, whereas it is originally within thinking. Actually, such power alienates itself within the inference, because one uses it, believing to have in the correlation of signs an agreement more concrete than what produces it. It is true that signs and symbols mark the itinerary of the relation, but such an itinerary is not the relation. The relation determines the itinerary all the way to the graphic symbols that indicate it. For this reason, the relation can retrace it. But its movement is to be sought not in the symbols but, rather, in the interval, or in the silence, that exists between symbol and symbol. It is the symbol's true sense.

If we look within the interval, we are led to behold thinking. This thinking, once beheld, escapes, insofar as it demands contemplative power, in order to be observed. It is a matter of possessing the deduction and its operations, so as to be able to abstract from their form, until following the thinking that carries them out. It forms part of the proposition of rigorous logic to recognize the demand of a specific discipline, so that from thinking there can spring what, above all, is required of it, namely, the immanent 'deducing,' as an expression of its inner nature, in which intuition and correlation coincide.

The thinking of analysis and of synthesis, of deduction and induction, is the force that is never seen and nonetheless always engaged. We are mistaken when we believe that we possess this force in its conceptual, or syllogistic, or inferential determination, because the determination is the product of such a force. It is not this force in its reality. For tasks that attend to human thinking, at least on the part of those who are called upon to give it a conscious orientation and logical form, such thinking must be experienced by means of the unique spiritual practice that it, itself, demands by means of its laws.

When we dedicate ourselves to a logical operation and we seek the relation between groups of symbols of concepts, we unknowingly appeal to an original thinking that springs from consciousness like an axiom from the form that is still undetermined, endowed with the power to identify with every possible form, namely a primigenial axiom, or principle of each legitimate axiom, from which we would like to move, but which in practice is avoided, because it is the *immediate* being of thought, to which the analytic *mediation* is dogmatically opposed. But it is opposed unconsciously, since logisticians, attracted only by its formal projection, ignore the mediation itself.

The possibility of a suprasensory experience of thinking, of a content that is identical to that of ancient mysticisms, is given and simultaneously taken away from the investigator of pure form. The most arid discipline of logic can be the doorway to a conscious metaphysical experience but, likewise, its absolute impediment. Naturally, the task of philosophers is not to renounce a meaningful rigorousness, but not to be deprived of what it presupposes as its own movement—the imperceptible bearer of the relation, of the form's life.

The fixed form is the form in which it is illusory to believe that one excludes the formative force. Meanwhile, it is a logical art to experience the very formative force that conditions the logical form, a force whose rules of formation can be known within the sphere of its 'appearing.'

Once the sense of idealistic philosophy was elaborated and the task of dialectics exhausted, it was precisely because preconditions were set on the speculative plane—so that the conscious perception of thought, as a further step, could be conceived, which would have restored present-day needs to perennial metaphysics and to ancient mysticism—that on the one hand, dialectics devoid of logos sprang up and, on the other, a logistic formalism, so as to prevent an experience of thinking from being barely conceivable as a model for pure experience: the one of which we continue to speak, but which we have yet to know.

20. THE SCHRÖDINGER–CARNAP CONTROVERSY

The presupposition implicit in the logical–analytical approach is the persuasion of the subjective and psychological character of thought.

There seem to be serious difficulties in imagining, for example, that the concept of the triangle is identical for all minds and that there do not exist different concepts of the triangle according to how many subjects think it. This is the limit of present-day formal logic.

Thought as a universal objective, immanent to the human mental sphere, is viewed as naivety by logisticians. It is a way of seeing in which the preconditions of the solipsistic state, or of involuntary solipsism, can be recognized, though not of that to which an idealistic extremism can deliberately lead. With the objective nature of thinking and, therefore, its original immediacy, easily excluded, logisticians cannot but turn toward recuperating objectivity within the discourse, that is, within the formal mediation—forgetting, however, (as we have shown) that, even in this way, they move from thought and that they establish normal values with the thinking that has yet to be formalized. With this, they elude the true communicative and correlative element of the various experiences of reality. Involuntary solipsism for them is inevitable, in a strictly psychological sense.

The problem of solipsism—which should however not concern logicians–mathematicians since it is excluded from the preconditions of their research– actually exists for them from a speculative perspective, semantically incomprehensible, and connectable to the question of "enunciated firsts," of original assertions, whose immediacy could be attained only because of a mediation that is experienced. But how can the mediation be experienced, so that the assertions do not presuppose logic and, nevertheless, are able to be recognized as true? In fact, once such preconditions are achieved, the logistic mechanism functions easily, it being a 'deducing,' which does not require anything that is not part of its own automatism. But the problem is precisely the "commencement." If this is ignored, there is no reason to worry about the solipsistic problem, even if there were such a problem, because only from the viewpoint of original thinking—consequently ungraspable by semantics—can the issue of inner communicability and the value of subjectivity exist.

The commencement is thought in its immediate manifesting, or pure thinking—to which the mediation itself is attributed, even what tends to organize itself in an exclusive and, therefore, formal dogmatic determination. The commencement is precisely the logos, without which logic and each and every formal system are not possible. Despite its rigorous organic nature, it becomes a coefficient of humanity's introduction to exact obtuseness, which knows how to translate everything into a logical discourse, without grasping an infinitesimal of reality.

An example of the disarming naivety of logician–analysts is the famous Schrödinger–Carnap polemic regarding the sustainability of anti-solipsism—a polemic considered to be an event indicative of the evolution of analytical philosophy. With 'physicalistic' coherence, Schrödinger managed to affirm the impossibility of establishing the homology of subjective experiences with regard to sensory 'perceiving.' It can never be verified, he said, that an individual's perception of the color red is identical to that of another who affirms seeing the same color—from which arises the limit of the experience's communicability and the justification for solipsism. This conclusion alarmed the world of scientific methodologists and philosophers, amongst which was Carnap, one of the fiercest, who having courageously risen to defend the antisolipsistic position and the cognitive objectivity of physical experience by means of a very ingenuous logical–analytical process, managed to reveal the scant validity of Schrödinger's affirmation and the consistency of the anti-solipsistic conception, based on the homology of the representations in the linguistic expression of various subjects with respect to the same perception of red.

It seemed as if, within certain limits, Carnap's analysis put things back into place, and the episode has passed on to the history of modern deductive logic. But the truth is that this episode is symptomatic of the clay foundations of the logical–analytical edifice, *a*) because, given the premises of logical empiricism, a series of propositions cannot prove, outside its linguistic function, something that is not an objective experience (no one, in fact, can prove that he or she perceives the perception of another person: otherwise we can, by forgetting the materialistic proposition, arrive at the "linguistic proof of God's existence," according to the fact that certain classes of individuals in specific places, or according to specific perceptions, can affirm being in communion with the Divine); *b*) because the question of the receptive modality of perception implicates the subject of consciousness, namely the "I," and is, therefore, metaphysical; *c*) because based on situations *a*) and *b*) logical–mathematical thinking should not have attempted to prove a fact that for it has no reason to be questioned; *d*) because none of the empirical–logicians seemed aware of the situations *a*), *b*) and *c*).

21. The Sense of the Communicative Function

What is the sense of this criticism toward modern deductive logic? We agree with it when it asserts that knowledge becomes communicable inasmuch as it is clearly expressed. But, at the same time, we believe that all knowledge must be graspable not only because of its rigorous expression but especially because of the thinking activity of the subject that apprehends. We must keep this in mind. Stairs can be built only for beings that have limbs to climb them. It would not make sense to build steps such that the movement of climbing them is avoided. The extreme clarity of discourse becomes flatness and obscurity, if the field of mathematical sciences is removed.

The thinking activity of someone who grasps a truth is qualitatively identical to the one thanks to which such truth is intuited by whoever expresses it. That is to say, it is real prior to being discourse, and it again becomes real beyond discourse. The most rigorously logical proposition is nonetheless understood thanks to an intuitive act. Precise discourse is the mediation of an inner activity that must again become an inner activity. Discourse is continually created so that it can disappear before that of which it is the vehicle. The difficulties of knowledge and, therefore, of culture and of civilization, are born when discourse becomes the ruler of knowledge.

We must not forget that discourse is valid for beings capable of making it rise again as thought, not for beings that lack thought, for which thinking must be replaced with word mechanisms that, within us, move what only we can move.

Apart from logical calculations for operations that can be reproduced for technical purposes, those who mathematically operate on the structure of discourse should worry about its communicative function. Discourse cannot be the vehicle of itself. Even when it intends to express linguistic rules, *it is the vehicle of a thought that we must be capable of thinking before it is given a discursive structure*. We must not forget that of which the discourse is a vehicle. That is to say, it is not so much the vehicle of a formal regularity, as it is of the thinking that must express itself by means of this regularity. This original content cannot be excluded, without the form losing its raison d'être. Though it is actually never excluded, we are unaware of not excluding it.

On the other hand, when logisticians believe that they operate toward the construction of verifiable propositions independently of the observation of facts, they fail to notice that they help themselves to a thinking that is already shaped by facts and that is not actually free of their imprint, even when they leave facts aside. That is to say, it is not that of the relation in itself, but of the relation already conditioned by the object, even if the object has been removed. The clarity of logical empiricism ends up being compromised precisely by our incapacity to distinguish between a purely formal relation and one that is particularized, or specific.

So that a real distinction can be possible, we would need to experience thinking to the point of noticing how it is inserted into the mechanism of perception so that perception can manifest. We thus notice how the effective relational force of thinking is not the one that already appears bound to perceptive contents, but the one that can be experienced free of them.

The incapacity of making such a distinction, which is effectively an act of consciousness, renders any linguistic structure inefficient in relation to the treated object, since it renders the distinction between "real" and "formal" ambiguous. Taking this distinction to the last resort, it turns out that present-day deductive logic—which is believed to be a formal science since its content is the form of logical discourse—is essentially a real science, because, with the form being identified with discursive mediation, the content cannot but be specific, even if the concepts of communication differ from those of every other real discipline.

22. THE REALM OF PURE FORM

Thus, we find ourselves before a given logic that narrows its field to a specific object, which is actually its not wanting an object. Its *realism*, in fact, is the very discourse as content, insofar as the form, identifying itself with the expressive mediation, renounces to be pure form. The expressive mediation, fixed as form, cannot constitute the formal norm, without contradicting the mediation's own reality, given that it, itself, presupposes a formal science.

Therefore, deductive logic cannot be a science of thinking, but only a specific chapter of logic as the science of thinking, which alone could be formal, to the extent that pure form is the thinking that operates logically according to its relation with itself, or its relational power, from which the logical determination can arise. The distinction between formal sciences and real sciences is not logical. There exist various "real" (or particular) sciences and only one could be formal, but not, if it does not bear, as the relational force, the metaphysical principle of its own analysis. Unable to bear this metaphysical principle, each system of formal logic is included within the limits of a particular science.

Naïve Realism Codified: The New Analytical Logic

We observe this, inasmuch as Nagel's expression, "Logic without ontology" should mean "logic independent of sensory experience," or logic that leaves out of consideration theories or statements of sensory facts, putting us into agreement with logisticians in ruling out the possibility that the concept of a sensory fact can be a "real" content, but according to a different motivation, given that we consider the determination of thinking (once drawn from the sensory fact) valid only in its internal identity.

But, it is thus shown that a pure formal science could not but be a science of the spirit that involves a special discipline of thinking, since—as has been seen—isolated concepts cannot pre-exist thinking. A concept exists because it is thought and, in being thought, it is removed from its temporary abstract nature, or particularity. The connections between concepts are the true formal movement, in that, if the contemplated concepts refer to sensory entities, their ideal connection, identified or perceived, liberates them from sensory constraint and leads them back to the realm of pure form: from which they were born, in relation to sensory perceptions and to corresponding representations.

If this "realm of pure form" is contemplated, we can legitimately turn to deductive operations capable of fixing given aspects of the methodology, and it will be possible to comprehend that there is no analytical operation that does not assume the form of pure thinking. Only the agreement with this form renders formal research legitimate and provides it with meaning, sparing it the realistic–primitive blockages and the corresponding ingenuities, now inevitable and truly dangerous because of their repercussions on human culture.

Sensory experience does not arise in order to bind thinking. Nonetheless, thinking can express its formative forces by immersing itself in sensory phenomena, inasmuch as it identifies with their formal genesis, which amounts to penetrating its own formal structure. Actually, we can say that modern thinking has no other means of grasping its own internal organic nature but that of following its own movement in the investigation of the structure of phenomena, assuming that this is still possible. It has nothing to do with the structure of words, nor of concepts, but of forms pulsating with life. We must discover what precedes dialectics, nominalism, and inference, in order to proceed from reality, whose principles cannot be thoughts already thought, but inner objective perceptions.

For the purposes of a real science of form, we must arrive at axioms that are inner experiences, primordial phenomena—the force of ideas. One can start from these. To depart from rational axioms or from definitions, however, means to establish concatenations of enunciations or regular progressions, but to create without a relationship to the foundation and, therefore, to fall into discursive automatism, where the creative play of thinking—true logic—is eliminated.

Just as the concept of a sensory object is formed based on its sensory perception, so too an original concept, an axiom, a primal enunciation, from which essential series of deductions can be derived, must spring from an objective inner perception. It is not a perception of abstract metaphysical entities, but of what is already experienced in deducing and is nevertheless unknown—namely, the principle of the deduction, immanent deducing, or pure thinking. The times are ripe for us to realize the urgency of this ulterior knowledge of thinking, in order to know thinking as pure movement, which can be experienced inasmuch as it, itself, experiences the sensory world.

The demand of empiricism, logically carried out, leads to the experience of its own original form, namely pure thinking. Empiricism demands to be consciously actualized to the point of being experienced. Only an obscure presentiment of this is had by present-day formal logic. The greatest consequentiality is the experience (empiria) of this very empiricism, which ends up coinciding with the initial emergence of thinking: the original experience, which only an obtuse rationalistic dogmatism refuses to admit.

The art is to carry out such an experience, there, where it demands to take place, at the peak of the dialectical scale, as a fact of the pure structural nature of thinking. Pure empiricism ends up being intimately connected to the logical construct, given that it is an agreement of the pure thinking form with the formal expression, which cannot be separated from the former except by way of conscious abstraction.

Each and every type of relation draws from such a pure form, in order to be truthful, even when it seems to occur by way of discursive consequentiality. The error of thought is the consequentiality that unknowingly detaches itself from the internal experience (*empiria*), by continuing to manifest on its behalf, according to the acquired discursive structure: mechanically. No discourse can be mechanical, without being opposed to thinking, to the very spirit from which it is derived.

23. The Ultimate Sense of Analytical Research

The objection that can be logically raised according to what we have, until now, been saying is that we allude to a transcendent principle of thinking that cannot be experienced, nor deductively verified, namely of the kind that modern analytical philosophy presumes to overcome. We have to admit that we are, in effect, referring to a metaphysical canon of thinking that we believe contains, within itself, all logical forms, including the possibility of the logical–symbolic form, whereas symbolic logic is formulated according to the assumption of its own mediation's self-sufficiency. We become aware, however, that logisticians cannot but refuse our statement, if they hold firm to the presupposition (without which the whole logistic edifice crumbles) that there does not exist thinking outside the one that can be expressed in words, for which exact discourse is the measure of exact thinking.

However, if what we affirm regarding an ordinary canon of thinking is true, the illogic of logical empiricism consists in adopting this original canon for its specific objective and of not knowing it or, better yet, avoiding imagining it.

Logician–mathematicians assert that for centuries mathematicians reasoned without becoming aware of the logical principles that were at the core of their thinking activity. They add that traditional logic and post-Kantian logic have codified principles that they really did not possess in conscious logical form.

We can advance an identical criticism today to logician–analysts. To arrive at the logistic codification, they appeal to a thinking that, from the point of view of formal objectification, is new with respect to the ancient syllogistic canon. They proceed according to a type of relation that postulates rules, whose exact normativity they themselves assert not yet knowing. They cannot know it, if this type of thinking does not become their conscious experience in relation to the empiristic demand, given that the logistic assumption must be realized. In this phase of being unaware of the determination, they inevitably move according to metaphysics, but according to an inverse metaphysics, since it is unknown to them. This is a situation furthest from the truth and, from a positivistic point of view, unsustainable.

Logician–empiricists cannot rule out the hypothesis that deductive science, brought to a mathematical rigor, requires a movement of thinking, which, because of its extreme precision, calls for a consciousness of indetermination more intense than that needed by the ordinary rational activity—an experience of the determination's becoming, or of the very movement of the inferring, which one should discover as the ultimate meaning of such research. But how do we become aware of the moment of indetermination, if the determination itself, in its abstract projection, is considered an original substance?

Naïve Realism Codified: The New Analytical Logic

To seek the canon of the inference is the beginning of a thinking experience that today we practically abort in the philosophical expressions that we go about realizing. We are unconscious of this abortion. It occurs and becomes known as a regular structure of consciousness. To seek such a canon in the calculation of the propositions and in their transformations into symbols is like seeking the reality of the reflected image inside the mirror.

Authentic logisticians could not but tend to comprehend metaphysics with renewed thinking, if they truly meant to reach the consequences implicit in their research. A pure formal logic that does not introduce the experience of pure thinking and, therefore, does not lead, in the form of a rigorous superconsciousness, to mysticism and to metaphysics, but arrests itself at the structures of discourse and at the relations between words, is a paralysis of thinking—therefore, a fact that is unconsciously psychic.

The essence of thinking is the nucleus of human 'functioning.' It is a serious reality with which we cannot amuse ourselves by way of reasonings borrowed from mathematical analysis, since the orientation itself of human culture is at stake. The thinking moment is difficult, precisely because of the unsustainability of a real sense of culture and because of the insufficiency of thinking in the face of problems that do not beset specific currents or categories, but the very structure of civilization.

There is no real thinking that does not involve the action of the soul, or noetic lucidity and, simultaneously, the discipline of an uncompromising assumption. Even though he was not endowed with the awareness of his intuiting, the person who understood this significance of the logical theme intuitively and, therefore, only sentimentally, was Wittgenstein, a solitary figure whose light was essentially mystical. It could not have been but mystical if, despite everything, he was capable of seeing ideal entities beyond the limit of the logical–mathematical formulation.

Part Two

The Path of Thinking

I

THE SEARCH FOR THE "I"

So that the principle of consciousness can be established—a principle to which we refer when, with formal determination, we each, consciously or unconsciously, say "I" to ourselves, and to which traditions over millennia with various names allude as if to the essence of individuality, in itself identical to the Divine—our most logical procedure today should be the subject's methodical search for how much within the soul becomes conscious in its name. This name is continually pronounced. What is strange is that we continue, concordantly, to know nothing of that to which it refers.

Given that the subject is always presupposed, in thinking and in discourse, its identification should be a logical requirement, as well as an ethical necessity. It should be the task implicit to the order of concreteness, which, at the present time, one intends to follow by means of precise paths of research, in all fields of knowledge, since this knowledge presupposes a series of conscious beings that produces it and a series that grasps it: or just as many subjects, or "I"s.

The problem is to understand how such research can be possible, which specific discipline it involves, and by way of which prejudices must it make its way, given that each current system is the product of the "I" of the thinkers and scientists that collaborate in it. And, by collaborating (insofar as they are provided with consciousness of the "I"), they should admit that there does not yet exist a science of the process more internally implicit in their investigation, and that it is thus necessary to identify a principle that would act within them without them knowing it. To bring such a process to light would nevertheless entail a new direction in the research, a real effort of impersonality, an attitude of responsibility, and a feeling of serving truth. Even if one of them asserted that the "I," or the subject of what they think, is not important for the purposes of their contribution, it would always be that individual—his or her "I"—to affirm something that would acquire value because of knowledge: since they, each, once again moving from their own individual "I," would reconfirm its authority.

Given that, in the philosophical sphere, the attempt to search for the "I" has failed in the West, they have come to misapprehend the impossibility and the uselessness of such a search—to the point of the absurdity of a civilization and a science being founded on the impulse of a new consciousness of the "I." But they are not to know this, because it would be superstitious or irrational or mythical to know it. It would be grave to think that somehow logic has something to do with the "I."

It would be helpful to explain to oneself why the consciousness of modern investigators does not manage to direct, toward itself, the capacity of observation that it knows how to direct toward what appears outside: (it is) as if, by turning to the external world, it loses the capacity to look at itself. On the other hand, we have seen (in the first part of this book) how present-day culture, for as much as it is produced by the consciousness of the "I," or by "self-consciousness," methodically excludes the "I," not so much by ignoring its own origin from the "I," as in its acquiring that systematic–analytical form that is so sufficient unto itself, so as not to allow access to a fundamental legitimization of its own process. We have seen how the linguistic systemization, becoming a path mechanically unavoidable, capable of movement only in the correlation of words, compels thinking to renounce its own intuitive movement and, thus, the possibility of manifesting original forces, which, as such, are identifiable as forces of the "I." These forces which, compelled to express themselves in a way that does not correspond to the level of their original content, cannot but appear under the category of unexplainable-ness, or under the form of incomprehensible events. In that sense, they besiege us evermore, without the possibility for us to recognize them in relation to their real content.

The impulse that governs knowledge in the present world now operates everywhere to cut the spirit off from culture, despite the fact that this culture is formed because of knowledge produced by the spirit. Moreover, the individualistic tension, expressed by means of ideologies that tend to protect an ethic–religious chrism from the unimpeded control of the instincts, is easily mistaken for the presence of the "I" in culture. Meanwhile, on the other hand, it is believed that an appeal to the fundamental nature of the "I" and to the need of a conscious experience of its principle, is a path of sublime egoism. The truth is that it is precisely the modern type of "individualist" that lacks individuality.

So-called individualistic tension truly has nothing "individual," which can manifest the values of the "I," for it is the expression of corporeity, or of instincts. It has to do with referencing everything exclusively to physical necessity and not to oneself. Naturally, even here, an "I" is indirectly called into play. There also needs to be a subject that refers the values of existing to one's own corporeity. It is the reflected consciousness of the "I," which mistakes corporeity for one's own being. The term "individual" is, in that sense, usurped. Of what is individual in today's human beings, there is only the awareness of their corporeal rights: to which they are now able to provide a spiritualistic context, as well as one that is methodological and progressive.

The culture of the machine is mobilized only for the body, the senses and the instincts, by means of structures that are technologically perfect. These structures, arising from the processes of consciousness, would have had the aim of rendering us independent of material necessity, so that we could amplify our own experience by means of additional forces of knowledge. Meanwhile, the opposite has happened. Among all peoples, these structures have become the instrument of subjugation of what below is against what is above. They have become the governing means of mediocre people, or of a humanity methodologically tuned according to the values of sensory semblance to paralyze the activity of the bearers of freedom and of the ultimate sense of sensory experience.

Through the nominalistic masking of its subversion of values, the culture of the machine irresistibly tends toward its intellectual codification, toward its ethics, toward its mysticism, toward its esotericism. For this reason, it programs culture. It organizes religiosity in a modern way. It draws from the metaphysics of the Orient. In that sense, it is a done deal.

It seems that some Eastern doctrines provide a technique to identify the pure conscious principle and to separate from it the alternating flows of the soul's life and its inherences to the sensory sphere. The "I" should surface insofar as it manages to be the silent witness, the *Sat-Purusha,* independent in the face of mental, emotional and instinctive currents, which, by virtue of this contemplator that breaks off the adherence to them, would calm down by arranging themselves as if around a center.

But Westerners that attempt such a path today—without knowing the forces that they set into motion in order to attempt it—while believing that they carry out that movement, actually do something else. They fall into unconscious dualism. They isolate themselves in a mental "zone" governed more subtly by the forces from which they presume to escape, since they believe that they recognize them as objective in another "zone" to which they are illusorily opposed: without noticing that they mistake a complex of sensations and correspondent representations for a picture of their own interiority.

By way of such a path, researchers do not escape the perceiving or the thinking, which correspond to the constitution of the present-day human being. However much we believe that we achieve by means of magical or yogic spiritual practice, we do not overcome the barrier of ordinary perceiving and thinking, which constitute the fabric of knowing from which we move. We ignore the degree to which we each articulate ourselves as an "I" in perceiving and in thinking. We cannot think nor perceive the "I," if it is indeed the "I" that basally perceives and thinks, and if we form the image of the "I," beginning with the conditions of the reflected consciousness of the "I." Our dilemma is to gather what on the plane of reflected consciousness can move independently of it, even though belonging to it—namely, its actual thinking.

Westerners who today attempt the path of ancient Eastern wisdom move inadvertently from the illusion of having at their disposal knowledge capable of comprehending that language, and of consequently realizing its content. Their initial movement of consciousness in that direction is that of which they should above all become conscious, in order to understand the limit that separates them from that content, and how it is a mistake to assume such a content without resolving the limit.

We can recognize this limit if we notice that the thinking of the "I" is not the "I" and that, however much we move within the thinking of the "I," we do not actualize the "I." It is as if thinking were a barrier to such research. The subject of such thinking is, at the same time, the "I" that we seek by means of it. Nonetheless, from the initial awareness of the investigation, we can discover that we must begin to observe thinking, if we want to find the point in which we still do not think, and yet it is the "I" on the verge of thinking. We could philosophize on such a task (which constitutes the theme of the second part of this book) to infinity, without leaving thought, without discovering the "I." Something similar happened to Western philosophies for which speculation on the "I" was more important than its perception. Therefore, that conscious philosophizing, which should have led to the experience of metaphysical thinking, was precisely what barred the path to it. Illusory idealistic structures served only to later furnish the discursive apparatus, necessary to the pseudo-philosophies of matter and to the logical forms of the negation of all metaphysics, all the way to structuralism, whose task today is to analytically devour them both.

It is the same reason for which present-day spiritualists and magicians, occultists, and traditionalists turn to an object by means of which they believe they penetrate into another sphere of being, upon which they actually speculate, without the hope of entering there, for they fail to notice their own 'speculating.' They do not notice being bound to the thought of an object, even if it is a metaphysical object: a closed circle within which they are inexorably compelled to remain. Whether the thinking is Hindu, or Buddhist, or Taoist, or Tantric, or Vedantic, or Theosophic, it is, however, inevitably thought and, as such, reflected, which paralyzes the "I" and nevertheless continually draws from it.

The real "I" cannot be identified with the thinking or the feeling or the willing in which it expresses itself, without renouncing to be the subject, just like the center of a circle cannot be the circle, even if it is its principle. The real "I" does not think. It does not feel. It does not will. Rather, it operates as if it thinks, feels, and wills. It identifies with thinking, feeling, and willing, without which it would not know how to experience itself as the "I." One must acknowledge, therefore, that the "I," in order to be, never is.

In identifying, with itself, the "I" does not think, feel, or will. But it needs to identify with thinking, feeling, and willing, in order to express itself in the world. The "I" still does not experience thinking, feeling, and willing apart from having to feel itself within them. It does not know what they are for it objectively, nor does it know how it can be the subject outside them—that is, the subject before them, the being that has the foundation within itself.

As if the "I" did not exist, thinking is normally sufficient unto itself. It thinks the being, things, facts, the "I," the soul, the spirit, and the Divine. It thinks everything, without really having anything of what it thinks. It reflects every aspect of being, every fact, but it has no power over them, or over itself. It is a thinking that rhetorically can arrive at the noble consideration, "I think therefore I am," because it limits itself to this statement, but the moment in which it should identify with the being of the "I," it carries on its movement in which there is no "I." It continues to be the thinking of the "I." It is the thinking with which we, as modern researchers, attain mathematical–physical or logical–formal certainties, not so that we can possess what we physically and formally take on, but so that we can realize in them a connection of reflected thought with the object, in which the shadow of thinking alone unites with the object's lifeless measurement, while we have the illusion of encountering the object's reality.

Researchers do not *create*. Instead, they *deduce* a type of neutral knowledge, which demands from them mathematical-ness and mechanicalness, rather than a living movement. Systematic mechanism, technology, structuralism and cerebral art are the current signs of this thinking, which does not possess what it thinks. It does not even possess itself, but only its own 'reflecting' that coincides with a contingent aspect of things, which it mistakes for the totality. This thinking—which identifies with its own reflecting and, by identifying, can also imagine the "I" and its being, and the supreme themes of the "I" and of being, upon which to philosophize forever, without minimally perceiving that upon which it argues and creates a systematic science—by continuing to ignore where the "I" is to which it inevitably makes reference, cannot be true thinking. Thus, the "I" that identifies with reflected thought cannot be the true "I," in that it cannot have life, nor movement, since it is compelled to adhere to the support by which thinking is reflected—namely, corporeity. The intuitive statement, "I think therefore I am," is insufficient to the act of consciousness with which it should coincide in order to be true, or more than a simple proposition. We can only suppose that Descartes intuited this principle at a given moment, experiencing remarkably the coinciding of being with thinking, as a life that can be perceived beyond the reflectivity of thought.

Reflected thought makes it such that the "I" feels identical to the body, closed within corporeal limits, without the possibility to conceive its own 'being' outside such limits. The "I" is compelled to think, to feel, to will, according to its adherence to corporeity, so as not to be able to experience the independence of the thinking that allows it to say "I" when it thinks, feels, or wills. Thus, the "I," continually taken to the level of normal consciousness by the current of thinking, feeling, and willing, believes that it is the experiencer, whereas, it is only the passive witness of its own dependence on them. *The "I" cannot know what they are to it*, since it is subjected to them as a result of identifying with them by not possessing its objective being as the "I." It therefore always has them in a muddled mixture.

Unable to be an independent "I" with regard to thinking, feeling, and willing, the "I" is limited to not knowing about itself except when it thinks or feels or wills. It is limited to not having itself outside such a moment, namely to not experiencing true thinking, feeling, and willing. For it is only conscious of itself in reflected thinking. Therefore, it can only acknowledge the conversion of reflected thinking as the initial condition of the real experience of the "I."

In reality, the "I" does not think, feel, or will, because it is the "I." It should continually experience itself outside of thinking, feeling, and willing, by not identifying with them, but by having them as vehicles of vision, just like it has the eye for sensory perception, for example.

Reflected thought alters such a possibility, because it needs corporeity, or cerebralism, to know about itself. It does not possess the force of being the support of the "I," or the vehicle of the "I," for it lacks the extra-corporeal life from which it arises. For this reason,

The Search for the "I"

the "I," by articulating itself within reflected thought in order to be conscious, falls into corporeity.

Even when it is unaware of it, the "I" believes that it is identical to the body, since it has no other means of perceiving itself, but corporeally. One with the body, it is forced to express itself in the alteration of thinking, feeling, and willing—namely, as ego. The search for the "I" cannot move from any condition other than the experience of the activities by means of which it manifests, namely perceiving and thinking: according to a method drawn from the penetration of the very process of such activities, not from an external reflection, which is already their product.

II

THE LINEAMENTS OF A NEW SCIENCE OF PERCEPTION

1. THE SUBJECT

Those of us who turn our attention toward the world actually observe it first. We know that observing it is not yet to understand it. Nonetheless, to understand it we must first observe it.

We, then, however, learn that we can observe the world—inner or outer—because, first of all, we perceive it. If we did not perceive it, we could not observe it.

Perceiving is the initial movement by which the world reaches us. We can even perceive without observing.

But, by proceeding in this act of attention to the world, we notice that such an act is possible as an 'observing' and, before that, as a 'perceiving,' and it will still later be possible as an 'understanding,' because there exists a subject of this perceiving, of this observing by means of perceiving and of a possible understanding by means of observing. This subject is the one that perceives, observes, and understands: the one being the "I." Even without the knowledge or science of the "I," as an entity in itself, it can know that it is the subject of its observing and understanding simply because it observes and thinks.

We also learn that our directing of attention to the world, our own observing, is a thinking applied to perceiving, a thinking that still does not form concepts and ideas, because it does not have an immediate need of them, since it is enough for it to follow perceiving, having the certainty of its movement in the support of perceiving.

Then, we lift this thinking inserted in perceiving—which is the observing—from its normal movement and have it as real thinking. With real thinking, we think about observing, about perceiving, about the subject of perceiving and of observing: which is the subject of the very thinking with which we think.

2. THE "I"

We cannot know that the "I" is the subject of perceiving, of observing, and of understanding from direct perceiving, observing, understanding, or from direct perceiving and thinking but, rather, by turning the attention, which we initially directed toward the world, to these activities: by thinking about them.

By thinking about our inner activities—perceiving and thinking—we are referred by such activities to an original point in which they have an author, or witness or subject. By means of thinking, we relate each movement to a subject, which no one outside us can recognize as such and, therefore, call "I." No one from the outer world can call it by that name, because individuals can each say it only to themselves.

We can move from this axiomatic thinking about the relationship between human beings and their conscious principle, by meditating on the objectivity of our original identity with the "I." The value of such meditation is not philosophical, but formative with respect to the means of knowledge indispensable to the subsequent moments of the investigation.

3. On Identifying with the Object

Only by leading 'perceiving' and 'thinking' back to their source by way of thought and by turning our attention to this source, can we as researchers intuit ourselves as subjects, and each say "I" to ourselves. At first, we must each have the perception and thought of the world's being, so as to be able to return to ourselves as the subject. However, we do not turn to ourselves by means of perception but, rather, by means of thought. Even if we have a feeling or a sense of the "I," this, too, is a perceiving, which we grasp by means of thought.

Nevertheless, once the idea of the "I" is acquired, this idea remains with us as knowledge independent of the process through which it has arisen, namely as thinking founded on itself: thanks to the foundation of thinking itself, which, in relation to the subject of the "I," has an initial way of manifesting. From this thinking—which (as we have seen) has an axiomatic value, not as a mere enunciation but, above all, as an inner act—the researcher can move, not so much in order to deduce, as to comprehend, according to the sense of its movement, which would tend toward identifying itself with the 'deducing.'

An observation necessary from the beginning is the following: in the act of perceiving and of thinking, we are each unable to observe ourselves as a subject. The moment we turn toward any object or theme, we are spontaneously prone to ignore ourselves. Such an aspect of the relation can be assumed as another postulation of the experience of thinking's immediacy, along the lines of the spiritual practice to which we refer. The temporary forgetfulness of the "I" within the object is to be recognized as a sign of its essential identity with itself taking place within the moment of perception and, thus, of knowledge.

Therefore, only by continually diverting attention from the world, can we consider ourselves subjects. Likewise, by ceasing to sink into perceptions or objective thoughts, we are called back to the sensation or the feeling of ourselves and to a thought of ourselves that depends on this sensation or feeling. It will be seen how our art as researchers, is to arrive at having objective perceptions and thoughts of ourselves.

By dedicating oneself to perceiving or to thinking, one forgets oneself, the "I," the subject—which nevertheless continues to exist, because of the profound identity with itself that escapes momentary consciousness.

But even when we are seized by a perception of ourselves, or by a feeling or an impulse whose intensity temporarily excludes thought, we are not present as a subject, we are not present as an "I," precisely because of this exclusion. We are led to a state of diminished awareness and, from the point of view of thinking, illogical awareness. We are led to *a perception of ourselves in which, even if we wanted, we cannot have ourselves as a subject.* Due to the logic of the previously mentioned non-*animadversio* (non-observation) of the "I" in perceiving and in thinking, we should each be able to refer to the "I" that is one with itself in the presence of its own movement. But this does not come to pass. For ordinary human beings, in most cases, this does not occur except later, when the feeling or the impulse have distanced themselves and we can only re-evoke them in order to comprehend which relationship with ourselves is put to us by such ordinary conditions of the soul.

We do not attain an effective perception of an impulse or of a strong feeling, because we are taken by their sensation, which, as an objective datum, escapes our thinking attention, or better yet, it is such that it tends to eliminate it. Thus, we learn that we cannot observe our own sensations and our own sentiments, or our own inner world, with the same objectivity by means of which we observe the world outside us.

In either case, by perceiving and thinking, we forget ourselves. We are directed toward something else. The object occupies consciousness. The subject exists, but it is immersed in something else.

It does not know of itself, precisely because it is the subject. But one thing is not to know of ourselves, to forget ourselves, by means of the perception or thought of something to which we direct our whole attention and with which we identify; another is not to know ourselves due to the incapacity to truly identify with a thing—as is the case with an invading sensation, or emotion, or impulsive movement, which impose themselves upon us as an inability for us to objectively perceive the object, so that we exclusively feel ourselves, alienated from ourselves in sensation, and we project this sensation onto the world.

The problem posed in this second case will be able to be resolved by those of us who grasp the sense of the first. In the first case, the presence of the "I" manifests according to an objective reality, while, in the second, it is precisely such a presence that is impeded. It is the impediment whose process we ignore. We will always ignore it, as long as psychologies incapable of penetrating the realm of the psyche presume to explain it by means of discursive analyses, leaving it to the mercy of an illness of which such discursive analyses are actually the expression.

Those of us who can grasp the process for which we manage to contemplate, as objective, the reality outside us, discover within us, a faculty of original perception that we can gradually refer to our own inner world, so as to have objective before us our own sentiments and our own impulses, as objects of the world. This is the real relationship of the "I" with them, a relationship ordinarily altered by the "I"'s insufficient awareness with respect to their manifesting.

As researchers, our art is to find, within us, the faculty of original perception, which operates unknown in everyday sensorial perceiving, since the sensory world manifests only as a symbol of the inner world.

4. The Original Immediacy and the Problem of Science

The "I," engaged in perceiving, engaged in thinking, overlooks itself. Immersed in perceiving, immersed in thinking, the "I" identifies with the object. It fails to notice itself. Does the "I" in such a condition perhaps fall short? Does such identifying lack a subject? It appears so, but the opposite is true.

The subject cannot be missing. Otherwise, this identifying would be for no one. It would, therefore, not be. The subject's non-presence is possible thanks to its presence at another level of consciousness. If the identifying is possible, it is so because an unseen author, the "I," can refer it to itself. The 'noticing of it' is an exceptional noetic act that cannot be substituted by its dialectical expression, which—for as much as it bears within itself the coincidence with the intuitive moment—cannot but bestow it reflected, by becoming its negation. The fact that the identification, or substantial correlation, of the "I" with the world escapes the "I," is, in effect, the problem that has shown itself to be unsolvable by any dialectic. The identification is an original act, whose effects we continually experience, without yet knowing its process, even though we succeed in imagining that it concretely exists.

With regard to being immersed in the other, it seems that there is no subject. The subject does not perceive itself because it is immersed in the other, which, in such a moment, is not the other but, rather, an indication of the "I"'s capacity to identify itself. The question is how much power of consciousness and autonomy is present to the spontaneity of the identification, ready to assume it. Because the identification, devoid of such intervention, cannot but become valid at its level and, therefore, invert the terms of the relationship with consciousness by grasping thought and controlling the forces of consciousness, until intellectually–rationally legitimizing its own alterity, or its own exclusion of the "I." This situation, as we have seen, characterizes the relationship of modern science with its object.

Different is the case in which, behind the identification with the object, the conscious forces of the "I" are present and functionally silent. In that case, there appears to be no subject, but the true subject, namely the one that does not need dialectical approval in order to be, actually operates. It is the subject that is all the more, the less it depends on such approval. Its forces are forces of self-consciousness. They are of the same nature as those active in the identification and, therefore, capable of taking on the experience according to an original power of integration or freedom.

In truth, the "I" actualizes itself more substantially the less it perceives itself in identifying with the object. The more it can be absorbed into something else, the more it expresses itself. Nonetheless, it can later measure this capacity of negating itself in something else, by reviving, within thinking, the immediacy of the identification. It encounters within it the forces of freedom that are so much more valid (if recuperated) the more they are capable of binding to objective necessity.

The bond cannot be accepted as a normal condition of thinking, assuming that a person is still capable of distinguishing such thinking from the phenomenon. The act of thought binding itself to datum, in the sensory experience, potentially contains within itself the principle of freedom, which demands to be recognized and carried out by means of a conscious unbinding. Renunciation of the unbinding determines thinking's dependence on the phenomenon and the projection of such dependence on a systematic codification: the situation of present-day science.

The art of the thinker is to actualize, in conscious revivification, the original identification's immediacy of life. The "I" is always one with itself. Therefore, it can identify with everything. But ordinary consciousness does not have the power to actualize the "I" as being one with itself. Rather, it adapts the "I" to itself, which is egoic presumptuousness. The "I," being one with itself, is drawn from normal consciousness, which is not the "I," but the reflection. Normal

The Lineaments of a New Science of Perception

consciousness, in order to actualize its profound identity with the "I," which is the possibility of its oneness with the world, should discover itself in this identity. In this way, only the objective alterity in which the world appears, can acquire meaning. Consciousness is thus actualized, there, where the alterity constitutes its limit, which, in reality, the "I" has already overcome. If the "I" had not overcome it, knowledge of the physical world, even in its narrow rational form, would be impossible. This knowledge, in its essential procedure, conserves or contains the movement of the "I," unknown above all to those who presume to identify it with scientific knowledge and expend it on such knowledge, by indefinitely extending its field of investigation, but avoiding its meaning.

In effect, consciousness has before it, continually completed, the act of superconsciousness, as the capacity of immersion that lives in beings, in things, in thoughts, in feelings, and in the will. But it lacks sufficient logical–rational power to notice it, at least to deduce it.

Therefore, physical sciences are arrested at the outer vision of the world. And what they concretely seem to edify is based on the poorest and most artificial aspect of reality. Scientists ignore what, from a scientific point of view, should be of greater concern, namely the *event* that unfolds at the scene of their consciousness when they become acquainted with the physical world, namely the event that cannot be separated from the investigation that they carry out, since it constitutes its meaning. And because it is separated from it, science is arrested before a limit that it illegitimately proclaims to be true and is, thus, the cause of a series of illusory positions. The modern scientist, in reality, by eliminating the "I" within perceiving and within thinking, eliminates the human being from the world of knowing, of technology, of human functioning.

5. Dependence on the Unknown Correlation

Therefore, considering that the dialectical "I," so to speak, disappears in perceiving, as well as in thinking, and given that, in real perceiving and in real thinking, the object absorbs the "I," the problem that arises is the experience of this immediacy, for only within it can the "I" be experienced. Nevertheless, it is not a philosophical problem, nor a psychological one.

The relationship of the "I" to thinking can be found within thinking itself. This is not so regarding the "I"'s relationship to perceiving, a relationship which initially can only be thought. In both cases, thinking, if it operates free of the dialectical state, enters, as we will see, into the current of the "I"—namely, into thinking itself, into perceiving. It moves as an original force that unfolds its objective being from the maximum power of informality to the maximum capacity of formal determination—from the world of the spirit to the world of the senses, and from this to that. In perceiving, the "I" is present without the percipient noticing this presence, or knowing how it manifests. The percipient comes to identify with the world, which thinking registers, but whose process it does not possess. This process, in its autonomy, is foreign to it. It is transcendent. Percipients must intervene with an act of consciousness in order to grasp the correlation of the "I" with being, as well as the independence of this correlation from thinking consciousness. But rarely do we at this point, as modern human beings, become aware of the sense of our own limit, that is, of our referring to the "I" because it is not the "I." This is expressed by means of a relation that essentially escapes ordinary consciousness, whose conception of an "unconscious" hypothetical is, thus, not a cognitive fact but, rather, the projection, outside itself, of the limit that is not recognized.

Therefore, none of us is the percipient "I," which we barely glimpse through thinking. Each of us is the percipient, but not in the way that the "I" receives perceiving. It is never the "I" before perceiving, but rather those who know about themselves, insofar as they are already seized by perception. Perceiving owes to thinking the awareness of its initial spontaneous encounter with the world, which is, therefore, the mediated encounter, in which nonetheless lies the secret of the "I"'s immediate correlation in the world.

The correlation, being immediate, is not conscious. Of this correlation, in fact, consciousness has merely its product, namely sensation and representation, thanks to which alone it is the consciousness of the "I."

For this reason, each of us who turns our attention to the world, does not observe the immediate relationship of the "I" to the world, which is 'perceiving' (itself), because we cannot observe it in its 'becoming' but, rather, as completed. The object engages the correlation, which we cannot observe within ourselves, as it is born out of the "I."

In reality, when experimenters observe, they do not observe 'perceiving' but, rather, the perceived. They do not observe the immediate relation between the "I" and the world, but the product.

The task is to understand how the correlation can be *dependency*, as long as it is a correlation unknown.

6. The Naïve Position of the Physiologist and the Psychologist

The physiologist and the psychologist, intent on penetrating the "mechanism" of perception, will always remain outside it, as long as their analysis is carried out on the basis of data—sensory organs, nerve endings and conductors, psychosomatic and mental processes—which are the 'perceived' that has already escaped them as the process of perceiving.

Those facts are not what can lead psycho-physiologists to explain perception, because psycho-physiologists can possess them only to the degree in which their 'perceiving' already assumes them. By means of such facts and, therefore, beyond them, they seek what they do not realize is already being expressed within them. This perceiving is what they should have as an object. But they cannot even conceive such a task, because they are unaware of the inner movement by means of which they continually enter into 'perceiving,' namely (the inner movement) on account of which they perceive. They imagine finding the content of immediate perceiving outside it, which thus shows that they do not know how to recognize the object of their investigation. Nor can they recognize the relation of thought already present within it by virtue of the fact that they perceive.

Perception actually lies within the person that perceives; and only in the act of perceiving can it be observed. This immediacy must be experienced, if we want to gather the real process of perception, outside the series of abstract ponderings on the subject.

But such a problem refers to the general problem of modern science, which unconsciously escapes the investigation of immediate perceiving, as well as that of immediate thinking. Modern science loves to act exclusively on the formal product of thinking, as well as of perceiving, the perceived and the 'already-thought.' It moves in the finished mediation. It avoids knowing who carries it out and how it is carried out. For this reason, it cannot, in any field, attain the certainty of starting from original premises, from real axioms.

Even from the preceding consideration, it therefore becomes obvious that we cannot conduct an investigation of the process of thinking or of the process of perceiving, which is not self-experience.

7. On Pure Perceiving

The art of seekers is to pinpoint the original mediation that is given to them by nature as immediate, the mediation that comes into being without them determining it, and that they are unable to observe as it comes into being, since they are one with it—namely, perceiving. This perceiving, as we have seen, postulates a subject that perceives, namely the "I." Through the connection of thinking, seekers learn that perceiving is the a-dialectical relation of the "I" with the world.

Such an a-dialectical relation turns out to be the fundamental encounter of the "I" with the world, that is, the only immediacy that manifests as pure mediation, according to a thinking that is autonomous in its immediacy: the non-transcendent bearing the force of transcendence. It is as if the "I" expressed itself in the perception of a thing by means of an original thinking, independent of ordinary consciousness and, therefore, of dialectical consciousness.

For this reason, experimenters that sought the "I," or their original thinking, could not but look for it in the profound correlation explicated a-dialectically within 'perceiving.' Such research, today, is fundamental as a gnoseological requirement, in order for the original correlation (dying out in its determinations) not to be transformed into deception. These determinations, in fact, continually alter its essence in becoming discursively cut off from their own internal identity, precisely because discursiveness can, by means of formal rigor, proceed on its own, feigning the presence of the contents to which it refers.

No 'perceiving' exists on its own. Someone perceives and is the subject of this perceiving, which we call "I." But the relationship of the "I" with the thing by means of perceiving actualizes a being of the "I" that we ignore, namely that we deduce and, nevertheless, is unknown to us. For we have no means to know it other than our own immediate relation with ourselves—namely, thinking.

Whereas the being of thinking reveals itself to us as the original immediacy within thought that overcomes its own mediation in a series of moments—wherein the mediation's precariousness inevitably recurs each time by way of dialectical necessity, and must be continually overcome by us (the method for the regularity of such movement is the spiritual practice of thinking)—perceiving is, instead, the immediacy that we can contemplate in the mediation itself. For we have it before us in its manifesting, but as an effective immediacy. There is no need to add anything to it. It is a gift that we receive complete. We unconsciously collaborate in its completeness, though we still do not really know how.

The art of pure perceiving depends on the ability to grasp this concept. In fact, it is the opportunity for what is contemplated to reveal how it manifests as one with itself: an impracticable occurrence in the normal process of observing the outer world. The object's identity with itself can be experienced by means of perceiving, in that it tends to manifest—in those of us who know—as our inner act.

A suprasensory element is drawn from the sensory object, an element that (as will be shown) we will be able to recognize as objective and identical to itself—namely, as a foundation. And, at this point, it will be helpful to remember how there is no foundation that can be experienced outside of us. If something is a foundation, it can only be so, because it becomes the perception of those of us who recognize it. Therefore, it becomes our foundation.

8. The Thinking Mediation

By means of thinking, we have the essential relationship with perceiving and, therefore, with ourselves. By means of perceiving we extend this relationship to the world. But both thinking and perceiving, in their immediacy, escape the consciousness of the "I," because this consciousness requires mediation in order to know. Perceiving is its mediation; thinking is its mediation.

We have yet to know true perceiving or true thinking. However, in thinking we have the mediation of perceiving and the mediation itself of thought. Therefore, the penetration of the perceptive content is an act of thinking that recognizes, within its own original movement, the immediate manifesting of the life of which it, itself, lives.

What manifests as our most earthly experience on the physical plane—i.e., sensory perception—is the kernel that contains the possibility of resurrection of our inner being, by manifesting as the objective content in which mineral consciousness and suprasensory consciousness coincide: the possibility of the communion (within the human soul) of the worlds from which they originate.

9. THE A-DIALECTICAL ANTECEDENT OF PERCEIVING

If there is a 'perceiving' in which the "I" has its initial encounter with the world—the immediate correlation, whose process is actualized insofar as it is drawn from observing, or from thinking, since it is later comprehended or deduced by thinking—it is obvious that the "I" carries out, within perceiving, a radical thought, which a-dialectically manifests its immediacy. In fact, it does not need to be translated into a concept in order to be, since it coincides with the object, but it is simultaneously the germ of representation, of feeling and of conscious thought. It actualizes an original thinking, which fades as an event of consciousness.

This alerts the person who at first observes the world, but it consequently cautions that the relationship between perceiving and observing and between perceiving and the "I" and between the perceived object and the "I" is established by thought. For this reason, the presence of the original thinking of the "I," inside perceiving, once recognized, becomes the petition for a specific functioning of thinking according to its own original immediacy.

As the connector between perceiving and the conscious subject, original thinking operates before we are able to recognize it as such, even if we do not recognize it. Its recognition is always possible logically, but the essential logic of that connection can only be experienced a-dialectically. As such, those who move exclusively on the dialectical plane ignore it. But not even its apprehension allows us to take a step forward in experiencing it.

The problem that arises with regard to perceiving is, therefore, the following: the world reaches the knower as an immediate relation within perceiving. Then, do knowers think and recognize their individuality as an "I"? Or is it not rather that knowers perceive and think because they are already present as "I" in the world—which is to say, in the world that arises as a relation of the "I"? Is there initially the world and then the "I" that knows it? And how can the world be a world that comes first, without the "I" in whose presence it appears and which only by ignoring its original correlation with the world can project before itself a "being before," of the world, which is, therefore, a "before" only for the consciousness of the "I," not for the "I," nor for the world?

Already responding to these questions is the observation that precedes them, namely the presence of a thought that in its immediacy has its logic, in that it manifests as one with the content of the 'perceiving,' actualizing the connectivity proper, for example, to the structure of a leaf, and therefore bearing, within itself, the capacity to be objective in what can be cognized. But this thinking cannot be identified by way of its rational or dialectical form, an abstract echo of its living connectivity. Having the "I" present within it, this thinking is an objective force that only indicatively can still be called thinking. It can be known by experimenters who, posing to themselves the question of the "I," consequently turn to the pure observation of the 'perceiving.'

The initial perception of the "I," in fact, is a sensory experience, a sense or a sentiment that is drawn from corporeity and only later, because of the elucidation of thinking, becomes idea. As an idea, it no longer needs a sensory stimulus. It is a force in which lives the "I." It lives thanks to impulses that it itself generates within the consciousness of the "I," for which this (consciousness) is led to find the foundation once again within itself. It is led to experience the a-dialectical antecedent of the 'perceiving' and of its 'taking on' the world.

10. ABSTRACT PRAGMATISM AND PURE PERCEIVING

The 'perceiving' is always about something, namely an outer object, a sentiment, an idea, or a sensation. It equally regards our outer and inner worlds. It is a mistake to believe that perception regards only sensory data, since it is an inner penetration, which one moment has the sensory as an object, then the non-sensory.

We must nevertheless observe that there are beings whose inner life is so identified with sensory experience, that they can barely recognize perception as an inner act within the sensory datum and, thus, acknowledge that the same act perceives thoughts or ideas, with an objectivity identical to that regarding sensory contents. Their habit of identifying with sensory perception deadens within them an awareness of the development of perception itself. Therefore, their realism is absolute abstractness. They believe that they touch what they think, and they are incapable of thinking what they truly perceive and, consequently, touch.

The thinking of those people, who undoubtedly constitute the greater part of humanity, is typologically "primitive." In fact, they are almost always dogmatic supporters of what is rationalistic, quantifiable, technical, and pragmatic. Their intellectualism is governed by the persuasion of a progress founded upon the perfection of the weigh-ability and measurability of reality. They recognize thinking only when its process is complete all the way down to the discursive form, so that they only have at their disposal a faint awareness regarding the original moment of the process. It is not a matter of making (out of this) an accusation against them, but only of ascertaining a fact. A law-biding majority has always eliminated those rare human beings whose task was to open the passage toward truth. The example of Socrates, in its singularity, can be recognized in every century.

Pragmatic–realists are led to negate the spiritual basis of thinking, because their waking state is not actualized in the zone where thought is born but, rather, there, where it discursively passes into cerebralism. Therefore, they are led to assert that the brain produces thoughts. Realizing their waking state on the plane of discursiveness, they are the diligent organizers of the formal structure of discourse. For them, discourse is essential, because without it, they would not know how to find thinking. They do not imagine that thinking can be followed in its movement before it becomes discourse and perceived as if we perceive something in the physical world.

What we, as observers, encounter of our inner world or of the outer one, without us yet adding thought to it, is our perceiving. Those who know how to grasp this can *understand how thinking, in its initial manifesting, is perceptible.*

Observers learn that, by means of perception, they can trace back to themselves as perceiving subjects. We have seen, in fact, that 'perceiving' is something only for the consciousness of the "I." Without this consciousness, 'perceiving' would not manifest, because it would lack a subject, as happens in sleep. But we have also seen that the consciousness of the "I" grasps it *a posteriori*, insofar as it observes and thinks: as if with respect to the internal nucleus of perceiving, it were in the state of sleep. Actually, the consciousness of the "I" has perception, to the degree that its observing and thinking do not turn toward its immediate act but, rather, toward the object of perceiving: in which the immediacy is the relation already realized. It is therefore realized in a state of consciousness analogous to that of sleep. The consciousness of the "I" is truly alien to such immediacy.

All that is perceived, manifesting by virtue of a-dialectical thinking—thanks to which perceiving is the perceiving of the "I"—is actually drawn from the consciousness of the "I." In fact, it is taken on as if the "I" did not encounter it in its objective manifesting, but only by means of that in which it is articulated for the awareness of itself—namely, thought. This thought intervenes in a relation already actualized and, by not noticing it as such, believes that it must establish the relation dialectically. In essence, what escapes thought is the relation that already exists and that resolves that alterity—an alterity, which, by contrast, exists because of thought and is codified by thought. The previously mentioned fact of the pragmatic–realist majority that today technologically tends to eliminate the spirit from the world is thus justified. The contradiction of technocracy lies in its being a creation of the spirit: in ignoring and contradicting its own principle.

Perceiving, taken on by the thinking connected to it, is the process that, in its original immediacy, is carried out within the human being independently of the consciousness of the "I," yet within the structure of the "I," which is the psychophysical human being.

It follows that the "I" is not present as an observer and thinker in perceiving, but it operates on the conscious and mental level, as if it were present. The consciousness of the "I" operates as if it possessed the a-dialectical relation of the "I" with the world. It mistakes the 'perceiving' for the perceived. It confirms the condition for which the percipient act lacks its noetic penetration. Thus, the world's abstract objectivity is born, which can be legitimately mathematized and likewise become the topic of all dialectics, with regard to a culture whose real function is to nourish the alterity, the unknowable-ness of reality.

This is the reason for which the sensory experience assumed by reflected thought normally excludes human individuality from the reality of life. It is as if it lacked the presence of the "I" in the world. We can think and theorize and construct systems of knowledge with relation to the perceived world, but actually we speak about something with which we have no relation, since the identity of the "I" with the content of the treated subject escapes us. It lacks the presence of the "I" in the 'perceiving' and, therefore, in what manifests as the sensory world. It lacks its being in the 'perceiving.' Therefore, such reality is also missing from logic, which, nevertheless, in its symbolic–mathematical aspect, it can legitimately do without. But, above all, it is missing from philosophy, which today is established as the ideal justification for the scientific experience.

For this reason, we see before us the world already made, without the "I" that nonetheless establishes the immediate relation with the world. And we believe that we have to grasp something that has been made without us, before us, outside us, namely a world from which we are effectively excluded.

What seems to have been formed before us is the "I"'s correlation to the world, which we do not yet manage to notice. Our unawareness of the correlation becomes, within us, a dependence on alterity, namely a dependence that leads us forward, without us knowing why we live and move in space and in time.

What is troubling is not so much the fact that we receive, as real, the immediate vision of the world (for what it is worth to our incomplete relationship with sensory perceiving) as the scientific and philosophical codification of such a vision, and the simultaneous exclusion of the forces of consciousness and of logical thinking, called to the codification, namely those forces that, indeed, contain the secret of the mediation.

One day, we will be able to discover how the legitimization of an abstract objectivity and alterity of the physical world results from the fact that scientific investigation is arrested in the middle of its task, because of the unconscious resurfacing, within it, of the atavistic impulse of an elementary religiosity, turned toward the deification of sensory phenomena, more than toward the perception of forces of which these phenomena are a manifestation.

In modern science, ancient idolatry, as a consecration of the material alterity, rises again in the guise of extreme regularity. A realistic science will, one day, through a rigorous analysis of phenomena and an objective observation of genesis and change in them, be able to arrive at their essences or archetypal forms, until establishing, on logical foundations, the illusoriness of sensory semblance, alongside the recognition of its temporary need.

11. THE PRESENCE OF THE "I"

Therefore, one thing is to observe the perceived, another is to observe the perceiving. The "I"—the original principle—is in fact present in the perceiving but it is ignored by the consciousness of the "I" that arises by means of the perceived. The perceived, not the 'perceiving,' is the support of consciousness. With the consciousness of the "I" being reflected within the perceived, the "I" is excluded. This exclusion is the source of error, which becomes existential normality. In fact, perceiving does not manifest without the "I" that perceives. Convergent movements of the psyche that seem to belong to the "I," but actually originate from the body, from the perceived, replace the action of the "I."

Within the perceived, the action of the "I" that made it possible, is excluded. Because of this, the outer world conditions human behavior. It is the origin of all the dogmatisms in scientific and logical guise, of all the errors of thinking, of all the illusory mechanistic formulations of the so-called moral sciences, namely errors whose consequences we must bear in order to notice them, without this nonetheless being sufficient to make us aware of the reason for which they occur.

In considering the perceived as an objective alterity, the action of the "I" is ignored in the 'emerging' of the form by means of which the perceived—and, therefore, the initial relation of the "I" with the thing, which makes the 'perceiving' possible—perceptively manifests.

It is the relation that is to be recognized prior to the perceiving itself. Otherwise, perception would not be possible: which is to say, perception is not what elicits the relation, but what communicates it in the form needed by sense-bound consciousness.

12. THE PURE EXPERIENCE

Based on the preceding considerations, it can begin to be clear how the investigation that regards perception attains real scientific value if it leads to observing the act of perceiving. Only from this observation can the content of sensory experience spring—(a content) that normally escapes consciousness and that we believe can be reconstructed by means of rational connections relative to the completed aspects of its process, which, consequently, require a "mechanical" recomposition. The observation of the perceptive act bestows the nexus of thinking that corresponds to the active moments of the process: not as the rational nexus but, rather, as the vital *continuum* of the same process. This is inner perception endowed with life, not concept. Regarding such perception, the concept can be formed after repeated objective experimentation. What matters most is the content of such a concept, namely pure perception as an inner content full of life. Pure experience.

To observe the 'perceiving' is to place oneself in line with the immediate relation of the "I" to the world. It is an extraordinary condition that we must will. Nature cannot lead us to such a condition. Instead, nature tends to detain us in the perceived, in order to possess human consciousness. The datum of nature reaches us without our initiative. It reaches us completed. Our initiative begins when, by means of observation, we become conscious of an operation that we normally carry out without knowing it, which is our participating in the manifesting of the datum of nature. It is an initiative that demands the activation of a higher level of consciousness within us.

"Traditional" human beings—in the sense that esotericism gives to this term—did not each need to place themselves as an "I" before the 'perceiving,' because, if they observed specific inner rules, they could receive suprasensory content within the perception of the immediate sensory one. The "I" actualized its metaphysical relationship with being, basing itself on a somatic support that it could attain, there, where it was penetrated by suprasensory forces. Knowledge of the support's metaphysical value was presupposed.

13. The Sense of Waking Consciousness

We have thus been able to show how, within perceiving, the "I"'s relationship with the object is already integrated, unconsciously. We must, nevertheless, ask ourselves what comprises the relationship: is it thought, or will, or feeling, or even a synthesis of these?

If it were such a synthesis, we must recognize that this relation would correspond to the essential nature of perception, because it conforms to its identification with the being that exists, outside cerebralism, or psychism, and outside intellectualist assumption. For it is one with the world. It is immediate. It is inserted in an objectivity to which it, itself, contributes. But precisely this essential wholeness is the sense of the "I"'s lack of awareness with respect to its manifesting, which is the manifesting of the world already made, not of the world in its being.

If the relation is the synthesis of the soul's forces in action, as a form of the original thinking of the "I," its 'escaping' ordinary consciousness is understandable. We must nevertheless observe that this movement, which, as a basic correlation, escapes ordinary consciousness, is not the "subconscious mind," or the psychoanalytical "unconscious"—a world (as has been seen) of a level inferior to that of waking consciousness and only experienced in its altering irruptions of such consciousness, and thus codified—but, rather, a form of "supra-consciousness," which is the virtual state of waking consciousness. We have seen, in fact, and it will yet be shown, that dialectical consciousness, in reflecting the act of thinking, without noticing it, and not even imagining it, is effectively a waking consciousness that is incomplete. For this reason, the correlation escapes it; reality escapes it. The reality, of which the scientist of today speaks, is, in essence, simply dreamed. It is the autonomous exteriority that is validated by the "I" but which excludes the "I," just as it is excluded from the body during the sleeping state. It is the exteriority not perceived directly, but to the degree that it is reflected in mental pictures and concepts, as the material of a dream. It is not direct perception, as is rudimentarily experienced in the contemplation of a color. The color is quality. The outer world of the scientist is quantity and movement—a movement of measurements and numbers.

14. Perceiving's Identity with Thinking

A thing is a thing because it is perceived. It manifests because it already contains within itself a relation with the "I," the most immediate: indicative, therefore, of the foundation.

We have thus considered how the immediate life of the "I," which is a relation, cannot be dialectical thought but, rather, an a-dialectical movement in which the synthesis of thinking, feeling, and willing are to be recognized as a 'manifesting' of the foundation. Therefore, recognition is the inner act, whose intuitive virtue cannot be drawn from any process, which is not the contemplation itself of the act, as a need of the foundation.

At this point, a methodological consideration becomes necessary. If it can be acknowledged that the immediate articulating of the "I" in consciousness is, first and foremost, an inner act, which then becomes concept and discourse, it is justified (for the purposes of experiencing the act) to admit that the direct 'articulating' of the "I" in perceiving is the same act, which, instead of expressing itself as concept and discourse, simultaneously becomes movement and form within the being of the thing perceived.

The problem, interwoven with that of pure perceiving, springs from the need to confirm if the thinking that becomes concept and discourse can be perceived as a concrete movement in itself before it becomes thought and discourse. Such a theme (dealt with in the following chapters) will explain the sense of the metaphysical act's identity in pure thinking, as well as in pure perceiving.

Those who experienced this pure movement of thinking would also experience the same force by which the "I" has its immediate relation with the world, in perceiving. They would experience a thinking that contains, in the pure state, the force of feeling and willing, namely the immediate being of the "I," as a movement of life.

15. REVELATION BY PERCEIVING

Recapitulating what has up to now been observed, we can say that each perceived entity, in being perceived, offers to consciousness its own relation with the "I." Such a relation, as we have seen, is the movement of the "I" within the thing, for which the thing is perceived. It is the movement that the consciousness of the "I" does not notice, because such 'noticing' rises up, provoked by its consequences: as sensation and representation. They are the production of the 'perceiving,' the *perceived*: from which the consciousness of the "I" moves as if from an immediacy, which is therefore a false immediacy.

We do not know our own *perceiving* but, rather, *the perceived*. As conscious beings, we depend upon our own relation to the world, since the 'appearing' of this relation escapes us.

Nevertheless, we can willfully turn our attention to a given perception, in such a way as not to be attracted by its immediate results, namely sensation and mental picture. By means of the "informing" (*animadvertere*) that the 'perceiving' arouses, we can prohibit ourselves of the form to which such informing normally gives rise—namely, sensation and mental picture.

Thus, as experimenters, we observe only the 'perceiving,' but we can only do this by means of the perceived. It is an act that we must deliberately demand of ourselves: in this lies its ascetic sense. We can willfully turn our own *animadversio* (observation) to the 'perceiving,' or to the "I"'s movement within the being of a thing, by contemplating the thing. We must have before us the perceived, the things of the world, so as to understand in them, in one of them, how the identity occurs, by virtue of an act that, though beginning with us, moves according to its own pure immediacy and, therefore, is objectified before us only when completed. We must contemplate the perceived as a fact to be retraced and not assume it as immediacy, so that, contemplated impersonally, it can reveal the movement through which it manifests.

Such an assumption is not artificial, but, if we observe, it corresponds to the logic of the perception. The content that must reach us from a thing cannot reach us from it, insofar as this thing is perceived and, as such, fixed in its determination. Rather, it must reach us from the act by means of which we can perceive, for the same reason a treasure chest is not the object that it contains. The task is to remain, with motionless but concentrated thought, before the perceived, so that, through a continuity of attention, it does not imprint immediate consciousness with itself, but gives that for which it is capable of imprinting on it.

The fact that the perception of an object demands thought, is a sign of it 'giving itself up' for something more than its appearing and what its appearing indicates, and *whose unfolding one can await,* before being translated into thought. What is thus gathered within the object moves from it, but on condition of resounding as an inner act of the 'experiencing'— namely, the most objective act.

It is not the specific being of a thing, not the perceived, that then draws the observer but, rather, the life of the "I" that manifests in the life of the thing, for which the perceived manifests as a symbol of the "I" that expresses itself in the world's being.

Normally, the materiality of things, their positing themselves as real in their alterity and as what conditions, results from the fact that the consciousness of the "I" is not present in the most immediate act by means of which it connects with the world.

The correlation of the "I" with the world does not manifest so that a dependence on the reflected consciousness of the relation can emerge, but so that the "I" can know its own presence in the world, through self-consciousness, which is formed out of an encounter with the world.

16. Semblance

We, as experimenters, cannot observe the 'perceiving' outside the perceived. We must look at a thing but, beyond looking at it, we must "see" it.

To be really present in the 'perceiving,' we must not identify with what "spontaneously" occurs in our physio-psychic being, as a result of perceiving. We must not notice what, within us, "naturally" leads to the perceived but, rather, what spontaneously can be given to us as a result of the awareness brought to the act of perceiving. We can realize this by contemplating the perceived until the moment in which this manifests to us in its a-dialectical movement. Thanks to a conscious inner attitude before an object, plant, flower, crystal, rock, or waterfall (the object of the mineral or vegetative nature, presenting the relation that corresponds most to the formal immediacy of the 'perceiving'), we must be able to distinguish "spontaneity," as the pure manifesting of perception, from apparent spontaneity, in which perception ordinarily occurs as a subjective mental–sensory fact. It has to do with two moments whose contrast is normally indistinct.

True spontaneity is the instantaneous moment of perceiving, not the moment immediately following that appears simultaneous to it and is already its subjective assumption, namely *the mediation assumed as immediate*. We can willfully observe the 'perceiving,' without altering its spontaneous process, by keeping to the moment of the immediacy, to the perceiving's initial manifesting.

In that sense, we begin to "really" perceive, because we do not interrupt an original spontaneous process, but willfully leave it be as it manifests objectively prior to its conversion into a fact of the physio-psychic organism, for which we can grasp it and continue it.

Normally, the spontaneity of such an act is illusory, because it is the prevailing of subjective necessity and the relation of this with itself, over the perceptive datum, which is thereby assumed according to an identity with itself for which it is not responsible, given that it is determined by the same subjective necessity. Therefore, the objective content of the datum—that which gives itself to the real identity of the "I"—is regularly lost and we human beings are cut off from the foundation of the world. We will always have the world outside us.

The fact that things occur to us as semblances is not derived from those things but from the dependence of sensation and thinking on a reflected relation, which is the unconscious negation of the original relation of the "I," of which the perceived is a sign.

Based on such a non-relation, present-day physiology and psychology conduct their investigation on the "mechanism" of perception and on the relation of this perception to the activities of consciousness.

17. The Experience of Form

We can willfully dedicate to 'perceiving' the attention that we normally direct toward its results. Then, within us, the observing (which moves from the consciousness of the "I") and the pure movement of the "I" in perceiving, coincide. Consciousness does not identify with "feeling" or with "mental picturing," but with what comes first, namely the immediate and motionless 'observing' directed at the perceived. It does not make sense for us to observe our own observing, which is the immediacy of the determination already in the act. However, it is essential that in the presence of the thing perceived we identify with the 'observing,' more than with the object of the 'observing.' In this way, we gather the original moment of the 'perceiving,' without allowing ourselves to be taken by the successive and apparently simultaneous moment, as normally happens, by way of the direct subjective process of the perceived.

The perceived must remain before us not as an object that imprints the mental sphere with itself, but as an absolute objectivity, with respect to which we achieve (even for the slightest instant) a state of stationary consciousness—owing to a more internal mobility that goes unnoticed—namely, the continuity of the 'perceiving,' insofar as it is the pre-sensory identity of the "I" with the object. Normally, in fact, we perceive and immediately feel or think. We do not know the 'perceiving' as an immediate identity. Therefore, we continually renounce the original relationship that the "I" has with a thing by means of the 'perceiving.'

This relationship, thanks to 'pure observing' and to its minimum continuity, is given to us, like the thing itself that we perceive. It becomes more important than the thing itself, because, for us, it is *to enter into the existing being*, with which the essential movement of the "I" is one.

Ordinarily, the eye does not perceive the tree, but the conscious subject inserts itself in the relation between the eye and the tree. The relation, however, is actualized by the "I"'s original identity with the tree. Such identity is obscurely felt by the primitive who, therefore, is led to deify the datum of nature, no differently than the modern scientist, typologically "primitive," is led to deify the physical phenomenon—the original act of the "I" eluding both, for reasons that are respectively different.

The appearing of the tree as a form founded upon itself is a symbol of the insufficient consciousness of the "I" with respect to its own original action. Such a symbol can be contemplated. The mediation of the form, which identifies with the appearing, is assumed by the contemplative act. The mediation is overcome, but not the form. The form manifests in the very identity through which it arises, namely the identity for which perceiving is possible, a perceiving, which normally goes unnoticed, since only the perceived is noticed.

There is a relation between the eye and the tree, secretly established by the "I," but that the consciousness of the "I" does not possess: yet it possesses its product (perception), not as the 'perceiving,' but as the perceived. Furthermore, it has been seen that consciousness ordinarily arises from being inserted into the relation, not by possessing it, but by undergoing it. Nonetheless, by means of pure observation, consciousness can work on itself, until noticing, within the relation, the force for which it rises as consciousness. The datum becomes the vehicle of such a possibility. We can gather the relation within the immediacy of the form, beyond the mediation in which it appears in order to be valid as 'appearing.' We have the inner resounding of the datum as the presence of the "I" within it, namely as an identity that is actualized. By virtue of this, alone, the datum is able to reveal 'its manifesting' as an objective being.

Therefore, pure perceiving is the resonance of the inner content of the perceived (which ordinary perception cannot give) and likewise, the initial experience of the "I"'s presence, within perceiving.

18. The Sense of Self-observation

To observe this perceiving is an extraordinary act that is not prompted by the processes of nature or by considerations conditioned by such processes but, rather, by the very canon of its own 'occurring,' if this can be contemplated, objectively.

It is obvious how such an experience differs from that of the physiologist or the psychologist, who presume to observe perception outside the center in which it appears, or outside one's own 'perceiving.' It is about an investigation possible only as self-observation. But it is a self-observation that in its objectivity involves a peculiar inner element of control and of discipline, for which it can be said that scientists, if they attempt such an experience, arrive at recognizing within themselves the limit before which modern research has come to a stop, and at comprehending how the way out of science, beyond its narrow horizons, is a "qualitative" path, so to speak. To pursue the investigation beyond that limit becomes a task of individual inner development, of a concrete relationship with reality, of a new meaning of research. It is the point in which the amplification of truth manifests provided that it coincides with the elevation of the soul.

The knowledge that we acquire today is knowledge that expresses the ordinary level, consistent with the limit mentioned. Thus, it does not require inner qualification by whoever produces it, nor by whoever grasps it. It demands only analytical intelligence and inactive apprehension. Knowledge beyond the limit, now urgently needed by human culture, is for the few who can understand how overcoming the limit depends on an ascetic activity that makes the perception of forces, abstractly seen as the laws of nature, possible. The knowledge of these few individuals can then be communicated to others capable of understanding it and, thus, rendered humanly practical.

19. Contemplation and the "Unconscious"

To observe the 'perceiving' is an extraordinary act, because it is to enter into a spiritual process that operates in nature, by consciously participating, within oneself, in its objective 'occurring.' We enter the very secret of life, because it is a 'perceiving' of life, not merely its measurable 'appearing.'

A thing is looked at as a symbol, not so that it can be taken on as a symbol, but so that it can be seen in such a way that it pronounces its own being by speaking its own language. One expects this to resound within the soul, by forbidding mental picturing and, therefore, any thinking whatsoever. It then operates with the power of that of which it is the symbol. The force of mental picturing, rendered quiet and motionless in the presence of a symbol, is led within itself to connect with its own inner source. In surfacing as the form's pure force, it actualizes a conversion, or a purification of its own original substance, decisive for the life of the soul, because it actualizes its own independence from the personal element that continually alters it.

The force of mental picturing, in becoming immobilized for pure perception, avoids, even for a slightest instant, degenerating into the ordinary automatism of sensation and of mental picturing. Due to the fact that it retraces the origin of pure form in moving according to the original identity, this force ceases to be grasped by "unconscious" impulses that, normally, unrecognized as foreign to the conscious life, appear identical to its movement.

The activity of mental picturing, by distinguishing itself from its usual alteration, which is its ordinary 'being grasped' by personal inclinations, becomes the force capable of distinguishing the real life of consciousness from the "unconscious" (the zone mythically represented by psychoanalysis, without any other experience of it but a series of representations and deductions, devoid of an effective perception of the psychic element), that is, from the zone in which physical processes irregularly influence the psychic life, or sensory processes are carried on in the neuro-vegetative system, for which, with respect to it, we are not the true subject, even though we undergo, by way of an arbitrary projection of images, the illusion of being it.

Only in a nearly somnambulistic state, or to the degree in which we are deceived regarding the nature of certain nervous disturbances, can we, as human beings, say we are moved by this "unconscious," which has nothing to do with our basic inner life, since this unconscious is a world of instinctive rubble, which tends to ascend to consciousness, by taking on forms of feeling and of the intellect, to the degree in which these are unconnected to the conscious principle. In reality, it can be proven experimentally that the presumed "unconscious" of psychoanalysis is a world of processes foreign to both consciousness and the sphere of perception, since they belong to corporeity and acquire a pathological character only

The Lineaments of a New Science of Perception

by drawing from their corporeal center and, therefore, by becoming known psychically.

In effect, we never have perception in the pure state. It immediately and continually connects with a subjective feeling–mental picturing, controlled by a sort of "memory" of an inferior kind, which is the surfacing of instinctive rubble by way of an associative path of the previously mentioned zone. Therefore, the less conscious we are, the less we react according to the objectivity of the perceptive act and of the correlative thought. Instead, we react according to the "memory" that immediately leads the perceptive datum back to its own significations, by tending to substitute the relation of the "I" with the object, until controlling thought in logical forms.

Through the breakdown of mental picturing, we undergo influences, which by their nature are adverse to the order of consciousness, with which we unconsciously identify. The subconscious action of such influences is possible there, where the "I," or the inner human being, is not present, since these influences are what tend to utilize the forces of the "I," which are not sufficiently conscious, and reduce such forces down to themselves, by managing (as we have said) to control thinking and, by way of such a path, to become legitimate in the guise of a psychological doctrine, among other things. The subconscious exists, but as a sediment of the dross derived from the elaboration of the real consciousness of human beings, which, by means of everyday experience, works toward its own independence from deviating influences. Consciousness truly has a whole other origin than that deposit of debris. It has to do with dross that would not be harmful if it settled in its natural corporeal center and did not rise to psychic values: precisely aroused in this, among other things, by the practices of false psychological doctrines and by the morbid vision that they, under the logical–scientific semblance, feed.

In immobilizing itself before the image–symbol of a thing, by means of the contemplative act, our mental picturing heals us of the influence of the so-called unconscious. It manages to distinguish its own pure movement from the outer influences that ordinarily operate to give meaning and value to the perceptive datum, according to the psychism they express.

Through the liberation of mental picturing and thinking from such unconscious influences, these influences are themselves freed and tend to settle in the physical being, forming part of a center that is their own and in which they return to being positive forces. Anguish, to which even a philosophy has been dedicated, is nothing but a corporeal fact drawn from its own natural center. Yet it tends to resound within the soul and even within the spirit, in such as way that not even a fierce philosopher such as Kierkegaard succeeded in recognizing its origin, almost certainly due to a lack of inner autonomy with respect to the processes of his own metabolic system.

Perceptive 'contemplating' is an original 'imagining' that is enlivened of the form of a thing and that, if it observes itself because of an intense correlation, is recognized as founded upon itself, independent of physical supports. It is, therefore, on the verge of expressing itself as creative imagination. By having the thing before itself, it grasps its living element and perceives within itself the essential identity of such a life. The living element of nature, like that of the psyche and of human culture, can only be found by such an imaginative power of thinking.

This is true thinking, which, from the inner intuitive element, receives the direction of its suprasensory origin. With respect to this, dialectical intelligence is the temporary reflected form, necessary to the moment of the limitedly physical and, therefore, mechanical experience of the world, but which, in establishing itself as the intellectual cosmos valid in itself, is a rhetorical structure opposed to the foundation. It believes that it opposes this foundation with a power of pride, justified not even by an effective rule of sensory reality, which it believes it possesses, and it behaves as if it did possess it, mistaking a limited action upon the outer and physical modalities of life for the action upon life itself. It is the rhetoric by means of which we, today, believe that we dialectically and logically create our own cosmos of intelligence, as an ironclad organicity of the ephemeral, by precluding ourselves from controlling the inner identity of such intelligence, and the dominion under which powers this rhetoric acts and the cosmos (which it seems to create) emerges.

20. PERCEPTION OF THE ESSENCE: THE NON-BEING OF MATTER

To get inside of the 'perceiving' means to encounter a fundamental thinking, which does not become a mental image, or discourse, but remains an intact movement of life, in that immediacy sufficient unto itself, which is the original relation of the "I" with things. It is the relation in which we live daily and which nevertheless escapes ordinary consciousness. The task, as mentioned up to now, is to gather this relation in the indeterminate moment of perceiving. This relation, in fact, does not arise from perceiving, since perceiving is not its cause, but its effect.

The relation, if known, ceases to be a reason of dependence, because the consciousness of the "I" finally moves within it. And, being able to move, this consciousness draws from the source of its movement, until becoming independent of it—so as to exist on its own. Therefore, it possesses the world not as an antithesis, but as that of which it is the essence, since the movement of thinking coincides with the objective movement of life.

Those who have followed the thread of these considerations, are able to realize how the world's alterity emerges as an objectivity seemingly identical to itself, from the weakening of the consciousness of the "I" to the original relation with its own being. Seeking its own being, it illusorily identifies it with the corporeal structure, whose modalities it undergoes due to the fact that this structure, in being employed for consciousness, becomes itself deprived of the relationship with the foundation, from which the need of sensory perception and the limit proper to its immediate mediation, arises.

The perceptive content, mediated by the sensory organ, has its own direct way of becoming dependent upon the mediation, which is not such, because it is temporarily unrelated to the foundation, but, actually, operative through it. From this, the need of the 'appearing' arises, which seems to have, within it, the content as a *substance* that it contains, even if it *invariably gives itself within the form*.

But, because of reflected consciousness, the form is confused with the appearing, so that matter manifests as if it were founded upon itself, in an outer "metric" aspect, which is its immediate structure, in keeping with a process that mediates it. This process operates as if it were actually physical—since it is devoid of the foundation's immediacy—and, therefore, as an 'appearing,' governed by laws which seem to belong to the level of its being as an appearing—namely, the mineral level. But it is the appearing that would not even be form without the immediacy of the foundation from which the relation is aroused. Thus, an unknown dependence on the mode of the non-real mediation arises, which hides the relation of the "I" to a thing, within perceiving: for which we have the material vision of things.

Thus, the consciousness of the "I" does not possess the content of the 'perceiving' but, rather, the form of its 'manifesting' within the sphere of the sensory world. The form, however, is movement, and the movement is one with the immediacy of the imagining: an immediacy that is imperceptible because its identity with itself can occur in the pure forms of images, of which our ordinary imagining is simultaneously the mediation and the arbitrary use. Within the correlation of the "I," instantaneous imagining operates unnoticed. The spiritual practice of perceiving is conducive to noticing it, because it suspends the mediation, be it even temporarily.

21. SUPRASENSORY PERCEPTION IN THE SENSORY REALM

The art of imaging is born in imaginative 'contemplating,' for which the thing perceived manifests temporarily as a symbol of the "I"'s relation with the world. The world, which rises up in sensory form, manifests as a series of symbols, thanks to a formal suprasensory movement that flows within the 'perceiving,' but it is never conscious. It dis-animates itself in becoming conscious. The transitory dis-animation—from which arises the need for a unilateral physical relation with the world and, thus, for science and for technology, as the abstract mediation outside the object, already mediated in its essential identity, but without the conscious capacity of this mediation—is what should not be assumed as definitive by the human being.

The language of the sensory world cannot but be symbolic. We can study and analyze the letters of such a language, but not so that the science of such an analysis can be established as an end to itself, but only so that—beyond the analysis—what this language really wants to say can be read.

The formal suprasensory movement can be encountered within the 'perceiving' (which it renders possible) and experienced directly, without mediation, since the process of perceiving is in itself independent of dialectical consciousness. This formative movement flows and operates as the structural force of living things. The form of visible things does not emerge in consciousness by way of its own power, but because the imaginative human element, containing the identical formative movement, identifies with it and receives from it the sense of its own formative power. This sense becomes extinguished by dialectical consciousness, so that form becomes the outer appearing that dialectical consciousness needs. However, *pure observation* can reascend from the 'appearing' to the form, and from the form to the formative force.

One thing is to say that the sensory world is the world of semblances, or *mâyâ*, another thing is to perceive the process by means of which the world manages to manifest as a scenario of semblances, and what it wishes to signify with this.

A-dialectical thinking, present within 'perceiving' as an imaginative activity, escapes ordinary consciousness, because similarly on another plane, the thinking that arises as an intuitive force before becoming concept and discourse is unknown to it. Nonetheless, contemplating the form of nature's entities as symbols of a reality about to manifest for more than its 'appearing,' trains thinking to feel, within itself, the original formative power.

The initial form of ordinary perceiving is the one from which the inner formal movement, the original correlation of the "I" with the thing, escapes. For it immediately passes away into a process of subjective consciousness, governed by subconscious memory.

The essential element of consciousness can knowingly connect itself to this perceiving, by taking on the relationship according to which it already operates within it. For the being of consciousness, to connect with the 'perceiving' means to overcome, within itself, the modal moment of sensory appearing, due to the structure of the sensory organ, which, as we have seen, can make its own mediation be one which conditions. For it can be assumed as immediate by the insufficient consciousness of the "I." Therefore, a sensory aspect manifests to which the perceptive movement (in itself suprasensory) seems to conform. (Precisely such an alteration, unrecognized, nourishes false memory, of which one barely has a presentiment, without the possibility of conscious knowledge from modern psychological doctrines.)

22. The Thing as a Symbol

The suprasensory process of the perceptive act cannot be experienced as such, if the modal impression that it picks up in consciousness (through the engagement of the illusory immediacy, owing to the structure of the physical organ and its "mechanical" function) is itself not recognized as a formal moment of the suprasensory movement, which demands to be realized by consciousness. Technically, it initially requires the symbolic engagement of the sensory realm, then afterwards the reading—or contemplation—of the language of symbols, which are things. Those of us who identify with our physical nature, and who want to build a culture based on this identification, are actually content with the prosaic, sensory datum.

It is not by chance that we speak of a "mechanical" function of the sense organs relative to their physical structure. In reality, by means of such organs, the inner human being is, so to speak, cast out from its interiority and led to see the world as an irrelevant outward appearance, because the conformation of such organs, in relation to present-day human consciousness, is such that, within them, the relation between formative forces and form is, so to speak, inverted.

The structure of the sense organs is such that the physical world in which they appear as mediators of consciousness has in them an essential prevalence provided by the same structural forces. These forces operate so that the physical element can put its own architectural demand forward to them. For this reason, the physical element functionally impresses the psyche with itself. Even physiology proves that within each sensory organ the structural physical element subordinates the vital, metabolic element to itself. Therefore, the human psyche, looking out into the world by means of sensory organs, is forced to perceive only the world's physicality. The corporeal nature of entities projects itself as a physical reality within the soul. The perceived world is assumed as a sensory world.

But it is a symptom of the insufficient presence of the "I" within consciousness and, therefore, within the psyche, since the "I" carries with it the possibility of an integral identity with the perceived object. Otherwise, perception would not be possible. The perceived object is a temporary mediation, not a fixed reality, as it appears. In effect, the world's scenario is not made up of objects, or things, but of symbols.

Perception is a true datum in its objectivity, but precisely this objectivity resounds without being assumed in the whole of its identity, which is its capacity to reveal itself as the mediator of that to which it is identical, as a living symbol, and therefore to pronounce its own being in consciousness, thanks to the original act of the "I"—with respect to which, consciousness normally is not awake. It is unaware of the force through whose virtue perception is possible, and it is possible in relation to the subject, to the "I," that perceives. The external datum is real for it, whereas it is only a symbol, or symptom, of a content with respect to which it still is not awake and that it consequently receives, almost in a sleeping state.

In this way, the world's objectivity is abstract; only abstractly is a thing an object. The object could be true, if the subject lived consciously within the content of which the object is a symbol, but normally even the subject is abstract. From the abstract relation between subject and object, there cannot but be born a realistic reproduction of the abstract objectivity—namely, the machine. This machine is, therefore, the dead symbol, or the symbol of what, fragmented, is recomposed with the semblance of organicity, which is to say, mummified. Though necessary on the level of outer reality, the machine symbolizes the powerlessness of consciousness to realize itself within the element of life which surfaces from perception by means of it. *Perceiving manifests to consciousness as the sign of a life that escapes it:* which it only abstractly conceives and abstractly reproduces.

23. THE NON-PHYSICALITY OF THE PERCEPTIVE CONTENT

The force by means of which we perceive, the immediate relation of the "I" with the world, despite becoming a vehicle of sensory engagement, is a non-sensory act, of whose real nature, we, as percipient beings, are unaware. For we become conscious by means of the sensory moment of perception.

The non-sensory content, if separated contemplatively from the temporary mediation (which manifests as a sensory impression), can be cognized as the object's fundamental reality. This contemplative act can be realized within the 'perceiving,' since this very perceiving itself spontaneously initiates it, and because we meet the sensory, not only with the senses, but with attention turned to what flows within them and does not identify with the specific sensory impression. Instead, it is gathered as a content in itself. This (content) is gradually realized and tends to reveal itself, according to the immobility and autonomy that can be developed in its presence. The relationship of the "I" with the object is experienced as the perception of a basic content that continually slips away into the ordinary perceptive process.

In conclusion, we can say: we normally receive, as objective, the physical image of the world, but the movement of our receiving is primarily the correlation of the "I" with the world, but unnoticed by consciousness, because, in itself, it is suprasensory.

The consciousness of the "I," which is normally enlivened within the 'perceiving' but receives the sense of self from the perceived, can turn to the perceiving itself and grasp, within it, the movement that renders the perceived form, valid. It thus manages to recognize that such a movement can occur because, in itself, it is non-sensory. The real content of the perception manifests in a form that appears "physical," but nothing physical lies within it. Perception is possible precisely thanks to the power of penetration of a non-physical principle within the physical.

In the contemplation of the 'perceiving,' we can draw, from the sensory datum, a spiritual content, which normally mediates the "I"'s relation to itself, to the extent that it is drawn from ordinary consciousness. Within this perceiving, we can recognize a vital movement of thinking, as an a-dialectical movement, identical (in its formative power) to the thinking that arises unnoticed within the soul, in order to continually become concept and discourse.

The consciousness of the "I" emerges within the perceiving, but it is realized as self-distinction on the strength of the perceived. It renounces the living moment of the 'perceiving,' in order to become abstractly conscious of itself. In the contemplation of the 'perceiving,' consciousness discovers the moment of its emergence, by experiencing the "I"'s living relation with the thing.

24. The Ordinary Relation

In pure perceiving, we gather the "I"'s immediate relation to the outer world, and we learn what the lack of knowledge of it means as the dependency of the life of consciousness on the sensory form of things. Simultaneously, we experience the independence of a life current, which is a synthetic 'thinking–feeling–willing' that continually identifies with the substantiality of the percept.

This essential movement of the "I" escapes ordinary consciousness, which, without being the "I," is nonetheless the only one to account for a formal presence of the "I." At this point, we can understand the sense of subjectivity's self-alienation (see paragraph 3) when consciousness sinks into a perception or into a thought. Consciousness falters almost as if to shed itself of its limit, but not because it undergoes a state of self-diminution, rather, because it is spontaneously led to let an act (even more concrete than what is normal to it) be carried out within itself, namely the operating of the "I," with which it begins to identify.

This point highlights the sense of the discipline of concentration, as the willed dedication of thinking to a theme, and of the exercise of pure observation regarding an object. The object ceases to symbolize the correlation upon which the consciousness of the "I" unknowingly depends (undergoing in such form the illusoriness of existing and its emotional–instinctive resonances), because this consciousness manages to willfully take part in the "I"'s immediate act.

The end of dependency in the "I"'s relation with a thing is the principle of a new scientific era, because it leads the seeker to perceive the limit of the alterity. This is already virtually overcome by the "I," in the perceptive act. Nevertheless, the 'overcoming' is unknown to the feeble consciousness of the "I," which believes to have before it, the objective world in its aseity.

In truth, the outer world appears much more objective, extraneous, and impenetrable to us—for which we, therefore, must find the exclusive physical–rational relationship with it—the weaker the consciousness of the "I" is before it. This consciousness is not fortified by strengthening (through logical–dialectical formulations) its position of reflected and abstract consciousness but, rather, by overcoming it. Concentration and meditation are each the art of overcoming it.

Pure observation is the conscious continuation of a cosmic process that occurs, by means of the human being, as the action of the spirit within nature. Sensory perceiving, experienced, can reveal the organizing presence of the spirit in matter. As experimenters, we can witness within ourselves the relationship that the suprasensory realm has with the sensory by means of perception. Thanks to pure observation, we can take on such a process and continue it.

25. THE PRINCIPLE OF A NEW SCIENCE

Whoever has followed our observations, can realize how the spiritual practice of perceiving is the foundation of a new science, which demands inner discipline, so that rational study and research can be the vehicle of truth. Without the impulse of such discipline, study and research will, nowadays, fail to arrive at anything other than a further 'technification' of existence.

Pure perceiving enables us, as experimenters, to encounter within ourselves a 'thinking–feeling–willing' in a pure living synthesis, which resounds within us from the real being of the perceived entity. Alongside the perception of the object's inner content, we realize within ourselves an independence from its appearing, by gathering the identity with it and the ultimate sense of its phenomenal nature. Simultaneously, we can harmonize the physical–mathematical experience with an original order of soul life. We begin to know the pure forces of feeling and willing, normally unknown, because we usually do not possess the 'perceiving,' the direct perception of feeling and willing but, rather, the perceived. For this reason, (as was said in the initial paragraphs), we can never be the subject, or the "I," before emotional–instinctive manifestations.

In ordinary perceiving, we do not realize the pure correlation of the "I" with the world. Therefore, we transform the non-consciousness of such a correlation into unconscious dependency, into a fundamental obstacle to freedom. Extraneous to the vital movement of the "I"—a movement that is the synthesis of the three forces in the pure state—we, by way of our subjective experience, separate, from such a synthesis, a conscious lifeless impression (thought) in the form of a *mental picture*, which is semblance accepted as truth, by connecting *sensation* to it, as the use of the perceived content according to the subjective necessity of feeling and of willing bound to corporeity and, consequently, to the values of semblance—producers, therefore, of all desire, attachment, emotion, passion, or of the dependence on a world which is not real in that form. It does not exist except for consciousness's lack of life, since this life is unrelated to the living movement of the "I" in perceiving.

As researchers, we can understand the sense of our subjection to a perceiving and to a thinking that are signs of the correlation of the "I," not the correlation itself, which escapes the weak, or reflected, or dialectical consciousness of the "I." This subjection becomes the source of scientific error—even of that (science) which is strictly physical–mathematical—since the immediate products of perceiving and thinking are not integrated by an awareness of the mediation upon which they necessarily depend, but, in their apparent immediacy, are assumed as values.

The fact that, at a given level, science and technology are true and necessary does not take away from the fact that they are the product of the paralysis of knowledge, of which science, in order to be consistent with itself, should become aware, so that scientism and technology cannot presume to include the whole of life within their power. On the contrary, an investigation of life, just beyond their limitations, is conceivable, thanks to the same conscious rigor that was necessary to develop within such power. Neither science nor technology should be renounced. Instead, the limitedness of their function is to be understood and the inner principle that renders them possible is to be found, so that this inner principle can reveal the sense of their achievements.

The experience of modern human beings, founded exclusively on the data of sensory perception and on the related rational activity, is falsified by the fact that the sensory content is not perceived as it is, nor thinking experienced as it is. It shall never be sufficiently emphasized that "traditional human beings" did not need *pure thinking, nor pure perceiving*, for they did not draw the certainty of their own vision of the world from the senses, nor from thought but, rather, from inner organs, by means of which they had a "direct perception" of reality, which integrated the experience of the senses and the thinking activity.

In light of the preceding considerations, we can realize how the products of perceiving and of thinking are not to be validated by the consciousness of the "I" barely surfacing. Rather, they are to be assumed as indicative of a task that awaits us as human beings, given that we are the bearers of consciousness: in this way, the ongoing correlation of the "I" becomes consciousness. The possibility for individual consciousness to be formed outside the unhealthy daydreams of psychoanalysis and of related pseudo-sciences has such a foundation. Meditating is the fulfillment of the thinking act. To contemplate by means of pure perception is to lead the world of the senses back to the spirit, but it is also the current model of contemplation. In both pure thinking and pure perceiving, we elevate ourselves to the "I"'s original correlation with the world. The correlation ceases to be dependency, becoming the restoration of direct consciousness that the ancient human being used to have independently of the senses and of thought.

Those of us who understand the meaning of such a path, also learn which task awaits us. In this way, we can know, beyond the earthly limit, a life to which sensory experience is simply a means, and we can cure the pain of a material alterity, which, as a tragic necessity, is projected daily onto the life of the soul. It becomes a psychological, cultural, social, scientific–technical value and thereby tends to mechanize existence, by enclosing it within very narrow horizons, never overcome by dialectical or technical means, and within a monotonous sensory sphere, never overcome by any spatial promptness—thus bearing the human being's identical subjection to the physical ghost of space, everywhere.

III

THE INDEPENDENCE OF THE "I" FROM THE SUPPORT

1. THE REFLECTED IMAGE OF THE WORLD

To operate within thought by means of thought, belongs to the logic itself of thinking, in that it brings to a conclusion a process that dialectics barely expresses and that it contradicts to the degree in which it expresses it. Operating in this way, dialectics turns out to be an objective indicator of thought—not thought (itself)—actually, as reflected movement, it is a negation of its original content.

At a given point of the research, we discover the world's reflected image to be the opposite of its reality. This reality can be reconstituted so long as it integrates the reflected image with another dimension of the world's objectivity, which continually manifests as the inner identity of that image. Yet, it demands a particular act of consciousness in order to be perceived.

New paths of science are indicated by the possibility of a conscious integration of the sensory experience. Without this integration, the reflected image, codified and transformed into knowledge, is the emergence of a world that has no relationship to the reality of which it believes to be the science, even if it has at its disposal, relative to itself, a systematic consistency of its own, that can be projected in a correlative technical–mechanical objectivity.

The technical–mechanical world is a negative mediation necessary to human activity that has become abstract, to the extent that its determination does not belong to the principle from which it unconsciously draws but, rather, to the consciousness conditioned by the reflected image of the world, namely to the consciousness devoid of thought. It is therefore a structure, in its organicity, that is provisory and that contradictorily excludes the principle of the thinking from which it arises.

Until now, thought has justified the "I." For this reason, it has never, from Thales onward, been able to be true thinking. Thales' last work, in fact, was the doctrine that denies thinking a foundation in itself, that is, it considers it a secretion of a substance that—without realizing—is itself thought to be a foundation: a crepuscular idealism, to which the negative unity of the rationalistic–mechanical world opposed to thinking is to be connected. It is the inevitable consequence of a millenary philosophizing that had living thinking only so long as it did not become conscious of it and as it began to become conscious of it, it moved only in the reflection: which, even if in certain systems it could not err, insofar as it conformed with its light, it was nevertheless the reflection, not thought itself.

From various indications, the moment seems to have arrived for the "I" to justify thought, so that thought can be experienced not in its subjugation to an "I," which, being reflected, does not manage to be itself without thought but, rather, as the essence of life, namely what always dies out as normal thinking and, as life, seems to come from corporeity, because of the alienation of the relationship to itself of thought, insofar as it is life.

Reflected thought reaches us from corporeity, but it originates outside corporeity, as real thinking. The reflected image of the world is thus provisory. It waits to be restored to its true reality by real thinking, which we can discover through the synthesis of the reflected movement of thought, within thinking itself.

2. The Foundation

The operating of thought is the initial manifesting of the "I" as a subject, within thinking. The subject that normally acquires the sense of itself thanks to an object already thought and, therefore, conditioned by content extraneous to thinking, begins to have life within the thinking unbound to an object, since it does not have, as a support, the thought of something, which inevitably excludes it but, rather, thinking itself, or its immediate support. Within this support, we can perceive our own being, according to the immediacy that we normally experience only in corporeity, without recognizing this immediacy as our own, by attributing it to the body.

The "I" begins to experience its own immediate being in its reality, by means of the thinking that willfully thinks a thought, which—even if it is initially a thought of something—in being observed as thought, becomes an object of a thinking that is unbound to any object and is, therefore, free.

Thinking that is free appears thanks to unfree thought, duly directed by drawing from the source of itself, because of the mediation that does not lose the light of which it is the alteration, at the level in which the alteration is valid.

The thinking that expresses its own real nature manifests as an activity independent of the processes by means of which it enters the sphere of necessity, because it can experience its own mediation by making itself autonomous with respect to it and, therefore, by realizing the immediate identity with itself, that aroused it. Its consciousness, in fact, is actually formed by way of the sensory path, but it emerges because it is nonetheless founded upon the original immediacy, independent of sensory processes. In reality, it can be consciousness only insofar as it does not assume (within its depths) the mediation to be the foundation, even if, by not perceiving the mediation, it possesses its discursive manifesting, or its reflection, as an abstract foundation.

Thinking can experience the mediation by converging (with unlimited attention) in any thought, which—being the mediation already created—behaves like the reflection that refers back to its own light.

3. THE INCORPOREAL SOURCE OF THINKING

To realize thought by means of thought is essentially the exercise of concentration. Even if carried out within the sphere of the thinking process, this exercise ends up being an act of willing, which, by means of thought, cannot but move from the conscious principle.

The "I" is normally conditioned by thought, to the degree in which this is conditioned by its own object. The reflected form of the "I" adjusts to the conditioning of thought, accepting, as immediacy, the mediation devoid of the principle of mediating, or assuming, as reality, the outer world and, consequently, physical corporeity. The subject thereby forgets, with respect to them, to be the "I" to which they give themselves. Forgetful of its own being, is the ego.

The situation of the ego is based on the incompleteness of the movement of thinking, which binds itself to its own mediations and which, thereby, obstructs the action of the pure immediate principle. We really do not know any other thinking except the one bound to its objects. The thinking that experiences itself free of contents would be the first real act of the "I"; (if one well understands) it would not be a philosophical or idealistic act, because removing the mediation so that the pure immediacy can be realized according to the mediation that does not fall into reflectivity, cannot be a philosophic description—as Hegel attempted (to prove), leading astray the pure thinking, attained, toward a further reflection of itself—but, rather, a logical a-dialectical operation, according to the canon established by the same pure thinking. But such an operation, in its pragmatic structure, ends up being an indispensable moment of an ascetic technique.

The Independence of the "I" from the Support

Thought, free of objects, insofar as it completely actualizes its own movement, turns out to be real thinking. But it can be experienced free of an object, to the extent that it can be extracted from an object. In our everyday experience, because of the reflected and, therefore, abstract determination of thought, the object manifests as identical to itself. By retracing the mediation, this thinking is restored to its immediate being, namely to the possibility of being reality, not reflectivity.

Gathering the force of thinking into itself by means of concentration is the operation by virtue of which thinking experiences oneness with itself. It ceases to be conditioned by its own object, and, by keeping its own movement intact, it does not relate to anything other than to itself. It is then experienced not as a determination of something that is outside it, not as a product of physiological processes, or of hypothetical "irrational sources" but, rather, as a reality founded upon its own essence.

Because thinking (when it is an activity in its wholeness) does not minimally depend on physical corporeity, it can appear as a certainty, if it becomes self-experience —upon this, alone, its subsequent reflective situation depends.

This experience is the inverse of philosophical engagement or of speculative activity, which invariably is thinking subordinating itself to an object, being yet again the search for explications and argumentations, which, indeed, engage thought, but they are not the experience of thought itself. For this reason, we can endlessly tell stories about the metaphysical, or the unconscious, or the instinctive, or the physiological origins of the thinking activity. The experience of thinking within thought truly cuts this storytelling short, because it grasps a process whose inner logic is precisely its need to be experienced.

With philosophy's motives having been extinguished and philosophizing having become analytical discursiveness regarding every problem, we no longer have the right to say anything about thinking that is not derived from an experience of thinking's identity with itself, namely from an experience that is not a rekindled speculation on a theme. Otherwise, the principle of the experience (*empiria*) and of the analysis goes up in smoke.

It is easy to philosophize on an experience that is not carried out insofar as dialectical thinking, in its abstract reflectivity, is mistaken for its movement, or its light. In that sense, each philosophical activity today arises as a sign of the powerlessness of philosophy to experience its own object. For this reason, it manages, on the one hand, to deny thinking the possibility of explaining the mystery of its own synthetic process, without which it would not be, and on the other, it resorts to thought in order to show its dependence on corporeal processes, or its non-reality and, therefore, its impossibility of being a synthesis.

None of these positions correspond to the content that it presumes to affirm. Such content, in fact, is nothing so long as it is dialectical, or annihilated by its reflected form, and only by ceasing to be dialectical can it be experience-able. But, at the point in which we have arrived, only by experiencing the thinking process can we restore meaning to human reasoning.

To experience thinking means to go to an original point in which nature does not control us by means of the soul. Rather, our fundamental being begins to manifest with soul forces that are independent of nature.

4. The Mediation Retraced: Pure Willing

To operate within thought by means of thought is, therefore, to enter the beginning of the determination, which normally alienates itself within consciousness and, thus devoid of foundation, conditions us, as if it bore the content to which it refers: as if it continued to have a foundation.

In reality, abstract reflection is an unfolding of thought without its initial ideal content. Accordingly, it acquires an autonomy of its own that is led to exclude the subject, the human being. Continually, the ideal determination, alienating itself from us in the reflective moment, with its unconscious consent, gives rise to the sense of its relationships with the world and the values by which we passively control ourselves, namely knowing everything by means of reflected explications but, therefore, knowing effectively nothing. The world, in fact, illusorily taken on by thought, does not cease to condition it. Rather, it becomes the legitimate condition.

To place oneself decisively before thinking is to ask this thinking to reveal itself, namely its very being, according to its limitless indetermination. Always the revealer of something other, thought is asked to reveal itself. Otherwise, the *other* that thought allows to be considered as objective opposite individual subjectivity, the *other* that it allows to rise up in mental images and in values, in motives of idea and of action, can be a deception. We must grasp what renders true what we believe to be true. A rationalist, a logician of today, cannot renounce such proof, which regards the consistency of systems upon which its certainties are based.

In order for the *other* not to be myth or hallucination, thinking must give itself to us, not as a form of what by means of it becomes true but, rather, as a content in itself, which, by way of an "initial perception," we can recognize as true, since it is the truth of everything that we can recognize as true. However, this "initial perception" cannot be the learning of reflective thinking through further mediation but, rather, the experience of the identity at the point in which it originates, for which it guarantees the objective manifesting of something that is not a given thought, but the movement's pure flowing, the movement's original willing.

This flowing is the genesis of the idea, which manifests as essence. Therefore, the 'assuming' of it cannot be itself the object of thinking, nor can it demand the search for a more radical act of certainty. Precisely because thinking by means of spiritual practice can, in its flowing, be looked at by us as something *other*, we can identify with it. The identity of thinking with itself becomes our experience of the principle that is one with itself. That is to say, the immediate being of the "I" expresses itself in its initial possibility of determination, as pure indetermination, on the verge of determining itself as willing.

The will is realized by means of thought. Within thought, we can perceive the will independent of nature, namely the willing that does not need to be thought, in order to be the original life of itself, or of thought. For this reason, true being is precisely the *willing itself*. But immediate willing, in which one is as an "I," is encountered in immediate thinking. In willed thinking, the original force of thinking is freed, which is willing. Willed thinking is, therefore, the beginning of the spiritual practice of thinking.

Each day, we are one with the thinking that we think, and this is our bondage to things and to the world, to myths and to alleged ideals, because that thinking actually remains unknown. We do not know where it comes from, or where it goes. By means of it, we are seized by everything that is 'other.' We have before us, as objective, the world by means of thinking that is active through the senses. Yet, we do not have thinking, as objective, because we do not identify with it but, rather, with its opaque determination. Even if we each say "I" to ourselves, we do not have the "I" but, rather, a reflection. We do not even have thought.

Only if we have objective thinking before us, do we willfully identify with the current of force from which it arises, and we receive this according to its reality. The reality of a color is that with which we can identify, because we have it before us. We do not need to think it.

Thus, when the concentration exercise is realized, we no longer need to think a thought, in order to have its real substance. In such a case, it has nothing to do with the *'already-thought'* but, rather, with the *being of thought* which can be contemplated, because the "I" that contemplates it does not need thought. Then, the being of thought is free and, as such, by soliciting the free being within the "I," it brings to the "I" its own original force.

5. Hegel and the Fatuous Bertrand Russell

In the free being of thought, the "I" experiences its own metaphysical freedom. The independence of thought allows it to experience thinking in its reality, as an objective impersonal entity, inconceivable to what is normally rational thought, and nonetheless realizable thanks to the conversion of such thought, which is the raw matter of the meditative work. For this reason, experimenters who, endowed with an adequate inner organ, arrived at the perception of the primordial ideas active within the structure of human beings and of the world and, then, intended to communicate that experience through a dialectical system, by adapting the immediate content to the meditative necessity of reflected thought, could not but express themselves as Hegel had to in *Science of Logic* and, particularly, in treating the "Philosophy of Nature"; then, in order not to be understood by whoever lacked such an organ of perception, but was assumed to be a philosopher, to the point of being mocked by a pseudo-philosopher such as Bertrand Russell, capable of seeing only linguistic structures.

The limit of Hegel was precisely the dialectical need to represent, reflectively, the retraced mediation. Therefore, the task of experiencing original thinking was indeed intuited by him, but, as an intuition, made dialectical, and therefore, not realized. In fact, it was excluded from the possibility of being realized insofar as it was made dialectical, since the realization would have required silence and the radical conversion of his philosophizing.

However, this philosophizing—in terms of an indication of the mediation's noetic experience and of the possibility of retracing and penetrating the reflective process, by virtue of the idea's original being—nevertheless remains, in the history of human thinking, an untouchable value, still not understood by the world itself of philosophers. Nor can it be grazed by the fatuous logic of a Bertrand Russell, so far removed from the majesty of that thinking, that he can deceive only those who do not know it and, nevertheless, today believe themselves to be logicians and thinkers.

It is symptomatic that a dialectic like the "mathematical philosophy" of Bertrand Russell arises in philosophy's twilight hour, when the world of ideas and of speculation has passed, and the breed of thinkers capable of using mathematics as a symbolic support for pure intuition is exhausted: when in place of ideas there arise discursive structures whose connective tissue is no longer thinking, but the outer relation convertible into arithmetical operations, and the world's very reality is assumed on the basis of measurements or numeric expressions.

Whatever the objective of mathematical philosophy, it cannot escape the limits of mathematics—which is to say, the limits of quantity. Whatever the determination of size or the algebraic game of the determination of various sizes and equivalences of sizes, they do not have the power to change an infinitesimal of reality, neither inner nor outer, if it is not thinking that makes use of mathematics, to express what it alone bears within itself, but that with philosophers such as Bertrand Russell it risks no longer bearing.

6. The Illusory Liberation: Krishnamurti

The secret of individual life and of the life of the cosmos, of human history and of the history of nature, is the transition from "I think" to "I am." It is the point in which thinking identifies with itself, and therefore, frees itself of the "I." But, in reality, the "I" frees itself of thought, by giving thought a way to express itself according to the force of its primordial nature.

Only by means of the thinking in which there reflects its initial movement, can the "I" draw what in its immediacy it awaits from

The Independence of the "I" from the Support

thinking. The path, however, is not to presume having the "I am" as an object, which would thus become its dull thinking reflection—like all philosophizing—but, rather, to begin experiencing thought according to the "I am."

Thought should not be passed over but, rather, grasped and discovered there, where, it is not yet a restriction to the "I," insofar as it ceases to be dialectical thought: thereby appearing as a pure force of thinking. We encounter our own pure willing, as the essence of thought and as the initial 'articulating' of the "I." But, here, since the nonentity of the individual limit connected to the thinking necessity is realized—given that the individual force is moved to within the research—the change of vision derived from the limit's nonentity is understood as a subsequent experience. Such a change is not arbitrary, but relative to the discovery of an original truth and of the meaning that this truth gives to 'existing.'

Thought should not be passed over. We, who presume this, will always have the illusion of freeing ourselves from a thinking activity, whose origin is unknown to us. By badly understanding a traditional teaching, or by allowing ourselves to be guided by cushy modern "teachers," with an Eastern tag, we remain anchored, in the depths, to reflected consciousness, that is, to corporeity, by deceiving ourselves of overcoming, or eliminating, what we truly still do not have the capacity to perceive—thinking. In fact, to act upon thinking, we must arrive at the point where it emerges. To arrive at the point where it emerges, we must possess its movement, and to possess its movement, we must know the art of concentration. But it is not enough to know the art of concentration. We must also actualize it, dedicating months and years, an entire life to such a task. And it is also essential that the art of concentration be the true one.

Whoever of us, in the depths of our being, rejects the effort to know the reality of thinking—of which only the so-called foundation can be experienced—imagines that we skip thought by eliminating "thoughts already thought" (which we believe to be thinking itself), in order to arrive at a "void," represented or dreamed. We project before ourselves a *being* of freedom, which we do not notice having as an idea, and from which we cannot execute a leap in order to enter into such a being, as if into something other than thought, or into an 'unthinkable' and nevertheless thought as 'unthinkable.' It is a contradiction from which we cannot escape, given that we cannot escape thought, by believing that we have overcome it. For we do not know where thinking is radically bound to corporeity and, therefore, where it can be freed and overcome.

The various forms of liberation recommended by J. Krishnamurti, for example, do not end up being inner acts but, rather, attitudes of liberation with respect to specific products of thought, or of thought and of feeling and of instinctiveness: nevertheless of 'thoughts already thought.' Behind these, their source remains intact and, therefore, ready to reproduce them, due to an unawareness of the manifesting of the mediation reflected by an instantaneous thinking which, continually called upon, inadvertently reproduces the mediation in its reflectivity. For this reason, the disciples of such teachers spend their whole lives freeing themselves from the products of an unknown thinking, products continually replaced by the contingent liberating attitude, which automatically reproduces them, since they are congenial to the psychic content of the attitude, or of the perception of themselves in a present that is imaginatively actualized and illusorily led outside the temporal dimension.

The psychic content is the radical non-will of freedom, inspired by a being other than the "I," feigning an easy liberation, the most sentimentally acceptable, which presumes to expel spatiotemporal conditions from consciousness, without wanting to know if it truly expels them and by what means. In fact, it concerns a representation of radical freedom, whose artificiality consists in being represented without one being aware of representing it: a temporary freedom at which we effectively arrive by means of a series of images of eliminations of inner conditioning states.

The Independence of the "I" from the Support

Even the elimination, itself, cannot help but be carried out by means of an image of the state to be eliminated. This state can, nevertheless, in certain cases, also really be there and the image of the elimination can function as an act that eliminates. But there remains the ambiguous presence of a thinking, which, by representing and imagining, actualizes these provisory transcendences without believing that it is thought (itself), because as thought, it, itself, has to have been overcome or eliminated. Such thought, therefore, remains well hidden, because all that of which consciousness becomes liberated is, in effect, not thinking itself, but, as we were saying, its dead product, namely the 'already-thought.'

Simultaneously being called upon eliminating are, therefore, an unconscious thought and the 'already-thought,' between which Krishnamurti does not show that he has the capacity to distinguish, regarding the subject of freedom. The question of becoming free, in fact, is posed only for thinking, not for the 'already-thought,' nor for all that is assumed at the level of the 'already-thought.' Being free of moods, or instincts, or the struggle against them, or assuming attitudes of freedom toward them—*by giving them a reality that they lack, except through the projection of reflected thought*—makes no sense. It seems as if Krishnamurti wants to free his disciples of this reflected thought, but he carefully prevents them from being able to conceive, as necessary, a method for this to be realized. For this reason, the disciples are always in a state of dependency on the administration of the viaticum of "conversations" in which reflected thought reflects, ever again, the liberation of itself and the redemption of feeling and of willing.

Actually, feeling and willing are already autonomous in themselves, but we do not know them as such, because we experience them by interchanging them with thought that is not free. We can have the right relationship to them if we can free thought, not by presuming to free ourselves of thought ahead of time, or mythically seeking something beyond it by drawing from the mental images that it provides in order to build for ourselves a being of freedom independent of it, which is to say, by organizing for ourselves a freed barren life, all modeled, in its liberating attitudes, through the most subtle weavings of reflected thought, which remains the secret ruler, for which freedom is truly dreamed. The liberation of thinking does not occur by eliminating specific thoughts, already thought, as Krishnamurti recommends, nor by monitoring the movements of reflected thought but, rather, by working to grasp thinking, there, where it is an autonomous movement founded upon its own source.

Pseudo-masters who advise against concentration and who recommend uncalled for freedoms from moods, today have the mission of taking away the remaining possibility of independence from naive disciples, because they deprive them of the life of ideas and, therefore, of ideas that rectify those moods, eliminating in those disciples the capacity to gather the reflected thought that provides such moods with life. In fact, concentration is the only path by means of which the passage from reflected thought to living thinking—namely, to the being of freedom—can be carried out.

We must cultivate the hypothesis that those who, today, by obeying a precise cosmic plan, have the task of preventing us from gaining freedom, possess a subtle means at their disposal to attain their objective, namely, to indicate paths toward freedom acceptable according to an immediacy that can be easily aroused by an esoteric–mystical language, and to thus divert our cognitive activity from itself, so that thinking can think the liberation from instincts, feelings, prejudices, the liberation from itself, but cannot grasp itself in the act of knowing. That is to say, it is unable to perceive itself by identifying its own alienation in reflectivity, from which it can never actually be freed.

7. The Ambiguity of the Practical Action

As we have said, the presence of thinking within us, as a form of anything else but itself, requires, from a person who truly thinks, that it reveal itself—not its *way* of revealing things, which is the object of philosophy but, rather, its own *being,* which no one yet sees.

To operate within thinking is to appeal to a pure volitional element inherent in it as an essential content, or as an original unity, of which it normally deprives itself in order to become the form of other contents, namely of various types of perception, sensations, feelings, impulses and, therefore, of the series of stimuli implicit in its relationship with the sensory realm.

From a normal experience, thinking receives a content that is not its own, but with which it inevitably identifies. Therefore, like thought becoming the mere reflected form of things, it does not seem to have reality within itself. With the discursive limits of thought being thus imperceptibly established, thinking can no longer have power. Meanwhile, discursiveness can embrace everything, without really grasping anything.

From such a situation is born (among other things) the conviction that when we express a charge of will, in organic and conscious form, we do not draw from a free will, founded on itself, but rather, from our corporeal nature, even when the corresponding thought is able to recognize itself as free. In effect, the discursive limitation removes from thinking the possibility of noticing the confines of physical nature and the independence of the *mediation*, next to which its immediate being seems to vanish. Meanwhile, this must continually manifest so that the mediation can be possible until carrying on as will.

It is the reason for which, according to current opinion, a vitality is attributed to action, or to activism, a vitality that we assume thinking lacks, since we do not manage to see, within the inner genesis of feeling and of acting, an ideal driving power: as if the movement were valid in itself, in its formal manifestation, and not as the movement of an idea, which, in truth, only in its original 'referring to itself' does the sense of movement and, above all, its possibility, lie.

No movement, or action, or willful act is actually valid, unless it is stimulated by an ideal content. Naturally, the task is to determine to whom such content belongs. The importance of recognizing its source is equal to that of understanding how, without it, no willful act is possible, nor is an action somehow able to manifest. There is no human fact that does not solicit its driving idea. "To act without acting" can therefore be intuited as the death of activism as a value, in view of the true action: which alone can take on visible forms. These visible forms always refer to a metaphysical content. But, contemplated as valid in their 'appearing,' they constitute the contemporary ideal of a "practical" conception that it deems to value in contrast to a theoretical conception: both being abstractions, apparently opposite one another.

The distinction between theory and practice is a modern abstraction, necessary to the mechanism of knowing, which excludes itself from its own source of thinking. Such a distinction does not reflect the reality of thinking, since it is itself the theoretic to which the respective practice—devoid of the principle to which it appeals and from which alone form can arise as an action—would be counterposed. Each theory, in that case, is not the internal thought of a concrete entity but, rather, the trace or the method so that such thought can be possible as the principle of the concrete action in which it intends to actualize itself. Thought has so confined itself to being the form of a reality extraneous to it, that we consider reality, devoid of the thinking by means of which it acquires formal objectivity, to be true. Nor are we more capable of attributing to thought a real being in itself, which is not a discursive content. The possibility of thought's inner identity is lost for the benefit of a formal and dialectical mechanism that, in every field, feigns the creative identity. For it does not possess this creative identity, nor can it conceive possessing it.

In such conditions, thought—to a prevailing contemporary mentality, especially in the field of psychophysiology—appears bound to corporeity, dependent on corporeity. It is believed to arise from the cerebral organ. But a conclusive investigation proves the exact opposite, namely thinking expresses itself dialectically by means of the cerebral organ, but it does not depend on this organ. The cerebral organ actually depends on thinking, on the profound forces of thinking, whose activity is found at the base of its structure, and which can be perceived by whoever arrives at the objective experience of thought.

To confine thinking to its exclusive form, essential for expressing sensory life, is not only the cause of the incapacity to perceive the independence of thinking from the cerebral organ, but it is also the cause of this organ's alteration (of which we spoke in the first part of this book) and of all bodily and soul illnesses. But it is clear that such constriction is unknown to dialectical thought, which nourishes it and expresses it. For this reason, those modern preachers who declare the need to eliminate thought, without even remotely imagining the whereabouts of what would be eliminated, deceive their disciples.

8. Independence of Thinking from the Cerebral Organ

Therefore, the independence of the thinking activity from the sensory support and its 'being founded' upon itself is not a hypothesis but, rather, a reality that can be known through experience. If such an experience is incapable of being carried out, it is superstitious to negate its possibility.

Of all the inner activities, thinking turns out to be the only one by means of which we can move from the foundation or from an original axiomaticity, since, experienced as thinking, it reveals itself to us as the content of all possible axiomatic enunciations and, consequently, as being founded upon itself, or upon a primordial essence independent of corporeity. In this way, we can prove to ourselves the objective existence of a suprasensory sphere. But such an experience is possible based on an inner discipline, whose methodology cannot be provided except by those who are able to completely possess the experience.

Feeling and willing, if objectively observed, cannot lead to their foundation, as they ordinarily manifest, since mere rational consciousness is unable to retrace their process, which is internal and unknown to it. The objective observation of feelings and of volitions or of instincts, assuming it is possible, is always arrested before a limit. In fact, they always lead back to corporeity, not because they belong to it, but because modern human beings, at the level of consciousness in which they find themselves, cannot but encounter them in the corporeal sphere, where they, in becoming subjective sensations, appear devoid of their original nature. The relationship of thinking to consciousness is different. Thinking—insofar as we immediately become activated of it, as conscious beings—offers its movement the possibility to turn toward its own foundation, within the very movement in which it thinks. It is a reversibility based on its primordial being. Today, human research demands the conversion of thought, as an experience of the means by which it unfolds. This leads to the foundation, due to its aim of being able to have before it, as a datum, its own 'manifesting'—namely, its own moment of life.

The reason why thinking can be experienced as the inner activity which, alone, has the foundation within itself, and why it can lead to such a foundation (if it is directly required of this activity and not its intellectual products), while feeling and willing always lead back to a corporeal support that ordinary consciousness is unable to identify and, therefore, overcome, depends on the fact that the conscious principle has, within thinking, its own immediate support, which, in turn, as a mediating process, has corporeity—the cerebral system—as its own support.

The Independence of the "I" from the Support

It is obvious that within the support of pure thinking—the most alive with creative ideation—the conscious principle can make itself independent of the corporeal support and, therefore, follow thought "directly," by being able to experience its process in reverse, even beyond the screen of cerebralism, in an incorporeal zone, where it can encounter the pure forces of feeling and willing. We cannot encounter these forces in their ordinary 'manifesting,' like we can with thinking, for they do not have the nervous system as a vehicle (as modern psychophysiology thinks) but, rather, other supports of the corporeal organism. And, ordinarily, only when they identify with such supports do they manage to echo within the nervous system, by means of which, feeling and willing are perceived in their final expression, or when no longer can anything other than the form by means of which they manifest be able to change in them. Instead, within thought, we can act upon its birth, if we are able to make the pure mediation coincide with the immediate being of thought, thanks to a specific inner technique.

Only by experiencing thought free of the senses and, thus overcoming the physical limit by means of which we initially become conscious of ourselves, do we open for ourselves the path to experience feeling free of the senses—which is the path toward a mysticism that renews, in new forms, the life of the ancient perennial mysticism—and to realize willing free of the senses, which is the path toward the renewal of ancient perennial metaphysics. This last one naturally includes within itself the first and the same intellectual spiritual practice. Nonetheless, it cannot precede these methodologically. Rather, it allows itself to be preceded by these, by operating through them, that is, by demanding to begin the transmutation of consciousness in its immediate vehicle: thinking.

9. THE CORPOREITY AND NON-CORPOREITY OF WILLING: THE FUNCTION OF THE SUPPORT

By experiencing the concept as pure immediacy, we, as researchers, can recognize the entity of thinking founded upon a suprasensory essence, in which the being of the concept is not yet determined, but it is the universal that has within it the principle of determination. Along these lines, the identity with the universal on the verge of occurring, inside the concept itself, discloses for us an area of freedom in which a higher life of feeling and a higher life of willing can be known, a higher life made up of the same universal substance of which thought becomes enlivened. We can recognize *the feeling and the willing that do not need liberation*, because they are already free within themselves, but as such un-manifested in the soul. The question of freedom, in fact, only regards the thinking that, in the conscious act, is bound to its own reflectivity.

Feeling and willing manifest according to the alteration or the non-freedom of thinking, therefore, in a form that does not concern their being, but our bondage to illusory necessity, which we allow to emerge from our own mental picturing. This is the sense of passions and of instinct, toward which any hint of an attitude of freedom is deceitful, since it ignores the radical bond of thinking and the futility of acting toward them, as if they possessed reality in themselves. Whoever understands this, possesses the secret of the harmony of the soul's life.

We can experience an inner reality independent of the bodily organism and recognize that such a reality is the soul's true being. We can understand how access to such a being is *initially* given to us by means of thought, to the degree in which we are not limited to having it as the immediate form of perceptions, but contemplate its movement independent of the perceptive content. We can have the objective immediacy of such content, by means of which we encounter the element inside of thinking, with which it normally identifies, so that perception can manifest. We can experience this

The Independence of the "I" from the Support

internal element of thinking within ourselves thanks to the capacity of contemplative differentiation, which up to this point has been able to guide us. It has to do with a 'feeling–willing' that belongs to the extra-corporeal sphere, which we can notice, insofar as we move at the same level in which thinking manifests its independence from sensory contents, namely from cerebral mediation.

Ordinarily, we realize the non-corporeity of thinking in a reflected and, therefore, unconscious form. Regardless of our physical–sensory situation, we can think independently of this. We can find ourselves in serious danger or in conditions of extreme uncertainty, and nevertheless have the possibility to objectively think that the sum of the angles of a triangle is 180 degrees. There exists in us the possibility to realize the autonomy of thinking in whatever sensory condition we find ourselves, but not the possibility to realize such autonomy as a real state of consciousness. This is because we do not know how the autonomy arises. We do not know which movement allows thinking to manifest as an autonomous being.

Our task, as experimenters, is to pass from virtual independence to real independence. In the first case, thought has an autonomy that is merely reflected, without life, in that it is still dependent on cerebralism. It is the thinking required, as a precise rationality, by everyday experience and by the processes of ordinary knowing. In the second case, thought turns toward grasping, within itself, its own element of life and, therefore, it acquires the strength not to depend on cerebral mediation in order to actualize its own movement. It thereby actualizes its own real being, as thought that has its own content within itself. It does not receive it from sensory nature or from its mental echo. In this content, thinking is one with pure feeling, with pure willing, which is to say, it is independent of the feeling and willing bound to corporeity.

The feeling and the willing that we know only in their sensory ramification, devoid of their foundation—insofar as their process, retraced, always leads back to corporeity—now become a non-sensory experience. They point to their foundation.

The importance of such an experience lies in the possibility to conceive a life of thinking, a life of feeling and willing, whose original reality is not to be sought in physical nature. We must now "prove" to ourselves the world's reality to which religions refer, not by means of dialectics, but by means of experience.

In the physical organism, we do not find anything that explains the life of thinking, the life of feeling, or the life of the will. The body only mediates an incorporeal life of the soul. The sensory view of the world is a soul experience by means of the corporeal organism, in which any physiological process accompanied by the manifestation of thinking, of feeling, and of willing, is foreign to their content, since it belongs only to the conductive function of such a manifestation.

Only the experience of the immediate being of willing in the form proper to it, can account for the relationship that willing has with the physical organism. Such a relationship cannot be observed in an organism outside the person who experiences, because one would always have the perceptions of someone else's organism, moved by a willing that only the corresponding subject could experience.

Investigators can only carry out the experience of willing within themselves. For this reason, they are able to observe, within themselves, which corporeal support really expresses willing. They then discover that it is not the nervous system, as modern physiology and, consequently, psychology affirm but, rather, another corporeal system that does not have a direct relationship to the thinking consciousness, which, instead, has the cerebral organ as a support. Yet, experimenters are able to arrive at a direct observation of this, to the degree in which they are able to have an experience of thinking independent of the nervous system, which allows them to look at the will's relationship to the physical organism that takes place outside such a system. In this way, they can understand that the function of this system with respect to the will is simply one of transmission, or of registering its sensory effects, according to the same process with which it mediates ordinary sensory perception.

Each alteration of this relationship, such as a trespassing of the forces of the will by their own corporeal support within the immediate corporeity and, therefore, as pressure on the nervous system, reverberates within the psyche as an instinctive emergence, or anguish, or fear. It is the alteration of willing, whose cause is to be sought in its physical support, not because willing arises from such a support, but because the alteration of this support involves an alteration of the manifestation of willing and, consequently, a typical series of irregular psychic facts.

Any presumed exploration of the "unconscious" meant to heal such psychic forms, does nothing but detain, within an inappropriate area, the irregular tension between willing and the nervous system and, therefore, confirms and nourishes illness. Meanwhile, the task of the psychiatrist or of the psychologist should be to consider the need of leading the psychopathic process back to the corporeal center, not by feeding any representation or interpretation of illness with dialogues, but by tending to eliminate its psychologization (*the true illness*) and to reinforce our willful autonomy as subjects, by means of simple thinking (or imaginative) exercises, so that the will, independent of the corporeity within us, finds the correct relationship to the corporeal support. Already the possibility of an objective experience of thought gives thinking the possibility to attain that independence from the cerebral organ and, therefore, from the nervous system, which places it in the state of not undergoing instinctive–emotive repercussions of the alterations of the support of willing.

10. The Immanent Transcendence of Willing: Logic as the Sleep of Consciousness

What has been affirmed can be experienced technically by way of the spiritual practice of thinking to which reference has been made.

The fact that the human being can make sense-free thinking and objective imagining arise willfully as the conversion of arbitrary imagining, in its appearing as a task neither imposed nor proposed by nature—while, if one observes, it is natural necessity that demands that we construct a "a civilization of machines," as well as the current type of culture—can show, to *those who intend on experiencing it,* how the human will does not depend on physiological laws.

Intuitive thinking and free imagination are the expression (by means of thinking) of a will unbound to corporeal processes. The immateriality of thinking can become the vehicle of the conscious experience of willing, which is its foundation. Today, real human success lies in realizing the point where free will becomes, by way of thinking, a fact of consciousness, perceptible as a content of life. Such willing is of the same nature as the forces that support the corporeal organism from an extra-corporeal sphere.

The living substance of thinking is this incorporeal willing, which, to become a rational activity, demands to be reflected as thought in the cerebral organ. Precisely because of this reflecting, it loses its own being, saturated with life. It becomes thought that is lifeless or reflected, because of cerebral mediation.

Therefore, the process of thinking is not to be sought in the sensory aspect of such mediation. No physiological investigation can grasp the nerve activity that lies at the foundation of thought, simply because this investigation, in any case, *finds itself before perceptions, not thoughts.* And if thoughts correspond to such perceptions, they cannot be but the thoughts of those of us who experience them. We should examine these thoughts within ourselves, not within the brain of another person. This means that we should be capable of the spiritual practice of thinking, in order to be able to gather, within ourselves, the relationship between thought and the cerebral organ. We could then ascertain how the processes physiologically graspable in the cerebral apparatus have actually nothing to do with thinking. Wherever they manifest, thinking cannot exist and, vice

The Independence of the "I" from the Support

versa, wherever thinking manifests according to its own autonomy, such processes are annihilated.

Because it is unable to manifest by rejecting such processes, thinking becomes a conscious activity. When, instead, living processes manage to influence thought, we cannot bring into it the real consciousness of the "I" and, yet, we can express ourselves with analytical organicity, insofar as we have at our disposal a logical procedure endowed with automaticity. Nature controls us without us knowing it, in that it holds us back at the threshold of waking consciousness.

This is useful for understanding how the activity by means of which logical determinations in consciousness are possible—since this activity is not to be consciously connected with these determinations, but, on the contrary, such determinations, in themselves, are validated as the typical forms of thought—corresponds to a sleeping state within us. It does not necessarily become conscious because it occurs in logical form. Before such a determination, we are in a state of sleeping consciousness, from which we can move to waking consciousness only by establishing a relationship of awareness with the act that gives rise to the determination. Deprived of such a relationship, we actually dream the content of what we see logically occurring outside. We cannot experience, logically, the connective forces of the logical process, because, for us, they occur at a level of supra-consciousness, with respect to which we, as discursive reasoning beings, are in a dream state.

We grasp reasoning to the extent that it has already entered a discursive form. For this reason, we are tempted to believe that, by formally arranging the discourse, we can possess thought, or truth. But with respect to true thinking, or to truth, we effectively dream. Therefore, the various logics of today, like the various dialectics, cannot coincide based on objective consonances. They will essentially always be in contrast with one another: each one experiencing truth in its own way, according to a contingent awareness of the object.

Logicians–dialecticians who seem to function in a waking state actually dream, because they see, in reflected images and in reflected thoughts, a reality that, as a conscious content, escapes them. They elaborate thinking from outside. They do not move it from within, by controlling vital cerebral processes. Rather, they unconsciously arouse them and lean on them, by way of the formal expression.

This explains, among other things, how dialecticism, even methodologically dignified, can no longer grasp truth. Therefore, simple "common sense" is superior to it. For example, we contemplate a missile with an awareness that is structurally valid, but we are incapable of contemplating, with the same awareness, a pumpkin seed that contains within itself, from a structural point of view, much more wisdom and power. It can give rise to another pumpkin, while the missile is unable to reproduce itself. The actual attempt to provide the power of truth to a logical discourse by means of its mathematical formulation is the sign of the fall of formal logic outside the synthetic movement of thinking, from which, alone, the inner connectivity of a logical activity, of a mathematical activity, can nevertheless spring.

Thus, nature seizes us again as thinking beings in a different way, insofar as in the sleeping state we make use of the will within conscious thinking to connect ourselves to the willing, by means of which nature operates within us rather than by means of us. For this reason, each of us thinks and believes to be the one that thinks; or we believe that the brain thinks; or we think of supra-nature as a power transcendent to us, not unlike the nature that we have impenetrable before us, because it is well shielded with notions and with mathematical–physical theories.

11. The New Spiritual Practice of Thinking

One thing is to be conscious of the thought of an object; another thing is to be conscious of thought that is without an object, which is the being of each thought before it becomes a conceptual form. The latter is a state in which thinking has the ideating power, intact, within itself—a power of which it continually deprives itself in order to become a conceptual determination.

If we become conscious of the being of a thought, we can manage to connect ourselves with its origin in an area where its immediacy can be perceived, without the need of reflection. This area is non-temporal and, therefore, precedes the process of reflecting, in which, by not having to be reflected, the presence of the "I" manifests in its identity with itself. Such an experience involves the temporal suspension of the mediation for which thought ordinarily passes over into reflection.

Ordinarily, thought's immediate being leaves the ghost of itself to reflection and, as a force, flows within the depths of willing, from which it corporally establishes itself as "something other" than thought. With the mediation suspended, upon the cessation of reflecting, the same pure mediation takes over as a function, given that it has no other object but its own principle, namely the immediate foundation, whose current of life becomes the fundamental will of pure thinking. It does not expire into a will, which, alienated from its own principle, always ends up operating as the instinctive force opposed to that current of life.

Meanwhile, in reflected thinking, the "I" is annihilated. It lives in the consciousness of the being of thought, as a power of will. It lives in the current of force that normally alienates itself in thought and that, consequently, we do not experience as thought, since this force is unconscious in every other movement of the soul's life. For this reason, it is not only the force of thinking within thinking, but within feeling and within willing, within perceiving.

The deception of psychoanalysis involves confusing, in the unique category of "unconscious," what is *below* and what is *above* ordinary consciousness, so as to lead us to the most tragic misunderstanding concerning our own inner life, because, through our lack of a distinguishing principle, the subconscious can legitimately invade consciousness. Nor is any rectifying experience possible, since supra-consciousness is mistaken for its opposite. Therefore, the possibility of an activity of consciousness according to its own principle is methodically suppressed.

The thinking-force is never experienced as ordinary thought. On the contrary, as rationality, or as dialectics or discourse, it is annihilated, and its dead form, in fact, is normally called thought. This empty husk is always filled by the *opposite* of what it originally is, which is to say, beneath name and form flow forces adverse to the principle of the force, unless the thinker is continually capable, through thinking, of giving them back to it.

Therefore, the thinking-force is not mental picturing or philosophizing, which are the typical activities of thought. But it can be experienced by means of thought, to the extent that we willfully abstain from rational or philosophical practice, and in given moments, train ourselves methodically to allow the whole capacity of thinking to flow into a single thought, so that thinking, in itself, becomes more internal than its dialectification, until coinciding with its own movement. In this discipline of thinking, its dialectical form is initially used as a means. Then, gradually, the means is reduced to a symbolic sign, devoid of dialectical significance, to the point in which only the perception of the pure thinking-force remains in consciousness.

This schematic reference to the spiritual practice of thinking is already a response to whoever objects that Eastern systems contain similar techniques of concentration and that we therefore go about giving modern form to a traditional method. Things can appear as such to those who, by refusing to experience thought in itself, accept *a priori* Eastern techniques and thus cut themselves off from the possibility of directly identifying the unconsciously implicit supra-rational element within their own present thinking and, thus, of recognizing it within the same Eastern techniques, so as to be able to truly make use of them.

According to these techniques, concentration is never used in order for the thinking-force to flow within consciousness by means of its determination, since these techniques lack (nor do they need) the experience of the typical determination of the modern mental sphere. Such techniques, on the other hand, see to it that thinking avoid every form of determination, by directly giving life to a given symbol, or image of a Deva, or a *mantra*, or a psychosomatic center. There is not a *sâdhana*, or *yoga*, that does not operate in function of a meaning, or of a vision to be attained, or of a contact with a force connected to the very object of the concentration. On the other hand, in the concentration to which we allude, the determination is the instrument, while the meaning is precisely what goes lost. The object is used so that its sensory content can be eliminated from it. In this way, the force of pure determination can remain within consciousness.

Thought is not the thought of which we must become free, but the one whose original power we need to let be expressed in its pure state—an original power that, for modern humanity (unlike that for ancient humanity), has manifested in individual form, by means of the sensory realm, until becoming objectified in a dead projection (even if exact) as mathematical–technical thought; and we succeed in doing so, to the degree that we are able to observe this original power, by gathering its non-sensory process, normally unseen. For, in the sensory self-negation of thinking, we can again find its supra-sensory content, by way of a willful conversion.

Normally, thought is aroused by forces interested in human expression, according to its physical nature, forces that we, as conscious beings on a physical plane, are unable to distinguish from ourselves, or from the movements of our own soul, above all in an age in which the task of regulating the things of consciousness—once entrusted to metaphysical consciousness—has been assumed by a deceptive psychology. While such forces cannot grasp the internal power of such thinking, its form is instead grasped and used by them. And, nevertheless, each of us believes to be the thinker. It is our task to connect with that inner power of thinking in order to have a real sense of what it accomplishes in the physical world. Otherwise, we unconsciously place ourselves against our own original order. We become the instrument of forces that grasp thoughts and the orientations of thought, of which we believe to be the authors.

As modern technical human beings, we are drawn by the effects of the movement of the internal power of thinking, by physical results, and by facts. We ignore the movement in itself and do not even imagine its force. Actually, we negate it by having a false concept of the force, by confusing this concept with the one that has physical potential, which we deduce from mere sensory notes. Such a concept, extended to everything, pits the product of the force against the force itself and, consequently, human beings against themselves, the being of the "I" against the "I." As we have seen, this contradiction has in "dialecticism," as well as in "logistics," its actual codification, given that both tend to exclude the "I" from thinking by way of a systematic path. They have already succeeded in excluding it from general human culture. In order for it to be noticed, its consequences have to be undergone for a long time.

IV

THE LOGIC AND TECHNIQUE OF CONCENTRATION

1. THE SPIRITUAL PRACTICE OF THINKING AND PHILOSOPHERS

Concentration is a willful act that, on the mental plane, actualizes the quintessential nature of thinking, namely its synthetic (essential) being, or the immediate manifesting of its light. The philosopher or the logician, partially and indirectly, always calls upon this synthetic being because of dialectical interests, but never so that the synthetic being can itself become experience and its immediacy manifest as thought. The philosopher and the logician, as well as today's common intellectual, are not interested in the light of thinking (assuming they can conceive it) but, rather, the light's shadow, the *'already-thought.'* Therefore, the structural culture of this 'already-thought' cannot have power over the reality of human beings. Instead, it expresses the limit of our thinking, as well as the lack of awareness of the limit. Decadent human beings have, within this structural culture, a means by which to affirm themselves as they are and to create "normality" out of their current state.

The philosopher's concern should have been—once recognized, thanks to critical philosophizing—the synthetic structure of thought, to have an experience of it, a direct experience, not a partial and indirect one that is implicit in the analysis of a judgment, of a syllogism, or of a proposition, according to a reflection unrelated to the idea's immediate being.

A direct experience of the synthetic power of thinking would have revealed the coincidence between the idea and its instantaneous 'welling up' from the very source of the forces of life and, thus, the integral nature of thinking—namely, it having its foundation within itself. It would have revealed the being of thought still unknown and, nevertheless, demanded by the times, as a force of knowing capable of responding non-dialectically but *pragmatically* to its problems. 'Philosophizing,' by renouncing its task, has allowed pseudo-philosophers, as well as dialecticians, and the mathematical tightrope walkers of discourse (the ultimate destroyers of the inner sense of thinking), namely those interested in the object of thinking, not its truth, or essence, to camp within the citadel of philosophy.

If modern philosophy had known how to better look at thinking than at the 'already-thought,' it would have avoided its own dissolution and realized its modern raison d'être, namely to indicate the path by means of which thought is the bearer of its own internal identity: the one that renders possible the process of knowledge, and logic as the science of such a process. It should have been its task to show, experientially, the reality of thinking's identity with itself, on this side of the forms of the reflective determination, from which it is thus possible to reascend to its immediate being. The concentration exercise would have ended up being the necessary act of the reascension to pure thinking from any particular determination.

The failure has been not to discover the only means needed by thinking to manifest its nature and its movement, namely the spiritual practice implicit to the awareness of the movement. It is concentration, not for a given theme but, rather, for the expression of the activity characteristic of thinking, namely its synthetic power, that is to say, this very power itself, not one of its determined manifestations.

Unfortunately, to destroy the last best chance for an art of thinking in the present day, a few preachers, with an Eastern tag, have come to the West to teach that concentration is a useless discipline, because it does not embrace, but excludes, the real being, for they confuse (due to insufficient noetic consciousness) the thinking act with its object and the being of thinking with its particular mediation. For this reason, thinking has been seen in its limited formal determination, as a thing that excludes others, according to an interpretation identical to that of so-called primitive realists.

In fact, no thought exists that is not illusorily bound to its own determination. The task is not to eliminate the determination, but to reascend from it to the thinking that is free, which negates itself in that determination. Concentration cannot but operate, according to such necessity intrinsic to thinking, at the point in which the determination is simultaneously the presence and negation of itself, always waiting to be realized, without ever being realized: like an operation continually left pending. Thus, there is no concept that does not have 'being' as an immediate relation to itself, namely the being that in the determination can appear as the most insignificant thing that is thought. There is no catharsis of thinking that does not occur, there, where it can be realized according to the very being of thought that renders it possible, since it is necessary. Concentration is truly the crowning achievement of the thinking experience.

2. The Function of Concentration

Concentration is the willful act that thought, insofar as it is reflected, does not normally carry out. For it does not set for itself, nor conceive, the task of experiencing its own synthetic power, prior to the reflective determination. Meanwhile, thought is capable of concentration that demands the action of this power regarding themes, which, because of their reflected structure, essentially contradict it. Such concentration does not bear the value of synthetic power, since it subjects it to aims that—if it had immediate expression, thanks to an awareness of the pure determination—it would not be able to have.

Normally, thought is incapable of spontaneous concentration unless it is aroused by an outer interest or by an inner necessity, namely with regard to a specific object, which, even if it is an intellectual object, not because of this, does it bind less to what is not thought itself. Therefore, an outer object always controls the consciousness by virtue of which it manifests and is thought.

Concentration, not willed consciously, or willed behind the stimulus of a given necessity, even if intellectual, is always a process that unfolds *by means of* thinking, but inevitably *in spite of* the original being of thinking, because of soul forces irregularly connected with the world's objectivity. From a certain point of view, one can say of them that they are connected too much or too little with sensory reality. Such a concentration can cease to be negative for the life of the soul, if the conversion of the particular determination of thought is continuously brought about by contemplating the independence of its mediation. But to this end, a particular activity of the life of the soul is necessary, which can only come from the concentration exercise.

By means of a willful act, we aim at controlling the ordinary thinking by means of which we think. The term "control" is to be understood in its literal sense. As conscious human beings, we decide to aim at such "control" by way of logical determination, since we notice that, on account of ordinary thinking, we are inevitably controlled by the object of thought, or by "entities" unrelated to the principle from which thinking moves and, therefore, unrelated to the real direction of the "I." These entities manage to control thought, by soliciting from it a concentration capable of giving a sense of security and of stability that seems to come from an intensified activity of consciousness, but actually does not belong to

The Logic and Technique of Concentration

it, since such entities are related to the reflected form of thought, by means of which they operate.

Thanks to the concentration exercise, researchers learn that true thinking is not that by means of which we normally reason and philosophize but, rather, its yet-to-be-determined content, which we can perceive with the force itself of the determination, since in its immediacy, it is in itself a higher ideational life, nevertheless knowable, which is valid, above all, outside its 'manifesting' as reasoning and philosophizing.

Just as the existence and the value of water is objective and knowable apart from the use that we make of it by drinking it, so too, is thinking originally valid apart from its 'adapting' to the human mental sphere and its 'assuming' the form under which, alone, the mental sphere knows it.

What philosophers have always sought was the thinking that gave them a way to reflect on the Absolute, on the "I," the soul, the world, space, time, and so on that they have always unconsciously identified with the object thought, for which they have never been able to possess the object, nor thinking. Rare philosophers have glimpsed this thinking in its pure non-determined state, but even in such a case, because of speculative need, it was more important for them to reflect it in pursued dialectical forms, than to experience its essence. The non-reality of thought, insofar as it could give rise to desired dialectical forms, has been, for them, more important than its reality. Such reality, in fact, would have deprived them of *philosophical desire*, namely what speculates on being, because it does not have being. It does not want being. It fears renouncing its own illusory being.

Nowadays, philosophizing could have meaning only as the capacity for restoring its original content to the concept, so that the coincidence of thinking with the non-sensory reality of the entities in ordinary knowing can be experienced, namely a real and perceptible coincidence, of which no philosopher, unfortunately, until now has been conscious. If such consciousness had been attained at least by a small number of elite thinkers, science would not have collapsed into technological nonsense, which, indeed, has a methodological foundation, but reveals the loss of contact with the object of technology.

The spiritual practice of thinking posits itself as the condition of a new 'philosophizing,' which moves from the foundation, from real thinking, not from its object, and that when it believes it moves from the object, it is aware of moving, above all, from thinking. The concentration exercise restores the possibility for us to experience *pure being*, given that it has, within thinking, the original 'manifesting' of being. Thanks to this, the millenary deception is able to cease, a deception for which we give value to a spiritual object as if it were the spirit, and, in the case of materialism, without the realization of treating the physical object as if it were the spirit.

3. The Autonomy of Thinking as Experience

Concentration has the task of restoring an original autonomy that is continually present in the act of thinking, but unconscious, because of the fact that consciousness identifies with the discursive determination. Today, this autonomy, corresponding to the purpose of individual self-consciousness, can be restored, provided that consciousness awakens, there, where it arises. It is the autonomy that renders the spirit autonomous in the presence of the world's objects, by revealing itself as the reason for the manifestation of thinking.

The concentration exercise is a way for thinking to be controlled, so that its nature can manifest in the soul, with the same objectivity that can be experienced by scientists regarding a physical phenomenon. The method cannot be but a regulating operation required by the thinking process, as it becomes immediately obvious from the experimenter's self-observation. Forces objectively developed by means of concentration gradually suggest the orientation of such a method.

The Logic and Technique of Concentration

Thought that can thus manifest its real nature later requires an attitude that can no longer be *controlling*, but *receiving*. As experimenters, we open up, in fact, to thinking endowed with the power of impersonality and of objectivity. This is not normal for us and cannot agree with the self-assertiveness initially required regarding reflected thought, which, by essentially turning out to be opposite the "I," requires being mastered.

Instead, we find ourselves before a thinking that does not need to be controlled and strengthened in order to manifest in its wholeness, namely a thinking, whose light and whose force are unknown to habitual reasoning. It is thinking that does not need to be grasped, because the 'giving of itself' distinguishes it all the way to the essence. The fact that ordinary thinking does not reach the essence of things is due to the fact that it is the alteration of its own essence, for which the mental image or abstract concept of the essence of entities is enough for it to believe that it knows them and reasons about them.

The alteration of thinking normally occurs in those of us who need physical support in order to be conscious of ourselves and thus create our dialectical activity out of original thinking. Meanwhile, the real "I," in order to be, does not need dialectics. In those of us who ignore it, it actually operates "indirectly" as the power of destiny. When it has thinking as a support, the "I" does not make it dialectical, but perceives it as the thinking of itself, or of the world's entities. Normally, however, the opposite occurs. The consciousness of the "I" is controlled by the world's entities, because it identifies with reflective thought, which, lacking its own original force, depends on the object. It models itself according to objective semblance.

We do violence to the reality of thought, by believing this thought to be *ours*. We distort the original being of thought and, thus distorted, we use it. Or better yet, we deceive ourselves of using it, because, by means of altered thought, the nature within us that uses thought becomes known. We are controlled by outer reality, which penetrates us by means of passive thinking and determines our feelings, our ideals, our desires, and our goals. Therefore, our task should be to control everyday thinking until we are able to have it free before us—freed of itself.

We can come to experience the autonomy of thinking to the point of perceiving this thinking as the creative force of nature, namely by not considering it our *own*, according to the contingent identity necessary to us, so that each of us can feel that we are an "I," without really being it, since we are unable to be the "I" in reflected thought. We must come to look at thinking as a being that bears its very own content. We must come to discover its initial movement that escapes us to the extent that we identify with it—so as to know it as pure life.

It is not this pure thinking that demands concentration, but dialectical thought, which always being reflected, is nevertheless structurally analytical, even when it expresses itself in judgments believed to be synthetic. In order for the true synthesis to be realized, and thus in order for the reality of thought to be restored to it, thinking needs to act willfully upon its own form, so that the content can flow within it independently of the determination in itself reflected, which is normally taken for its real content—namely, so that the real content can finally manifest.

4. The Concept and the Thinking-force

The concentration exercise, regardless of its object, is an imaginative exercise. Even when concentration unfolds by means of a sensory object, it arouses the internal imaginative power of thinking, the sensory form thereby manifesting precisely as an image. In *pure perceiving*, which was dealt with in the second chapter, this imaginative power is enlivened to the point of (becoming) an objective determination, because the experimenter prevents it from being converted into sensation or into abstract representation.

The difference between thought and imagination is not significant. Reasoning is normally an abstract thinking, while imagining is thinking by means of formal elements drawn from sensory experience and connectible in an arbitrary way. Therefore, it bears within itself an element of life, normally unconscious, of which rational thought is deprived in order for the conscious abstract form to manifest.

The concept is normally abstract. The spiritual practice of thinking tends to restore to the concept the element of life that flows spontaneously within the image. The concept, as a synthesis of representations, is an archetypal image, deprived of imaginative content, because it is abstract. But the concept can be experienced as an archetypal image, if the element of life that renders possible its manifesting by way of rationality, is brought to consciousness. It has to do with retracing the process of rationality until perceiving and resolving the abstraction.

Thanks to a specific conscious act, thought can discover the element of will—or of life—of which it deprives itself in order to become a concept: which is to discover the essence. For this, it needs to actualize, within the very concept, its original relation with itself by making use of the mediation in which it occurs by way of an object. Through this object, thought, converging indirectly toward its own immediate being, operates within the mediation itself. It realizes, within it, a continuity, which is a limitless attention that arouses its volitional element, namely the same volitional element that, as a structural force, normally flows unconscious within the image.

By means of concentration, thought tends toward its pure essence, not by aiming directly at it, not by being able to pass over itself but, rather, by nourishing itself of the imaginative forms in which it moves, as an unknown volitional element. The concept of "flower" can be directly expressed by normal reason. But for it to enliven itself of the life that is extinguished in the sphere of conscious reason, it must nourish itself of the series of images of different flower specimens and pursue such images by drawing from the objective idea present in each of them. In this way, however, the idea is itself still not experienced directly, as are instead the images of the different flowers. The idea becomes cognitively noticed.

Thinking can grasp itself only by means of the forms in which it already manifests. It does not manifest in the pure state, but only by means of themes and contents. It must therefore discover its own activity by observing any one of such forms. Since the concept is always a synthesis of representations, it must reconstruct the series of representations that form a concept, in order to discover, in the concept's vivacity, its own living activity.

Thinking is concentrated on an object and intensified, so that a concept can eventually arise from it, alive, like in its immediate manifesting. Thinking dedicates itself exclusively to such an object, avoiding any possible association with other themes that essentially, by removing it from the initial proposition, would tend to pose the relation to it that it already has with the chosen object. But since the concept, or synthesis, to be reconstituted and kept before consciousness, contains, within itself, in its particular determination, various representations that involve relations with other concepts and, therefore, with other groups of representations, thinking must be concentrated in such a way that it does not abandon itself to any consideration that does not necessarily regard the proposed theme. That is the very reason why the theme or the object must be particularly simple, so that it does not bring about a conceptual analysis, of which, for the practical purposes of the concentration, there is a need only within limits required by the reconstitution of the concept.

It is not the analysis that matters, but the intensity and the insistence of thinking that actualizes—by means of 'converging' into a point—the wholeness of its movement, namely the possibility that in the most simple determination of thinking there flows its maximum synthetic capacity.

This activity is the same that is particularized in each thought, not changing level for the fact that it can think "universe" instead of "chair," but solely because it can actualize its own movement independent of the object, which is to say, independent of cerebralism. It is as if from a reflection one passed to the source of the light—the true change in level.

5. The Unknown Content of the Idea

The concentration exercise is, in any case, an imagination exercise. In fact, a series of mental pictures is needed to reconstitute, by way of their inner animation, the idea that moves them. Such an idea is present in each one as its raison d'être, but it is not identifiable with any of them in particular. Since the idea is their original unity, each of them in relation to itself, is its abstract negation.

Ordinary 'mental picturing' is an abstract 'imagining.' In concentration, it is turned unambiguously toward a theme and, therefore, indirectly led to enliven itself of the will from which it moves. Through such enlivening, it was lifted to its real nature, discovering its noetic function, namely the mediation between sensory forms and archetypal thought, the idea.

An idea's creative vitality can be consciously experienced, notwithstanding the philosophies and empirical logics that have decreed its vacuity and subjectivity: not unjustly, given that it appears to them as such, since that sort of conceiving is founded upon the very incapacity to conceive the experience of ideas.

It is helpful to realize that we are normally capable of ideas and concepts, only insofar as we direct them at objects, inner and outer. We never experience the conceptual and ideal activity in itself. This activity appears in us as long as it is not what we come to know but, rather, provides the formal determination. If we want to imagine the conceptual activity itself, we must reduce it to an abstraction, that is, we must express concepts and ideas, provided it identifies them with the discourse of which it clothes them, by excluding their life. In that sense, indeed, the art of formal discourse has arisen, illusorily autonomous with respect to thinking.

The deception of philosophizing has been to proceed always by means of ideas, but not to turn toward the direct experience of their movement, and, at a given moment, no longer know that we operate by means of ideas. In this way, we come to doubt their life and the possibility that such ideas are the foundations of reflection. Meanwhile, to codify such doubt, we must still proceed by means of ideas and always have ideas as a foundation. The fact of not knowing this has led the latest philosophers to form (by means of ideas) the foundation to entities that are not ideas but, rather, things, or perceptions or logical propositions, which rise to the dignity of the foundation only by being valid as ideas, yet without being recognized as such. Thus, they become myths, on the basis of their abstract discursiveness, or according to their negation of the idea as a foundation. It is a process of mythicization that no philosopher has been capable of discovering—only a few of glimpsing—for which, in the end, philosophy was unable to avoid giving rise to its opposite, to the negation of the spirit, which was its aim, the initial reason for its 'speculating.'

6. Thinking as Informal Power

There is no 'imagining' that is not founded on the idea. An 'imagining' founded on itself does not exist, except for mental picturing or arbitrary daydreaming, whose irregularity consists in being the imaginative activity subtly controlled by corporeity—the typical subservience of thinking to the psychosomatic element. The negative unity, here, finds in individual nature a temporary foundation to its own contradiction—temporary, insofar as it is willed in its non-reality, with the force of the real foundation, whereby imaginative and unreal wrongly arrive at being equivalent.

Whatever the thinking exercise, concentration or meditation, it is always an imaginative exercise. We cannot arrive at concentrating on pure thoughts, if initially we do not pass by way of forms themed with a conceptual content, or by way of the series of analytical representations, drawn from the sensory world or from its mental echo. But the pure concept, if realized in its internal identity, manifests with the living power of the image: as an archetypal image.

'Imagining' is the means by which to pass from abstract rationality to the world of pure ideas, or living ideas. It is a means, not an end. 'Imagining' is exercised and kindled, because, from within its form, living thinking operates as an informal power, which we are not yet able to experience directly as a formative force.

If within the synthetic manifesting of the conceptual activity, living thinking did not operate as immediacy identical to itself, concepts would not be possible. Current philosophy tends to eliminate the concept, to replace it with the word, so that the immediacy (identical to itself) cannot be of the concept, but of the object to which the word corresponds as a surrogate of the lost concept. Therefore, imagination remains only within its limits of arbitrary activity, devoid of life, extraneous to its own foundation, without idea. It is cut off from reality and drawn only from corporeity or, more precisely, from cerebralism, as is witnessed in so-called modern art.

7. Imagination Exercises

The imaginative activity is the means both for the concentration that tends toward pure thinking, and for meditation.

It is the formal pure movement, necessary to the spiritual practice of thinking, until it identifies directly with its own original content, independent of name and form, which ordinarily enables it to be reflected in sensory consciousness.

We tend to experience independence from name and form by means of mental pictures, which, thanks to their restored imaginative autonomy, gradually cease to correspond to sensory contents, to which they are necessarily bound from the beginning. Imagination is to be freed from sensory contents by means of imaginative meditation.

For this reason, there exist concentration and meditation exercises that are carried out by means of imaginative activity, and likewise exercises capable of rendering objective the activity of 'imagining,' so that it can be the preparer of what Spiritual Science calls "imaginative consciousness," capable of perceiving suprasensory reality in images, thanks to the presence, unseen, but operative of a consciousness superior to it, of which it is the vehicle. In that case, just like a sensory entity is seen by means of its form and its color, so too does the suprasensory image arise not per se, but as a form or sign of a spiritual entity. From this, we can understand how the experience of imaginative forms is not an end, but a preparatory phase of the direct perception of pure spiritual contents.

One thing is imaginative spiritual practice; another is imaginative consciousness. The former is a preparation for the latter. While imaginative spiritual practice consists in the series of exercises directed toward the activation of pure imagining, imaginative consciousness is the attainment of a super-individual level in which pure imaging is objectified as the support to spiritual essences or entities that it receives in symbolic suprasensory forms.

Imaginative consciousness, though superior to normal thinking consciousness, is not yet such as to support the extra-formal power of entities and of suprasensory essences. Therefore, it initially grasps this power in images. Such images are temporarily true. Their form is objective and proves to be identical for each experimenter, when the imaginative spiritual practice is carried out according to the laws of the spirit.

It is the mediating form of a cosmic language whose transcendent sense does not undergo form, not even suprasensory form. Therefore, in order to manifest, it demands the annihilation of the substantial mediation in which it is gradually reflected: essential only as a structural phase, for which the imaginative mediation of the original content is temporarily willed as real. The inability to understand this orientation provided by The Master of the New Times[3] has allowed a few frivolous writers of esotericism to attribute visionary finalities, or the opposite of his teaching, to the imaginative path indicated by him. With this, however, they have given a measure of value of their expositions to whoever, in spiritual research, wants to realize how things *truly* stand.

8. The Technique of Imaginative Liberation

Imaginative exercises initially have the task of freeing the imaginative faculty from an element of arbitrariness by means of which it is normally altered and of which it is nourished. Without a precise technique of this "liberation," the 'imagining,' despite every other discipline, remains the vehicle of sentient consciousness. In that sense, it can give rise to an ulterior form of the subjection of thinking, namely the unconscious autonomy of reflected imagining: which is to say, *mediumship*.

Only genuine Spiritual Science can teach the imaginative technique. Yet, not even the possibility of drawing from this Science is enough to immunize us, as disciples, from the danger of sliding into a spiritualistic arbitrariness or into a subjective visionary state, if a lack of dedication and coherence dulls in us the logic of the teaching's original determination, as the gist of concentration and of meditation.

As was said, in 'imagining,' an unconscious will element is present, so much more alive the less a reflective determination insists on its unfolding. Nevertheless, for the purposes of the imaginative spiritual practice, the conscious principle, by means of special thinking techniques, must operate so that the current of willing proper to the 'imagining' can depend less and less on the instinctive zone. And even when this is achievable, the art of the disciple is to recognize the instinctive element that tends with renewed power to appropriate the imaginative current, once this current is awakened and capable of autonomous movement.

'Imagining'—which, as a faculty of representation is normally identified with objects of the physical world, or even corresponds to personal sensations and feelings—begins to free itself of such contents and to possess its objective movement, thanks to the imaginative exercises. This is the moment in which, if a rigorous work of thinking has not been prepared, profound and subtle instincts that project themselves in the most deceptive form for us, can make use of the imaginative activity, for such instincts correspond to the nature to which we are still bound by way of an identity unknown to us.

No one can be spared such a test. Spiritual Science technically foresees it as a crucial point of our preparation as disciples: a decisive moment for a change that invests our whole life. Having given autonomy to the imaginative activity, without developing an adequate faculty of conscious control, we, at the initial 'manifesting' of the imaginative world, can fall into the illusion of finding ourselves before the objective suprasensory world, while, in reality, we have nothing before us but the spectral projection of our own dependence on nature, at a level that awaits to be known and overcome by us, so that the real suprasensory experience, beyond, can be possible. Believing such a temporary vision to be suprasensory—a vision which, given inadequate preparation, can appear to us with forms that satisfy our egoity—we enter a state of spiritualistic vanity. We can presume to teach the path of freedom and seduce many weak people.

9. The Object of Concentration

Concentration is practiced by means of an object. For today's human being, it is a mistake to presume practicing a concentration without an object, or to contemplate themes of a metaphysical order, without having at first radically experienced the thinking that manifests only by means of an object. Modern human beings initially cannot gather thinking except in the object, be it a physical thing or be it a speculative content. We must move from this object, if we wish to free thinking from it and fundamentally know thinking. For only at the root of thinking can we free ourselves of this object.

The object, which simply needs to be re-evoked by becoming an object of concentration, gradually ceases to bind thinking to itself, because it is not what grasps thinking. Instead, this thinking operates within it. The object becomes the means for the restitution of thought to a level that is proper to it, or better yet, is its real state—which, consequently, only exceptionally, by means of the will and spiritual practice, can we restore. By experiencing it, we recognize it as the flow (in conscious form) of thought that operated unconsciously on the original structure of the human mental sphere, which is to say, we recognize it by the purity and by the super-individuality of its force.

Within the form of the concentration, the restitution of thinking is realized indirectly by means of the process of mental picturing and imagination solicited by the thinking consideration of the object. A series of images is recalled to recompose the integrity of thought, which eventually manifests in its reacquired conciseness (essentiality), as original thinking.

If the object is a physical thing, made by a human being, it must be simply re-evoked in order to become thought's point of convergence, until it restores, independent of itself, the thinking that thought it, there, where mineral and vegetative nature is to be contemplated in its physical 'appearing'—this belonging to a particular order of perceiving exercises—so that perception can communicate the living thinking that it conceals within itself.

Nature truly has thinking within itself. This is not the case with a human-made object, whose outer form expresses a relation that is merely abstract, in that it is not within the object, but within the human mind. Meanwhile, the object of a mineral or vegetative nature is the immediate form of a thought present in perception. Our task is to notice it.

A physical thing made by us mechanically or by hand, must be evoked in concentration. To perceive it simultaneously makes no sense, since its outer form is indeed correlated to thought, but it is not its direct expression. It is a manifestation of human thought, but not of formally creative thought, like what operates, for example, in the plant. For it is not an organism but, rather, an outer appearance organized or mechanically ordered. The thought of this organized outer appearance, by means of concentration, is identified independently of it and, therefore, brought back from its reflected state to the original conceptual moment.

Whatever the type of concentration, the 'imagining' becomes the movement of thinking, toward the prime idea, or the living concept.

In ordinary life, we continually make use of concepts, but only in function of the objects to which they correspond. We have the experience of the object, but not of the concept by means of which that (object) can become experience. Nevertheless, the experience of the concept is not a philosophical operation but, rather, the possibility to extract the inner content from the object, by reconstructing its objective life of thought, so as to be able to have this content as an object.

10. Typical Exercise of Concentration

This exercise can be executed in due parts. We must acquire mastery over the first part—which in itself is already a complete exercise of concentration, capable of giving to thought the force of its own reversibility—to be able to pass, after a given period, to the second. Having come to this, the two parts blend into one.

Part 1. One evokes a given physical object—something human-made—that is familiar and that because of the simplicity of its workmanship is exhaustible in a brief series of representations.

The simplicity and the minimal importance of the object pertain to the technique of this type of concentration. Since the activation of the volitional element of thinking (normally excluded from the rational process) is its goal, the object must be such that, it is not its meaning that arouses thought because of emotional–volitional stimuli. Instead, it is thought that expresses itself willfully by means of it. The thinking activity must respond not to spontaneous urging but, rather, to self-determination.

One describes the object with precision, avoiding lengthiness. One briefly produces its history and individualizes its function, until reaching an image-synthesis (or concept), which finally can remain before consciousness with the same vivacity by means of which it initially arose. Thanks to its acquired objectivity, it can thus be contemplated for a few moments, unlike when it is initially evoked as a theme still inside of consciousness.

The reconstruction of the object all the way to its image-synthesis, or concept, is the true and proper exercise of concentration. The ability to dedicate maximum attention to this typical synthesis of thinking, with regard to a theme of limited meaning, develops the most intense will within the vehicle of thinking. It is important not to be distracted by anything, even for a second. If this distraction occurs, we must retrace the extraneous association, until it can lead back to the point in which the distraction intervened.

As was said, this first part of the exercise is already, in itself, a typical concentration exercise of fundamental value. If supplemented at other moments of the day by special exercises of feeling and willing, it is sufficient for the purposes of liberating thought. In its simplicity, such concentration leads thinking to a point in which it can proceed without dialectical support (but only imaginatively) by drawing its own force from itself. It is not the complication or the dialectical refinement of the exercise that matters but, rather, its legitimacy from the suprasensory point of view, or the intensity of attention that can be developed by means of it.

Legitimacy from the suprasensory point of view is provided by the thinking that directly actualizes itself as immediate, according to the pure axiomatic nature of which it is woven and that it alone can consequently confer to any enunciation, insofar as it draws it from itself a-dialectically, by drawing from its own original forces, namely those that render truth knowable.

One thing is the thinking shaped by a physical object that we illusorily believe we have as an object of thinking, another is the thinking that, in order to really think the object, frees itself from the impression that it bears of it, through the intensification of the content by means of which we think it. Thought discovers, as its own, the force with which the object opposes it as the 'already-thought.' Then, it can direct this force (that is free) to any worldly object. This is an art that the investigator of the sensory world has lacked.

Part II. The image-synthesis, or concept, of the object is contemplated by realizing its objectivity, namely by impersonally giving it life, as if it were produced by way of its own power. The image must remain before the inner gaze, without the need to exert effort so that it can exist animated and autonomous.

Persistence in the concentration at this point has the function of letting the object's sensory form fall away completely. In its place, a sign, or symbol, of its ideal living entity remains, which, by feeding on the contemplative act, identifies always less with the initial conceptual meaning of the object. It begins to be something more in another sense. It is always the identical concept, but the enlivening of it by means of its own inner life frees it of its particular determination. It tends to manifest in its original power, the life of every concept.

The freeing of the thinking activity from the cerebral support, namely the initial manifesting of real thinking, or the conversion of thinking from the reflected state to the state of metaphysical assertiveness, corresponds to a given moment of the contemplative concentration. We must, nevertheless, observe that such thinking is still not experienced in itself directly, since it flows unseen: the attention being concentrated on the inner object. If we tried prematurely to divert attention from the inner object, in order to contemplate pure thinking, this thinking would be rejected. Its manifesting would be interrupted.

11. COMMENT

It is helpful to emphasize that Part I of the exercise is already a completed form of concentration, typically sufficient unto itself, for the spiritual practice of thinking and the introduction to the experience of the "void" (or, of the conscious and, therefore, willful annihilation of the activity thus attained, through the surfacing of the original forces of consciousness). In that sense, it gives rise in another but not dissimilar way, to overcoming the residual formal element of the theme, which is specifically required of Part II.

The first part can lead in and of itself to the liberation of thinking, if it is practiced with regularity and continuity, given that its intensity manages to objectify the inner content of the theme. Along the same lines, the second part consists in having as an object the enucleated content of the first. In the one and in the other, the sense of the theme is led to exhaustion, so that in its place the aroused thinking-force can surface.

The distinction of the two parts is useful for becoming gnoseologically aware of the exercise—and, therefore, in relation to the need of going back, now and then, to insist upon the preliminary analytics of the first part, or even to suspend it temporarily.

It can be said that Part II is the completeness of Part I and that Part I, if achieved in its entirety, contains Part II within itself. In the end, the exercise is one. Its completeness can lead us, as experimenters, to the thresholds of living thinking, or to the possibility of contemplating the activity that is aroused from the depths of the consciousness soul, in two parts, which is no longer a thinking, or a thinking contemplation but, rather, the beginning of an inner perceiving.

Such perception occurs as the possibility of receiving in the guise of the objectified thinking activity and, therefore, in imaginative form, the suprasensory contents of things, if granted by persistent practice and by the awareness of its ongoing function within the soul. It has to do with an indirect and temporary communion that has the task of preparing us for direct communion. Along these lines, we can continue our spiritual practice, having a way to concretely consider the needs of our research, which now come to us clarified by the initial connection with the suprasensory world. The technique now obeys an inspiring impulse.

We find ourselves before a reality that lies beyond the 'manifesting in images' of the suprasensory world, of which each form that gives itself to us is simply a sign. Such reality, in order to be known, at a given moment, will demand from us the stillness of our thinking activity and the extinction of the imaginative forms attained, but it will simultaneously require from us a thorough independence from the corporeal ties of the soul, together with the strength to endure its grandiosity and the unexpectedness of accommodating it, by manifesting as the perception that overturns the meaning of the ordinary values of existing, since it is the reality at their foundation. This perception will not be able to manifest except by means of the inner forces of the "I," aroused by concentration. The "I" encounters, as its world, the world's invisible foundation.

The fact that such an experience overturns the sense of the ordinary values of 'existing,' even through the vehicle of painful experiences, does not mean that we have to distance ourselves from 'existing,' but that we finally can have an objective relationship with it and develop understanding for other beings, since we are no longer impeded from meeting them with limitless brotherhood.

12. The Esoteric Sense of Concentration

It is useful to insist on one point. Why is a pin or a glass recommended as an object of concentration, and not a mystical symbol, a *deva*, a *chakra*, a sacred name? As we have mentioned, the reason is simple. We, modern human beings, who concentrate on one of these noble themes cannot help but think it with the same type of thinking ordinarily used to think a pin, glass, chair, and so on.

The mental state of normal human beings today is such that it is not the nobility of a theme that can determine a change in the level of thinking but, rather, the opposite. The nobility or the special meaning of a theme psychologically condition thinking, in that they subtly stimulate feeling and the will as they exist in their immediacy, by strengthening in them that instinctive predominance over thinking, which they have in manifesting by means of corporeity and expressing personal nature.

Thinking directed toward a simple physical object, instead, renders itself independent of the psychological mixture. It is realized as the initial element of autonomy with respect to the life of the soul. It moves from its connection with the sensory datum, in order to overcome it within the datum itself, independently of feeling and willing, by attaining that impersonality of its own movement, which is realized but not possessed by the modern scientist in logical and mathematical operations. This impersonal nature does not belong to the thing or to the mathematical operation but, rather, to thinking, which can discover it within itself, by means of them.

We must change thinking, not the object. We must operate within the thinking that has become bound to the sensory realm and not strengthen this thinking with spiritual contents, which serve the vision of life according to which it has conformed. Overcoming the sensory limit is possible within our thinking experience of the sensory object, not of the presumed "spiritual" object, the whereabouts of whose spirituality is still unknown to us. Nor can the liberating activity, despite the spiritual object, come from thought that does not know its own original deficiency, given that it is reflected thought.

We must add, however, that even the art of concentration, in order to be operative according to its principle, at a given moment, must connect the experiencer to *the source of the teaching* from which the knowledge of such an art springs. It is an agreement whose necessity and function regarding the perception of individual limits and of what can overcome them, can gradually be recognized by us if we develop the correct orientation.

The source of the teaching cannot be identified or confused with another that is similar, except temporarily, in the intellectual phase of the research. During this phase, the force is not so important as the knowledge, or the orientation. The force is already present within us and becomes dispersed by us in various forms, because we lack knowledge with respect to it. It is not a matter of depending on a given school but, rather, of connecting with the spirit from which the research ordinarily moves and which, for a long time, we risk not knowing. It demands free recognition, in order to be operative beyond any pretense of the spiritual: each pretense being, moreover, the test necessary for attaining freedom.

This spirit does not identify with a written work, even if a written work can reflect it and indicate a method for recognizing it. It so happens that some beings do not seem to change level through the fact that they have specific works available or even succeed in understanding them.

13. Psychosomatic Prejudice

The concentration exercise does not allow distraction, not even when we believe that we notice qualitative changes within ourselves. If these occur, they must not be observed during the concentration, but eventually afterwards. There must not be, at the center of consciousness, anything but the contemplated object—as a thing evoked, or an image–idea reconstituted.

Least of all, we should not allow ourselves to be distracted by sensations unrelated to the task that we have proposed for ourselves, or sensations provoked by its possible psychosomatic repercussion, even if it takes on a "positive" form.

We must not call on concentration or meditation for somatic attainments or healings, because this, if ever, occurs by way of

The Logic and Technique of Concentration

another path, thanks to correct thinking itself being realized, without the need of a request. This request, in fact, if accompanied by an ascetic exercise, subjects this exercise to itself on behalf of a whole other spirit than that of the pure spiritual practice. It is the attitude that tends to bind the forces evoked to corporeity, obtaining results that, even when they appear positive, are very quickly lost, because they are not imprinted onto the physical by forces independent of it. The non-request is the art of disinterest in the meditation, which makes it possible for transcendent extra-corporeal forces to operate, according to their norm, in corporeity.

The forces evoked in concentration and in meditation are not experienced directly, because they belong to an order that rules the sensory realm. They would not be able to be evoked directly, because the ordinary thinking from which the spiritual practice inevitably moves—at the level in which it initially finds itself—rejects them. For this reason, we resort to the mediation of the object or of the meditative content, which avoids the presumption of a direct contact with the forces, namely a presumption which, if it has free rein, leads to corporeal zones in which we encounter the alteration of forces, and mistakes, for a suprasensory experience, its opposite: from which the destruction of physical and psychic health begins.

We must not place tasks upon the suprasensory realm regarding its action on the body, because such action belongs to the suprasensory realm, not to the ego. We can identify an error of thinking at the root of such a presumption. It is the reason for the interest in *yoga* at the present time, or the affirmation of a psychosomatic ideal longed for by the individual subjected to a false self-image: precisely the one that simultaneously, by means of *yoga*, we would aspire to redeem. It is always the ego that tries to draw forces unto itself, so as to subject them to its aims.

Corporeal healing and the harmony of the inner life ensue from the ability of such forces to operate free and unseen within the soul, according to the moments of thinking's liberation. This is an individual act possible only to the experimenter, who must be able to insist on it. The rest is the work of forces that are evoked, not necessarily simultaneous to the moments of the inner discipline.

The devotion itself, as the inner mood of the spiritual practice, rises unwilled, as logic of the fidelity to rightful thinking, of persistence and of courage, which need to arouse, within consciousness, the perception of its real nature.

These considerations, therefore, also regard the present tendency to render current the psychosomatic aspect of the exercises of ancient *yoga*, whose technique conformed to an inner constitution that differed from that of the modern human being. This technique rightly took advantage of corporeity, because this corporeity did not participate in the ascetic or magical *opus* as mere physical corporeity but, rather, as an entity governed by spiritual processes. Only outwardly did *yogis* take advantage of corporeity, cultivating the science of the breath and ritual postures. Their 'functioning' was essentially extra-corporeal. *Yogis* were intimately connected to the cosmic powers that support corporeity.

14. Outdated Techniques

Today, the danger of renewing the techniques of ancient spiritual practices—assuming that they are accessible in their original writing—consists, above all, in the fact that they are devoid of the content of which they were the instructive expression in specific traditional forms. And, therefore, they no longer arouse the forces to which it is believed they appeal. Even the most prepared individuals are unaware of the danger, since possible esoteric callings do not remove the limits of ordinary consciousness, which demand to be recognized within the sphere itself of consciousness, by virtue of an activity that, though belonging to it, knows how to find within itself the point of transcendence and, to devote to this a specific discipline: a discipline that, therefore, contemplates (in terms of consciousness) what the metaphysical principle demands from the obtuse, modern mental sphere.

Today, we are unable to perceive what we set into motion when we appeal to our own consciousness, in view of an extra-normal experience. Even when the form of our spiritual practice is intellectually "regular," the content that we identify with specific names and representations cannot correspond to it, since we lack the accord between consciousness and the forces that render such content knowable.

When a purely intellectual "regularity" operates, the danger consists in being able to unconsciously "compel" the forces evoked to divert toward the subconscious, because of an inability to establish a relationship with them by means of the only element of reflected consciousness, which, by virtue of self-activity, can attain its own independence from it—thinking. Those forces, unable to be met by the autonomous movement of the consciousness soul, once evoked, flow in the underlying zone, within the life (or etheric) body, no more no less than how it occurs in a mediumistic experience.

The process is also identical to that for which such forces—aroused otherwise by the affirmative and agnostic attitude of today's human being—failing to encounter, awake, the willful element of the soul, itself desirously taken by the sensory forms of existing, are forced to flow during sleep in the living corporeity, or in a "zone" unforeseen and, therefore, irregular, where they transform into their opposite, operating as germs of an arbitrary and corrupting mental activity. Such a deviation, corresponding to the level of cosmic forces adverse to the liberation of the human being, manages to assume in practical life the semblances of a scientificity particularly evolved, that promises a world of further physical conquests, capable, in their artificiality, of binding the human being evermore to the idolatry of the sensory.

15. THE NEED FOR AWARENESS OF THE LEVEL

Exercises and rituals carried out by us today evoke forces that, in order to be positively operative, need to encounter the soul, there, where it is not subject to corporeity. Unfortunately, as modern human beings, we do not possess a soul capable of extra-corporeal consciousness. Rather, we possess a discursive soul. Our consciousness soul today is reduced to a discursive organ, even if refined. Its real forces are thus led to flow into an inferior "site" that does not exclude its vitality. They descend into the "zone" of instincts, where they change aims and, as such, are led to govern the individual being from the depths. Ordinarily, this individual being is capable of willing something tenaciously and organically, and thereto it mobilizes the type of dialectics necessary. Yet, such willing actually does not come from us but, rather, from the sphere of the alteration of original willing, namely from the sphere of desire and of instinctive tensions.

To find agreement again with the suprasensory realm, we should, above all, know ourselves and become aware of the level at which we find ourselves, so as to in fact begin operating on this. We must avoid beginning with exercises and rituals that we arbitrarily apply to ourselves, since they, actually being processes unrelated to the demand of our inner condition, strike our imagination or excite our vanity.

If, by being unaware of our own level, we devote ourselves to exercises and rites that are not required by our true condition, we evoke forces that we cannot yet encounter in the suprasensory sphere, but only in the instinctive sphere, to which we effectively still belong and within which we unconsciously attract them, since the sensational repercussions, or the obscure emotions that we can draw from their evocations—connecting, there, subjective magical, or occult, representations—are sufficient for us. Beneath these mythical sensations, spiritual forces (altered or irregular) actually operate, which can appear to be those evoked, that is to say, they manage to pass themselves off as them.

As we have indicated, the same willful tension of modern human beings, forms part of the picture of such a phenomenology, in another way. But, in particular, for the spiritual researcher, there cannot be a training of thought or of meditation, which is not destined for such corruption, if the exercise does not correspond to the canons described, whose regularity depends on the possibility for thinking to be recognized as the spirit's potential means within the consciousness that is nowadays constitutionally opposed to the spirit.

The exercises indicated correspond to the spiritual practice that contemplates this function of thinking and, therefore, the initial need for its reversibility, or for its conversion from the reflected state to the original state, which is the actualization of its freedom now simply "virtual." Each exercise that does not aim at such a conversion, but excludes it with mirages of strengthening techniques of the will, according to magical and yogic schemes, cannot but be harmful, since it does not appeal to the forces of the foundation of consciousness but, rather, to that egoic consciousness in need of semblances, whose earthly tensions are that for which pain, sickness, and death are still necessary to human nature.

16. Meditation

One turns to an image that is the expression of an objective inner experience and, thereby, recommended by Spiritual Science, or drawn from a text of ancient Wisdom. For example, "Every stone has its thunderbolt."

There is no reason to analyze the concept of "stone," or that of "thunderbolt," or the idea that unifies them. Rather, we need to take on the image that immediately manifests by means of the words, namely by means of their pure 'resonating,' which evokes what corresponds to them within the soul. We need to leave intact the life by means of which the image initially rises up in the soul, without taking any of it into consideration.

Usually, we do not contemplate an evoked image, but there is the tendency to immediately translate it in terms of rational understanding. We must oppose this tendency. It is a matter of avoiding any intellectual digression on the theme and of insisting on the spontaneity with which the image appears, so that it lives within consciousness, intense and animated with feeling, as it does in its initial 'surfacing.' It makes no sense to reflect on its possible meaning, since the reflective process extinguishes the living element that its form bears. Such form must speak for itself, unaltered by any interpretation.

Like any image, it inevitably has a form drawn from sensory experience, but in that form flows a suprasensory content, which we must allow to surface. Therefore, the less it has intellectual meaning, the more it bears a transcendent content and, with this, it gathers unknown forces of the soul. It is the intensity of such forces that matters, not the rational assumption. This assumption inevitably eliminates such forces in the discursive projection, which in relation to the adopted task makes no sense.

Therefore, in the image's sensory capacity there does not flow subjective imagination but, rather, the formative power of the image, the spirit that it potentially incarnates.

Such an experience can allow us to understand the meaning of the oral or written communication of contents that derive from direct metaphysical experience and that can be taken on by us as listeners or lecturers, so that we can transform, into our own inner perception, the intellectual activity initially aroused by the dialectical form of such contents. What was once an initiatory preparation by means of an ascetic–ritual law, in modern times—with the intellectualistic impression of human interiority taken into account—is carried out by means of communications that we can take on in their dialectical form, or simply comprehend, but also penetrate and contemplatively enliven. In that case, they lead our thinking activity to grasp within itself the suprasensory force that they contain.

What is communicated in an esoteric and cosmological way by those of us who are truly bearers of the suprasensory experience and not of a scholarly language that feigns its existence, does not have the function of an eccentric and mythical knowing but, rather, of soliciting an inner capacity of perception that exists inside us, nevertheless, without us being yet aware of it. Whoever objects that receiving such communications creates a state of dependency, insofar as it demands passive reception, must try to better understand what has been said. It is not a matter of *believing* something, but of *experiencing* an inner content that, if it exists, must reveal itself, beyond intellectual meaning. Whether or not it corresponds to what is dialectically considered logical or true is not important. Instead, it is important that certain conditions of the meditative technique be observed.

17. Meditative Spiritual Practice: Exercise I

One type of meditative concentration can be the following. A specific triangle is thought, e.g., an equilateral triangle. We keep its image before our awareness, with utmost simplicity and continuity. Then, next to it, we imagine another triangle also equilateral, yet bigger, and we then contemplate it by comparing it to the first one. We observe how the one and the other are, in effect, figures of an identical archetypal image.

Such thinking must be simple and possibly a-dialectical and, nevertheless, involve the following consideration: that the matrix of the two figures is one. Big or small, the triangle, having identical form, does not pose for thinking a problematic of space but, rather, solicits the intuitive relationship, for which the form's ideal oneness with itself is possible, beyond dimensional differences. In effect, the enlivening of the image's informal content transcends the differences. This extinguishes its residual sensory inherences—i.e., its residual 'depending' on cerebralism.

We keep this non-dialectical thinking awake by imagining other equilateral triangles of various sizes, always reducing them to one, the initial one, which we contemplate as being identical to itself beyond all dimension, at the conclusion of the exercise.

18. Comment

This type of concentration contemplates forms that do not exist in outer reality, except in a symbolic objectivity. It therefore appeals to pure imagining, or to the immediate synthetic virtue of thinking, which, as has been explained, initially does not manifest directly, but needs forms that we imaginatively provide to the informal or inspirational–intuitive content of a thought.

A mathematical, or logical, or metaphysical theme can also solicit this type of thinking in scholars intent on a specific investigation, but in that sense, the relationship that thinking has with the object is the opposite of what the meditative exercise tends to establish with it, since for scholars the theme is the end to which they subordinate the movement of thinking, while the meditative act tends to specifically liberate the movement from the theme. This movement, in fact, is implicit to it and, nonetheless, is not even put into question by scholars, despite the fact that it has to do with a content that is more concrete than the theme itself.

The pure mathematician and philosopher, if they are thinkers, can, in most cases, appeal to this inspirational–intuitive thinking, without yet imagining its existence. The fact that they, by sometimes examining their actions, know that they have intuited something, does not mean that they perceive the intuitive force that has come into play. On the contrary, we can say that this (force) can operate precisely to the extent that they do not possess it. Their possibility of drawing from intuitive thinking demands—as an inner condition—that they be unaware of its surfacing or of its disappearing.

Such a situation in the modern era has, until the end of the past century, constituted the limit to pure intuition and to research. Today, research has even lost this possibility of intuition, so that such developments of thinking applied to technique or to dialectical discourse—or outside our own intuitive life—are considered creative advances. In every field, "production" is confused with "creation." A technical or philosophical or artistic product gives the illusion of thinking or the spirit progressing, while, in reality, it is about the product of the life of thinking's arrest in the area of the "simulacrums of things," through the establishment of a world of artifices and pretenses of values, endowed with its internal logic and with its ironclad technological necessity.

We must grasp these distinctions of the merits of intuition so as to understand the sense of the exercises mentioned, which are urgently needed where human *intelligere* (understanding) is bound to cerebralism and is, therefore, arrested as a creative faculty. In truth, thinking appears humanly productive precisely, there, where it ceases to be effectively creative.

Realistic logic should lead the researcher to recognize the priority of the task of training the typical thinking of research, namely the thinking capable of an activity independent of the cerebral organ and, therefore, of an intuitive connection with its own inner forces. It should understand and construct the method that gives original thinking a way to work at the transformation of its own organ and to be humanly productive. The brain does not have to grasp thinking. Yet, thinking, free and connected to its very own essence, must be the force by which the brain allows itself to be transformed.

19. Meditative Spiritual Practice: Exercise II

We can then concentrate on a triangle. Now, the object of our thinking is not a specific triangle, isosceles, or right-angled, or equilateral, and so on but, rather, the triangle-type, as a concept–image, which contains all of them, without being any of them in particular.

The exercise involves keeping awake, before consciousness, the image-type, through an a-dialectical awareness of 'its summarizing' all the forms of the triangle. In order for the "form" of this image to correspond to the content, it cannot be fixed, but it can have within itself, as form in movement, the presence of its own indetermination. The indetermination is the principle of 'its manifesting' as an image: which does not need determination in order to be mediated. The art of the spiritual practitioner is precisely this, namely to be so aware of the determination's mediating value, so as to be able to overcome its process.

20. COMMENT

No image of concentration or of meditation can have an outward or fixed character, like a thing of the physical world. Even what we imagine to be immobile, inevitably manifests enlivened in its immobility, continually arising from an imperceptible formative force, which is itself informal and, therefore, non-temporal. For this and other reasons, we deliberately avoid the term "visualize" widespread in modern spiritualistic language, according to an assumption of the imaginative act, which tends toward a type of reproduction of physical seeing that subtly binds the forces of imagination to the materiality of things and, therefore, to the cerebral organ, from which, instead, they should be freed.

In the second exercise, the triangle as an original form, in which all the sensory forms are present and transcended, becomes the object of concentration. The image is now, in its absolute immateriality, a pure sign, independent of formal determination. It is the symbol of the suprasensory form of the triangle, not the suprasensory form itself, namely, the imaginative movement of the idea, not the idea.

By contemplating this movement, the pure idea, or archetypal virtue, whose specific feature is the independence from temporal, as well as spatial, determination, solicits the inner forces of the human mental sphere in imaginative form.

Our art, as experimenters, is to not come to a stop at any particular form of the triangle, which would lead it back to the sensory level, where imagination is conditioned by cerebralism. Imagination frees itself to the degree in which it moves according an inner ideal essence, which governs the form inevitably woven out of projections of sensory impressions. The limit proper to this projection nevertheless remains, even if governed. It remains because imagination does not yet have the force to free itself of the formal mediation drawn from the sensory world and, therefore, it cannot offer, to the inner experience, the pure imaginative vestment that it objectively demands. Such mediation is overcome in the third exercise.

Regarding the second exercise, the synthesis of the forms into one must not call forth speculative issues, which would not make sense, for the synthesis corresponds to the objectivity of a necessary inner experience, whose purpose is merely to reveal itself.

21. Regarding Pure Thinking

The first two exercises can be considered an *indirect* experience of that exceptional state of thinking called "pure thinking." It must be remembered that we cannot access such an experience, unless we place ourselves before thought as if before a content in itself, and not before the thought of something. Such thought must be willed in accordance with the experimental attitude that has nothing in common with that of the philosopher, theoretician, dialectician, inclined solely toward the expression of a content that subordinates thought. If anything, it is the opposite. The required attitude is that of not wanting to convert anything into knowledge but aiming exclusively at perceiving the being of thought, by means of a "picturing" that solicits its pure formal power as content.

Therefore, the exercise of "pure thinking," to which we are alluding, is not the simple possibility of speculative thinking, that abstracts from objective contents but, rather, the possibility of willing thought, by means of the concreteness of an object, which, by revealing its formal inner structure, can further lead to the indeterminate intuitive content, the foundation of such a structure, which consequently can be contemplated just as the object was previously contemplated.

22. Meditative Spiritual Practice: Exercise III

The mastery of the two preceding exercises introduces the possibility of the third. In the first, the form of the triangle, freed from the determination of spatiality, solicits in the 'imaginative vehicle' its substantive independence from metric space. In the second, the form of the triangle tends to be the conceptual image independent not only of spatiality, but also of temporality, because in the form–type all the forms are present and gathered into one, namely those forms whose diversity, or reciprocal opposition, not only involves space but also a temporal succession.

With the third exercise, the *pure idea* of the triangle is evoked.

In the first two exercises there exists the form, which is led back to its pure movement. The movement, here, is to be understood differently than what can ordinarily be conceived in the physical sphere. It is to be seen as an act, devoid of space and time, which actuates the form. This form, again being the form that appears, is overcome, or extinguished, in the third exercise, insofar as its movement (which is its pure being) is itself contemplated, without an image. We can concentrate on the content–essence of the image–type, to the extent that the ideal–formal weaving of the representations of the two preceding exercises is contemplated with regularity.

The image–type disappears, but its idea remains, the idea of the triangle, which, unseen, enlivened the image–type as movement.

The Logic and Technique of Concentration

Form and name must disappear, and the ideal content must nevertheless exist, alive. *It is like concentrating on a nothing*, which, nevertheless, is the essence—the true reality.

When the idea of a triangle is evoked, for an instant it is gleaned as an imperceptible that does not need representation to be what it is. That instant escapes normal consciousness, whose immediate relation with itself awakens opposite the formal element of the image–type, or before the determined image. The moment of indetermination, which is the creative informality, escapes it. Likewise, when a train of thought, or an event, or a text that is familiar to the intellect is remembered, there is a moment in which it is present in its entirety, without form, in the act of ideating–remembering, namely a moment that is non-temporal, as well as informal, in which the train of thoughts, or event, or text, rises up in its totality. But in order to express what it thereby evokes, we must deprive ourselves of that moment and convert it into a series of representations or concepts: and, thus, it is stretched out in time.

The non-temporal and informal moment of the idea that normally escapes consciousness, which is awake only in the formal act of thinking, can become a conscious experience. It is the beginning of the possibility of living thinking: what our present culture has lacked.

As long as the act of thinking has a form, however much it can, as an act, call itself *"pensiero pensante,"*[4] it is always reflected thinking, conditioned by cerebralism. It is not the reality of thinking, but its transitory projection, in which we can nevertheless philosophically recognize its instantaneous coincidence with itself, as the act's tangency with its continued existence. But this recognition is not the experience or perception of the thinking act.

The perception of the creative moment of thinking involves something more than a mere philosophical authentication. In order for that instantaneous perpetuity not to be illusory, thinking must not be assumed simply as a philosophical *"pensiero pensante,"* but it must be experienced (in accordance with the technique described) as a primordial current of life, independent of name and form. This can even operate in the form as a modifying force of the organ by means of which it expresses itself.

23. Obstacles to Meditation

An analysis of the technique of concentration can be studied and learned for the purpose of the regularity of a spiritual practice, upon which nothing can be affirmed that is not the experience realized according to the immanent laws of the spirit: the true Tradition.

Outside such a spiritual practice, the texts of ancient wisdom no longer have anything to say. Yoga is no longer Yoga. Zen is no longer Zen, The Vajrayana is not the Vajrayana, and it is rhetorical to speak of it. Not because they do not conceal within themselves original forms of truth, but because there is no longer a thinking capable of movement and, therefore, of identity with them, outside the reflective mediation.

With thought devoid of the intuitive element, modern individuals can nowadays become interpreters of those doctrines, further veiling their meaning, precisely by presuming to interpret it in present-day terms. Except that they do not know the art of thought's conversion, which we have dealt with up to now. It can be experienced within the process of thinking that normally appears in the normal rational experience, if we have the power to turn to it directly, according to the canon of its original movement, capable of identifying the limit that, today, is to be overcome in the mental sphere.

The most formally abstract and analytical thought conceals within itself, the force of what it is as pure essence, all the way to its suprasensory source. Those of us who have the capacity to retrace the current of thinking as it appears in the ordinary rational thought process discover the levels of consciousness we lose during the descent from an original intuitive consciousness to lifeless rationality. The conversion of present-day thinking leads us, as experimenters, to unforeseen experiences, which we can recognize as what the perennial metaphysics requires today in relation to the times.

Nonetheless, our analysis would be unproductive and expire into dialecticism, if it were mere learning and did not become practical guidance. We must point out that none of the described distinctions must intervene in the unfolding of concentration and meditation. Such distinctions are necessary to prepare thinking and to later clarify the meditative exercise. This meditative exercise must however actualize absolute independence of its own content during its development, namely an independence even from the rules according to which it was learned. The distinctions do not have to be brought into the meditation, because this meditation, by wisely opening up to its own movement, is on the verge of metaphysically actualizing and transcending, within itself, each and every rule.

If we observe, the content's independence is realized not with regard to the substance of the rules but, rather, relative to their dialectical expression, which, if it is recalled in a moment of the meditation, operates as an obstacle. The content correctly realized is followed a-dialectically, during the meditative act, as what has value in itself and not in what we eventually attempt to remember. Remembering must be assimilated in the act of contemplating. Any tactic that wants to be remembered with regard to the content of the concentration, leads outside it. It is conducive to a relapse into the usual thinking. If this occurs, it must be noticed so that the diversion can be reascended consciously.

An analysis of the meditative technique must be studied before or after the exercise. This analysis cannot be introduced while this exercise unfolds, because the technique itself, to which this analysis refers, is in the act, in its real form, which does not suffer intellectualistic intrusions, or discursive problematisms.

Meditating or thinking, without any recollection of rules, without distractions or reflective interferences, is everything. *Reflection and memory are the obstacles to the meditation.*

Those of us who understand meditating, or thinking, as absolute acts, independent of any sensory, or psychic, or mental interference—each interference being unable to not be contradictory as thought that opposes the thinking that trains itself to express only itself—those of us who understand the possibility of realizing, in a single movement, the whole of our imagining or thinking, like when we are unconsciously drawn by an object that has the power to spontaneously polarize all our attention, so that we do not make an effort, but have only the thinking that flows according to thinking, are on the true path of meditation.

V

THE "I AM"

Individuals can each say "I" with regard to themselves, but no one can claim to possess the sense of such an expression. The *"I am"* is the term whose content can be real for whoever encounters the "I," insofar as one finally encounters what one says one is.

We who discover the "I," discover nothing behind us, which is not the reality upon which we nevertheless lean, since we are ordinarily led to seek outside what we, within ourselves, already are. We know that we do not have to change anything within ourselves. We do not have to pass onto another level of being, but we must have the strength to be who we already are in the depths.

Those of us who discover the "I" do not encounter it as thought, or image, or feeling but, rather, as our very being, never before known, which we glimpse as the principle of what we always are. Secretly identical to that principle, we nevertheless do not see it. We do not feel it. We do not actualize it. We do not allow ourselves to rest on its unlimited fundamentality. We do not make use of it as the absolute source, because normally we believe ourselves to be one with what we think, feel, and will in the world of finite things, even though we each say "I" with regard to ourselves.

For this reason, the ordinary "I" does not live of itself, but of its own finite image. And to this it binds itself, by ignoring its own being, devoid of ties. It does not realize that it binds itself in order to know things by not arriving at itself: at the one who actually does not need to know things.

As a being that is never known, the "I" cannot be imagined as it is, and, in becoming known, it ceases to be what it is. In reality, it cannot be known. Who of us, in fact, can know it? Nevertheless, self-experience, for the "I," is initially a process of knowledge. It is a matter of understanding its sense and limit.

Self-experience, even if it involves the initial process of knowing, demands a conversion of this (knowing) according to the a-dialectical-ness of the "I." In common knowing, the force of the "I" is carried out, unknown. As researchers, we can experience this to the degree in which (according to the technique described in the preceding chapters) we free it from the form of finite things by means of which it manifests, but which is really not it.

Freed, such a force inevitably manifests by means of a movement opposite to that of ordinary knowing. For this reason, it can lead to the "I." We needed to experience the law of such knowing, in the sensory sphere, so that we could recognize it by way of its rational manifestation, as an original force that tends to reestablish itself, and understand the task of retracing its movement: which is to *invert its movement*, by freeing it of opinions generated by its validation of the sensory realm. Our test, as researchers, is to endure the nullification of human opinions, to which the resurrection of thinking gives rise, if we bring about this resurrection. From this nullification arises the sense of thinking's relation to the sensory, without contradicting the original relation, needed at its own level.

The more we bind ourselves to what we are not, or to what is outside us, the more thinking needs to be logical, because a series of rational relationships need to replace the synthetic perception that we once had of reality. Logical thinking, however, is not identifiable with its product: logic. The error of thinking lies in establishing its own logic for itself. Meanwhile, the logical forms, as has been shown, should be its instruments for specific analytical–technical operations. In the thinking freed of its logical products, we have the principle of a power of re-ascension of the thinking process by means of which it descended from the heights of an original intuitive consciousness to the level of dialectical–abstract consciousness.

Rational thinking, regardless of the doctrine in which it is established, leads away from the "I." Therefore, it cannot attain human wisdom. Its culmination is the common feeling, which can appear as sublime intuition in an amorphous world of automatic 'logicism.' The more intelligence takes root, the more it leads away from the "I." The inversion of its movement is the thinking of the "I," the beginning of wisdom.

The form by means of which human thought manifests has nothing to do with thinking as an original force. This force, freed from the form of finite things, is the identity by means of which the consciousness of the "I" is led to realize its foundation. As experimenters, we each encounter our own principle in certain moments of thinking's independence from the psychosomatic support. We do not experience such independence as our own, but flowing from a principle to which it is inwardly identical. We perceive this independence as *external*, at the boundary of consciousness and, nevertheless, we cannot but experience it within ourselves. Thus, we encounter the secret of freedom, experiencing as immanent what we must first perceive as transcendent. The vehicle of logical thinking in this experience is essential as the capacity to distinguish the formal movement of thinking from the discursive form.

If we, as experimenters, were identical to the principle that we encounter, we would each be able to say, "I am," with regard to ourselves. But we cannot yet say it because our first incorporeal identity is the movement of freed thinking, namely the support of our free being, not its freedom. We can only recognize the independence of the "I," to the extent that, in the vehicle of pure thinking or imagining, we come to see it as the principle at the boundaries of the consciousness in which it now exists.

To perceive this independence, transcendent to us, is to realize it. This is the secret. We do not become free of it if we do not transcend what we are. But we are what we are precisely because we are nothing. We are an abstract mental image filled with sensations. We are not what we radically are, because we do not transcend the image of ourselves. We are closed within it. The art is to perceive what we are beyond the limit, just like the outer world is perceived beyond the limit of the physical person. But what is beyond the limit is inherent to those of us who perceive it.

If we encounter the "I" as the principle of present-day consciousness, we acknowledge it and feel expanded in the limitless being in which it continues across transcendent levels as a principle, but that we truly can begin to receive with our 'discerning' and feeling.

Initially, the boundary of consciousness is still real for us as a sign of the "I," but also as a limit. Nonetheless, we know we can look at this limit (which we previously did not see) and, thus, beyond it. The limit has no other meaning. We receive within ourselves a life that does not come from nature, but from what precedes it. And we know that even this life becomes corrupted as it flows into us, because we function according to the reflection of the "I," not according to the "I": according to its finite image, which is the ego, not according to its infinity.

The vision of the boundary is the principle of its overcoming, because that boundary is temporary. We recognize it as the projection of consciousness bound to the sensory, which disappears through the strengthening of consciousness, through the liberation of thinking. As experimenters, we know that this boundary, crossed owing to the rediscovery of the "I," leads us toward what we do not yet know how to see, because an organ of vision must be formed in order to focus on it. We then know that before us lies the mystery of the world's being—namely, the Logos. The "I am" is the name of the Logos.

We can find the "I" that we each say we are—the foundation from which everything is reclaimed and brought back to truth—if we raise, within ourselves, the "I." Only the "I," to the extent that it actualizes its independence, can connect itself to its source, the 'I am.' Independence, alone, is, for the "I," the possibility to identify with the Logos, with the "I am."

We can have access to the experience of the "I," without yet realizing it. We can enter there by liberating thought. Yet, for this liberation not to be a culmination continually lost and irrevocable, for it to become instead a conscious act and give rise to the perception of the world's 'becoming' that thinks, we must connect ourselves to the principle that is the "I am."

There is no new or ancient spiritual practice that can realize the inner human being, unless it connects to the knowledge that springs from the intimate encounter with the being whose transcendence is the only immanent one. And this is the point: that it draws so much more profoundly from itself, the more (by correlating its own research to the "I am") it feels its transcendence to be immanent: which is its 'forgetting' to affirm itself as the "I," or better yet, losing the affirmation of itself in the outer world, since the "I" does not need this affirmation, insofar as it already is an affirmation of itself. Each validation of the "I" in the sensory world has nothing to do with the "I," whose dominion is suprasensory. For this reason, it already governs the sensory. It operates in the sensory without being grasped by it in any way. But in order to know this, it must first be grasped by it.

One does not encounter the "I am" by means of faith, or the mediumistic abandonment of oneself, but by converting thought according to the original power of its movement, so that its life can be taken on by the one who, by means of it, expresses itself and finds within it the way to be consciousness (unto itself): the "I."

As we have said, it is not enough to be aware of the movement of thinking, if there is no connection to the *author* of such movement, which demands the absolute independence of the being that operates in its name. Spurious freedom is that in which the "I" is removed from the 'I am,' namely the freedom with which, even spiritualistically, the "I" (believing itself to be the "I") operates, moved by earthly necessities.

If there is to be a connection with the original "author," we must initially train ourselves to discover where it is expressed in the correlation with the world. We begin to enter the secret of things, by forgetting the "I" and perceiving the prime substance of crystals, of plants, of the forms of entities: perceiving the relation with the "I" in front of them. This is recognized as a relation with the one that knows no opposition, or limitation, namely the "I am," in which lies the origin of their being, of their appearing and disappearing.

The "I" is not to be sought outside the "I." Its absoluteness is not an image. It is not a philosophical impulse. It is not a ritual, nor a magical path. Rather, it is it itself, its being, which we are in the depths, if we know how to enter into the depths of ourselves.

It is not enough for the "I" to be. We must be the "I." We must encounter, at our very root, a being in which not only the soul has its foundation, but even the body: which is the substantiality of the soul and of the body that expresses itself in their movement, more than in their form. With respect to it, we each say "I," but we continually contradict it, because its independence is contradicted. We use this independence in order to depend on what it is not.

The "I" that we each say we are, is not the "I," because we speak of that in which the "I" is reflected, essentially making the reflection absolute, by not knowing where we truly begin to be the "I."

The "I AM"

We would be the "I" only, there, where we encountered the 'I am,' which is the "I" that already is, namely whose freedom is its very being. For this reason, it does not need freedom. Meanwhile the "I," as an "I" that thinks, feels, and wills needs to be free, in order to be the subject of what it does: in order to be the "I" according to the I am, in order not to be against the I am.

The "I" that acts as the free "I," though bound to thinking, feeling, and willing, cannot but corrupt these soul forces and, as philosopher or esoteric teacher, give doctrinal form to such corruption.

The "I" that cannot know its need as the need to articulate itself within immediate thinking and that, therefore, cannot experience the autonomy of thinking as a vehicle of its autonomy, cannot be free.

Thinking is to be liberated. The "I" is already free, but the bond of thinking prevents the 'actualizing' of its freedom. The autonomy of thought manifests the autonomy of the "I," but it is not this. The autonomy of thought that operates as the autonomy of the "I," is not authentic. It becomes deceitful, if its relation to the "I" is not perceived.

The autonomy of the "I" is to be contemplated as what, in itself, is already realized. The deception is not to notice what manifests such autonomy as thought. The deception is to believe that we are free, there, where being free is used in order to bind ourselves to sensory things. The task is to notice how freedom is rejected and where the autonomous being lives unconditioned by what is the completed structure of the body and of the soul. The task is to contemplate such autonomy.

Not to see the presence of the autonomous being in thinking is to escape the contemplation of reality. Each time that we think an object, in the thinking impersonally correlated to it we have a movement of the spirit. But we ignore this movement and lose it, by binding thought to the object and losing thought's element of freedom. It would be enough for us to look at such thought, so that it could reveal to us how it expresses and suppresses our freedom.

Freedom is the urgent demand of those who are not free, because they are not free of themselves. It does not concern the "I am." Only the "I" bound to corporeity can conceive the task of freeing itself, in order to realize its own being, since such a being cannot manifest itself but as independence. The independence can be contemplated, there, where it already is, but there it can be indicated by another name. Contemplation of the independence is the principle of its realization in the one who contemplates. The one who contemplates the being of the "I," is the "I."

We, who are not free, seek freedom, but we are not free in the part of ourselves that we believe is free and use as if it were free.

The ordinary "I" is always in keeping with something. Nevertheless, continually referring to itself, it turns as if to the one that is on its own. But it is never on its own. Its contradiction is to believe that it is the "I" and, nevertheless, to behave as if it were not, namely to affirm its 'being free' where it makes no sense to be free and to remain bound to an outer appearance, which demands from it, freedom's illusory 'expressing' of itself.

In order to know its force, in order to know where it can free itself, in order not to reinforce the bond by believing itself to be free, the "I" must draw from its own original being, namely from the "I am." It must conform to its not being bound to anything, to realize, as a free being, its presence in the world.

It must contemplate what it claims to be, and what operates within it in essential solitude, that is, what operates unknown. If it did not operate unknown, it would not be able to reveal itself. It would not be able to begin the liberating work.

To conform to its own original being within its inner depths, to receive its inspiration and life, is not to depend. It is to discover the ultimate support, for it is not the support but the origin itself, which is restored from the depths: for which the support is no longer necessary.

The "I AM"

The misunderstanding of letting go of the "hold" that we imagine but we do not know, ceases. There is no letting go of any hold. Any support that acts as the vehicle of the "I" in earthly experience, is actually a limit. It is not a support, but an object that the "I" has renounced having before itself, in order to perceive, in order to know. Operating as the support of the "I," it is the error. The "I" inheres to the earthly, to things, to events, to sensations, to thinking, to feeling, to willing, because it is not itself, but the principle that fails itself, by leaning upon them, by needing them as a support in order to be. Meanwhile, they await to be its object, its experience, so as to be reconnected with their origin. *Each and every support is not a support of the "I," but of what obstructs the "I."* The deception is continuous, above all, thanks to the images given by the bearers of false freedom.

There exists a gang of teachers, of the left hand, of the right hand, of the center, of the center left, and of the center-right, apparently adverse toward one another, whose task is to mislead the research of present-day disciples, by holding back their consciousness in one of the supports and indicating apparent freedoms, plausible transcendences. As long as the true limit is not glimpsed, we surrender to the unknown support, for which we continue to say "I" without being it.

So that we do not fall into the temptation of seeking the "I" demonically, mystically, or philosophically, the "I am" operates unknown, revealing itself only in the contradictions of thinking, as in accordance with the independence of the "I" from supports when encountering the sensory world. As long as the "I" believes that it can operate in the world by way of its own power, it will mistake for its own force what illusorily comes to it from its identification with the psychosomatic supports. It will mistake arbitrary acts for free will. It will not be the "I" that acts but, rather, the powers that grasp it by means of supports. Its affirmation will be its subjection, equipped with all the justifications of culture. But even this will end up being necessary as the crossing of darkness on behalf of those who have to mistake it for the light, in order to discover the light.

With this, we did not demonstrate but indicated how the discovery of the "I am" can be the measure of the "I"'s liberation and how every other form of liberation is abstract and deceptive. Only the Logos can be present within the human soul as a measure of its being the "I," at the center of itself. Only the "I," insofar as it rises free, can attain within itself, the "I am."

Measurement regards earthly work. Only those of us who encounter within ourselves the principle that is the "I am" can harmonize our inner experience with the series of human tasks. We realize, with this, the ultimate sense of 'existing.' We realize the Spirit of the Earth, without which the Earth is a kingdom of death, with mechanical semblances of life. By virtue of this identity, its work can have the continuity of freedom.

The support will always grasp the human being, as long as we do not know that we are each, within ourselves, an "I," which, only by realizing its own independence, can be one with the "I am" and, therefore, with the reality of the Earth. Error and disillusion, desire and aversion will always control us without us noticing it and noticing where it begins. They will control us all the more, the more we believe ourselves to be religious, or mystical, or majestic, or initiated, so long as we do not know our "I" to be illusory, if we are incapable of not depending on anything that is not its original identity: the "I am."

Whoever does not know the mystery of the Logos and the vanity of every vague desire for knowledge or for the affirmation of the "I," cannot discover the "I."

Rare human beings that succeed in discovering the "I," would discover it the world over. These rare individuals have to overcome the test of falling short of their task, just so that they can really begin to be free. They must be aware of the temptation to use the spirit's initial movement, or freedom, according to earthly ties still unknown. The "I" has within it the power to recognize them. It has absolute authority to create, out of each earthly element, the substance of its action.

If the contribution of those individuals fails us, then no human religion, or philosophy, or logic, or science will be able to avoid the confusion of terms of each and every problem. The likelihood of gathering the truth of situations will always be less—even if there exist dialectics and logics that specifically presume to penetrate them.

Those who seek truth, seek the spirit. If they seek the spirit, they seek the "I." But they cannot arrive at the "I," if they do not cognize its very being as a presence that accounts for itself, inasmuch as it accounts for every assumption of truth.

Only the Logos is able to say "I am" with regard to itself. "I am" is the name of the Logos just as "I" is the name that only those who say it can give to themselves. Those who reach the "I" discover the Logos to be the foundation of the "I," for which they can say, "Not I, but the Logos within me," which is true freedom, since it does not appeal to any condition but only the foundation. Identified with this foundation, they can operate in the world.

Those who turn toward seeking the Logos can actualize fraternity on Earth, because from the depths of the soul, they are united, according to the true word of the "I," within the principle that can say of itself: "I am."

Notes

1. *"tutte le vacche sono nere"* (all the cows are black): a reference to the *Phenomenology of the Spirit* in which "Hegel refutes Schelling's conception of absolute knowledge in terms of immediate intuition and feeling, a conception which dissolves the rich differentiation and determination of empirical content into a 'night in which all cows are black'." (Taken from a running commentary by Yirmiyahu Yovel from *Hegel's Preface to the Phenomenology of the Spirit,* Princeton University Press, 2005 pp. 248.)

2. *empiria:* an experience understood as the origin of knowledge or even as a practical 'acting' or functioning; all that regards the experience or has a relation to it; the sum of experiences, free of theoretical preconditions and extraneous to speculative meditations.

3. The Master of the New Times—i.e., Rudolf Steiner.

4. *pensiero pensante:* Please refer to the "Translator's Note" in Massimo Scaligero, *A Treatise on Living Thinking: A Path beyond Western Philosophy, beyond Yoga, beyond Zen* (2015) or in *The Light (La Luce): An Introduction to Creative Imagination* (2001).

Glossary

acephalous	no longer having a head; headless.
aseity	the quality or state of being self-derived or self-originated.
axiom	a statement or proposition that is regarded as established, accepted, or self-evidently true.
axiomatic	evident without proof or argument.
axiomaticity	the characteristic of being axiomatic.
cerebration	the working of the brain; thinking; cerebral automatism.
deduction	the inference of particular instances by reference to a general law or principle; the action of deducting or subtracting something.
gnoseological	of or relating to *gnoseology*.
gnoseology	the philosophic theory of knowledge: inquiry into the basis, nature, validity, and limits of knowledge.
identity	oneness; a close similarity or affinity; sameness in all that constitutes the objective reality of a thing.
induction	an act or process of inducing; the act of causing or bringing on or about; inference of a generalized conclusion from particular instances.
mediation	intervention in a process or relationship; intercession. (Scaligero: "…both thinking and perceiving, in their immediacy, escape the consciousness of the 'I,' because this consciousness requires mediation in order to cognize. Perceiving is its mediation; thinking is its mediation.")
monoideism	the domination of a single idea, as in certain mental disorders.
paralogism	a piece of illogical or fallacious reasoning, especially one that appears superficially logical or that the reasoning person believes to be logical.

pleonastic	the use of more words than are required to express an idea; redundancy.
problematism	the doctrine that philosophy is a branch of inquiry aimed only at clarifying problems and examining their significance and that of their components but not solving them (A. Pablo Iannone, *Dictionary of World Philosophy*, Routledge, 2001). "*Discursive problematicisms*" here refers to discursive incursions that intrude during the meditative act and one's attempts to analyze "existential" issues.
propaedeutics	an introduction to a subject or area of study.
sophism	a fallacious argument, especially when used deliberately to deceive.
solipsism	a theory holding that the self can know nothing but its own modifications, and that the self is the only existent thing.
syllogism	a deductive scheme of a formal argument consisting of a major and a minor premise and a conclusion (e.g., *all dogs are animals; all animals have four legs; therefore all dogs have four legs*); *deductive* reasoning as distinct from *induction*.
synthetic	limited to the essential, to the only elements that take on a particular importance or meaning; attributing to a subject something determined by observation rather than analysis of the nature of the subject and not resulting in self-contradiction if negated.

A Note from Lindisfarne Books

SteinerBooks and its imprint Lindisfarne Books comprise a 501(c)(3) not-for-profit organization, incorporated in New York State since 1928 to promote the progress and welfare of humanity and to increase public awareness of Rudolf Steiner (1861–1925), the Austrian-born polymath writer, lecturer, spiritual scientist, philosopher, cosmologist, educator, psychologist, alchemist, ecologist, Christian mystic, comparative religionist, and evolutionary theorist, who was the creator of Anthroposophy ("human wisdom") as a path uniting the spiritual in the human being with the spiritual in the universe; and to this end publish and distribute books for adults and children, utilize the electronic media, hold conferences, and engage in similar activities making available his works and exploring themes arising from, and related to, them and the movement that he founded.

- We commission translations of books by Rudolf Steiner unpublished in English, as well as new translations for updated editions.
- Our aim is to make works on Anthroposophy available to all by publishing and distributing both introductory and advanced works on spiritual research.
- New books are publish for both print and digital editions to reach the widest possible readership.
- Recent technology also makes it efficient for us to make our previously out-of-print works available for the next generation.

SteinerBooks depends on our readers' financial support, which is greatly needed, appreciated, and tax-deductible. Please consider a donation by check or other means to SteinerBooks, 610 Main St., Great Barrington, MA 01230. We also accept donations via PayPal on our website. For more information about supporting our work, send email to friends@steinerbooks.org or call 413-528-8233.

www.ingramcontent.com/pod-product-compliance
Lightning Source LLC
Chambersburg PA
CBHW021803220426
43662CB00006B/166